DOMESTICATING REVOLUTION

GERALD W. CREED

DOMESTICATING
REVOLUTION

From Socialist Reform to Ambivalent
Transition in a Bulgarian Village

The Pennsylvania State University Press
University Park, Pennsylvania

Library of Congress Cataloging-in-Publication Data

Creed, Gerald, 1958–
   Domesticating revolution: from socialist reform to ambivalent transition in a
Bulgarian village / Gerald W. Creed

        p.   cm.
   Includes bibliographical references (p.   ) and index.
   ISBN 0–271–01712–0 (cloth : alk. paper)
   ISBN 0–271–01713–9 (pbk. : alk. paper)
   1. Agriculture and state—Bulgaria—Case studies.   2. Post-communism—
Bulgaria—Case studies.   3. Land reform—Bulgaria—Case studies.
4. Agriculture, Cooperative—Bulgaria—Case studies.   I. Title.
HD2043.C74   1998
338.1′8499—dc21   96–46712
                                                                              CIP

On title page: Clerical and administrative staff of the Zamfirovo cooperative farm
on a brigade stacking straw in 1987.

To my mother,
Ruby Speer Creed,
who taught me to make the most
out of what you have,
and to the residents of Zamfirovo,
who always did just that

НА МОЯТА МАЙКА,

РУБИ СПИР КРИЙД,

КОЯТО МЕ УЧЕШЕ, ЧЕ ЧОВЕК ТРЯБВА ДА ИЗТРЪГВА

ВСИЧКО ОТ ТОВА С КОЕТО РАЗПОЛАГА

И НА ЖИТЕЛИТЕ НА ЗАМФИРОВО,

КОИТО ВИНАГИ СА ПРАВИЛИ ТЪКМО ТОВА

Things come apart so easily when they have been held together with lies.
—Dorothy Allison
Bastard Out of Carolina (1992)

Contents

List of Illustrations

List of Tables

Preface and Acknowledgments

This book presents a collection of interconnected paradoxes, analyzed in paradoxical ways. I set out to capture the difficulty of Bulgarian village life with an argument about the amelioration of rural socialism since the 1960s. I credit villagers with achieving this transformation but posit no concerted program of resistance. I suggest that the improvements, rather than the difficulties, caused the system's collapse, and that the collapse, of all things, provided the catalyst for a socialist revival. The socialist revival was a defense against the excesses of transition, but it eventually made the crisis worse. My goal is to account for this trajectory of transition, yet more pages are actually devoted to the village experience with socialism. While the latter is intended to improve our understanding of socialism as a distinctive social system, it does so by periodically invoking similarities with capitalism. I argue that one such distinction was the continuing centrality of agriculture under socialism, but my evidence comes from a village that was significantly industrialized. In short, nothing is exactly (or only) what it seems, and the contradictions themselves are the crucial keys to understanding. The attempt to explicate the legacy of socialism, then, is much like the socialist system itself as described in the following pages: analyzing one contradiction exposes another dilemma, which reveals yet another, until, after several such detours, you realize you are back to the paradox with which you began. The most important insight is not what you learn pursuing each new lead but the configuration of paths you have to travel in the process.

While traveling these paths for nearly ten years, I am afraid I have acquired as many debts as insights, and I would like to discharge them first. As a believer in the centrality of economic forces I will start with the organizations that have financed my efforts. The Fulbright Hays Research xiv					Preface and Acknowledgments

Abroad Program, the National Science Foundation, the Research Awards Program of the Professional Staff Congress of the City University of New York, the International Research and Exchanges Board (IREX), the Wenner-Gren Foundation for Anthropological Research, and the Joint Committee on Eastern Europe (of the Social Science Research Council and the American Council of Learned Societies) each provided funds for a crucial portion of the research or writing. The latter three underwrote multiple portions of the process. I am extremely grateful for their contribution and faith.

Numerous individuals in the United States and Canada have provided the personal and intellectual counterparts to funding. Prominent among them are Daniel Bates, Elizabeth Brusco, Donna Buchanan, Barbara Ching, May Ebihara, Lyubomira Gribble, Karen Judd, Donna Kerner, Aisha Khan, Gail Kligman, Margo Matwychuk, Mieke Meurs, Carole Nagengast, Linda Nelson, Allyson Purpura, Claire Riley, Elizabeth Sheehan, Sydel Silverman, Maria Todorova, and Terri Vulcano. In addition to their unique contributions, many of these people also read and commented on parts of this book. Thank you all. David Kideckel, Susan Lees, Jane Schneider, Carol Silverman, Katherine Verdery, and Eric Wolf read nearly the entire manuscript and helped me improve it significantly. It is my good fortune to call them mentors. Timothy Pilbrow deserves special mention for the difficult job of indexing. I am thrilled to have the final product published by Penn State Press under the trusting guidance of Peter Potter and Cherene Holland.

My contacts in Bulgaria at the Institute of Sociology were crucial to the completion of this research. They fulfilled any request, answered all questions, and provided a collegial atmosphere during my visits. I want to single out Veska Kouzhouharova Zhivkova, Vladimir Vladov, Svetla Koleva, and Stanka Dobreva for being especially helpful. I must also thank Ivan Ilchev and Velislava Dimitrova for making me feel at home in Sofia. Of course, my greatest debt in Bulgaria is to the villagers of Zamfirovo, who put up with my prying presence and my broken Bulgarian to provide me with insight into their lives. Several did more than just put up with me, actually incorporating me into their families. These included Ivan and Maria Kostovi (Shilovi), Kiril and Yordanka Pelovi, Todor and Yordanka Todorovi, Emil Slavkov, Filip Filipov, and Petur Aleksandrov. To these, and the many others who helped me out in so many ways, I offer the book itself as my acknowledgment.

Finally, I must thank my family for a lifetime of support. My mother deserves special recognition: she inspired my intellectual curiosity, imparted the sensitivity essential for an anthropologist, and provided me with the sense of self-worth needed to withstand the assaults of academia. It is only fitting that I also dedicate this book to her. Gene Oyler has provided every conceivable type of support to me and this project over the past fifteen years; all the remaining gratitude goes to him.

Before turning to the analysis, I must add some final words about words themselves. I have avoided using Bulgarian terms whenever possible. When it was not possible, my first choice was to use Latin forms commonly employed in Bulgaria (for example, in maps and English-language publications). In the absence of alternatives I transliterated words myself, following the scheme outlined by Richard Crampton (1987:xiii). Problems with English words were not so easily resolved. I use the term "revolution" for the arrival of communism in Bulgaria and for its collapse because both events brought revolutionary change. As is clear in the brief historical descriptions herein, neither event depended on popular rebellion. In effect, they were both joint products of the Soviet Union and the Bulgarian Communist Party. Still, in the years between these turning points, the everyday efforts of Bulgarian citizens to improve their lives pushed the Communist Party toward its 1989 abdication.

The subsequent electoral successes of the Bulgarian Socialist Party (indeed, of socialist parties throughout eastern Europe) rendered the designation "postsocialist" potentially misleading for the 1990s. The postcommunist alternative implies a prior condition of communism that neither the residents nor leaders of east European countries claimed to have achieved—their societies were technically socialist, on the road to communism, guided by the Communist Party. Furthermore, any designation including the prefix "post-," like the term "transition," violates the desire of people who lived in this period to have a time of their own—an era that is meaningful in and of itself rather than for what it follows or precedes. "Transition" is also problematic because its common usage implies a temporary condition and an inevitable result. The social characteristics of transition may be quite enduring, and the outcome is certainly not predetermined. In the absence of a more precise alternative, then, I use these words interchangeably to indicate the period since 1989 when communist and socialist ideologies lost their official monopoly over society, although not necessarily their social currency. In this sense there was indeed an evident transition, although what followed was not invariably capitalist democracy. Having made this concession to conventional terminology, it seems moot to maintain a rigid distinction between communism and socialism for the period from World War II to 1989. Although I appreciate the distinction, the two ideas were ideologically linked throughout the period. In general I believe the descriptions in this book reveal the ambiguity of all these terms, and thus I am not overly concerned about their discursive power in this case.

INTRODUCTION

As often happened during my stays in Bulgaria, one summer evening in 1994 I was invited to dinner with the family of a village friend. The meal started late since it was a peak period in the growing season and every hour of daylight was precious, but the lateness only enhanced the atmosphere of deserved respite and celebration. After a few hours at the table eating, talking, and watching television, when the surfeit of homemade wine had taken a toll and the grandfather had fallen asleep in his chair, his son offered a summation of the country's desires: "We just want to be normal. Not backward, not communist, not in transition, just to live like they do in normal countries." I suppressed an anthropological urge to challenge the concept of "normality" and allowed him to continue:

> Just look back. We have always been in some mess, either under Ottoman control, clients of the Germans, part of the communist camp, and now in transition. And what is this transition? During my whole life we have been in some kind of transition: the transition to socialism, the transition to communism, and now the transition to capitalism. We are always in transition. The goals change, but we stay in transition. This is our fate, to always be on the road to someplace we never reach. In my opinion we never even achieved socialism, not to speak of communism. Do you think we will do any better with capitalism or democracy? I doubt it, I really doubt it.

The irony and ambiguity of his observations haunted me. Although this fifty-year-old man grew up entirely under the socialist regime, his view of the world was so strongly defined by Western capitalism that his own experience, indeed all of recent Bulgarian history, seemed abnormal—a mere aberration. Yet, at the same time, his critique of "transition," a concept closely associated with Western standards of normalcy, was stinging and insightful. It revealed the very emptiness of the concept in a historical context of seemingly perpetual transition. In these observations my friend shows just how complicated the communist legacy is—here ephemeral, there determinant; but in so doing, he takes us toward a better understanding of that very complexity.

This book is an attempt to apply such insights from Bulgarian friends and acquaintances, mostly of rural origin, to scholarly models of socialism and transition. Their experiences provide more than local color—they teach us essential lessons often missing in scholarly analyses. They show that what ordinary villagers ordinarily did significantly influenced national outcomes during socialism and afterward. Indeed, I argue that village actions transformed socialism in ways that both facilitated the transition and then restrained it. Listening to villagers also verifies that socialism was an extremely variable experience, both across the society and over time, and that these differences variegated the legacy of socialism as well. Finally, villagers remind us that the impact of socialism shifts in response to the transition itself. As the transition unfolded, current events began to influence villagers' attitudes and actions, albeit still in concert with their socialist experiences. Thus, while the socialist background significantly determines the outcome of transition, it does so in indeterminate ways, with the particulars being shaped (and reshaped) by local and personal experiences. Consequently, any attempt to make sense of the transition in Bulgaria must revisit socialism through lived experience.

While many commentators on the transition attend to the socialist legacy, they often begin with models of socialism developed without in-depth ethnographic engagement. By problematizing only events since 1989, this transitology risks translating misconceptions of the past into inadequate explanations of the present. For example, there is a trend to blame limited progress toward land privatization on old communist leaders or technocrats protecting their privileged positions. This follows almost lockstep from previous authoritarian, top-down models of socialism that blamed bureaucrats for obstructing reforms and granted limited roles to the masses unless organized into resistance movements on a par with the Hungarian Revolution or Solidarity.

When we look at Bulgarian villagers, however, we see instead that ordinary people, from factory workers to tractor drivers, devised viable strategies under the conditions of that system. More important, their everyday actions forced the state to adjust in ways that gradually ameliorated the entire socialist system. By simply doing what they could to improve their difficult circumstances, without any grand design of resistance, villagers forced concessions from central planners and administrators that eventually transformed an oppressive, intrusive system into a tolerable one. In short, through their mundane actions villagers domesticated the socialist revolution. Villagers themselves noted the improvement, tracing it back to the late 1960s when the benefits of economic development and early reforms started to be felt. But domestication was not an event; it was an ongoing process.

Ironically, the system itself helped make domestication possible: the totalizing nature of socialism amplified everyday peasant resistance (Scott 1985) into a more transformative force than is often the case under capitalism. Istvan Rev (1987) has documented this dynamic in his important essay on Hungarian collectivization and the subsequent reforms achieved by peasant resistance. In Bulgaria, however, I see similar transformative possibilities in rural *compliance* as well as resistance, and I view such changes as a more integral and ongoing part of socialism's systemic operation. While socialism may have politicized mundane actions (Rev 1987: 341), daily life as the motor of change rendered the process less noticeable to observers and participants and less likely to provoke state backlash, even as it moved toward the 1989 revolution.

The household as a space of social interaction was crucial to this outcome. Many of the local practices that slowly transformed Bulgarian socialism revolved around the possibilities and constraints of village households (obviously conferring further relevance and meaning on the term "domestication"). As David Kideckel (1993) demonstrated convincingly for rural Romania, the household, while never truly "private," was virtually the only arena that retained any ideological or political autonomy from the socialist state. This limited autonomy helped depoliticize the economic maneuvering carried out in the domestic spaces of Bulgarian villages, keeping the transformative actions of villagers closer to compliance than resistance. The fact that villagers domesticated socialism at least partially through actions perceived of as compliance made socialism more attractive after 1989 than if the whole process had been cast as resistance. The story to be told here, then, is a moving testimony to the power of everyday practice to reconfigure the very conditions that inform it. Unfortunately, this domestication also established constraints to subsequent change.

Let's be clear: the domestication of socialism did not transform the village into anybody's ideal. As Millar and Wolchik (1994:4) point out, positive changes under socialism had negative counterparts, and the latter eventually overwhelmed the former. The following pages give ample evidence to this effect. Bulgarian village life remained difficult: most men carried the double burden of subsistence farming and wage labor, while women added on domestic responsibilities for a triple hardship. Consequently, rural life was devalued culturally, economically, and politically, while villagers were prevented from escaping it by migration restrictions. Numerous other examples could be presented to demolish official propaganda about the glories of socialism in the countryside. Still the gradual process of domestication had its own impact, an impact not captured in positive and negative accounting. The point here is to break through the binary discourse of "good" and "bad" to suggest that rural socialism in Bulgaria was both extremely difficult and increasingly tolerable.

It was for the latter reason, as well as the lack of options, that villagers were willing to "live within a lie," as Václav Havel (1985:31) characterizes socialist complicity, or help "paint" socialism, as Burawoy and Lukács (1992) describe it. Domestication also helps explain why so many Bulgarians voted for the Socialist Party in the three parliamentary elections between 1990 and 1994, twice electing a socialist majority. Many were supporting a domesticated socialism that was tolerable if not ideal. Their experience of domestication over the previous twenty-five years of reform (especially since the late 1960s) had convinced them that socialism, while rigid, was malleable—a feature likely to increase in the wake of 1989. They were understandably hesitant about embracing and promoting new arrangements that threatened past concessions and identities, even if they advocated democratic capitalism as a political philosophy. Others were simply weary of change or, as Bruce Grant (1995:39) puts it, were "exhausted by the macronarratives of the state." For them, domesticated socialism was better than starting over on another cycle of transition. In general, I believe early postcommunist actions in the village reveal an attempt to protect and continue prior improvements, to use the concessions and arrangements achieved under socialism to domesticate the revolution of 1989 as well. The early transition, however, proved more intractable than late socialism.

Certainly many Bulgarians never reached any accommodation with socialism, or found the resulting arrangements intolerable. They will likely object to the idea of domestication. Intellectuals and literati, for example, often felt their very identities censored along with their works, so it is not surprising that they provided the vanguard of the early antisocialist movement. Other cultural workers, such as the professional musicians described by Buchanan (1995), were more conflicted. Thus, domestication was not a uniform outcome; it depended on particular experiences with socialism, but not always in obvious or expected ways. For example, villagers were arguably the stepchildren of socialism, abused by a paternalistic state in deference to its "real" proletarian offspring. Abuses included collectivization, forced requisitions, paltry wages, low priority in the distribution of goods, and cultural devaluation. Yet in postsocialist parliamentary elections the countryside exhibited the strongest support for socialist candidates (Stokes 1993:177, Troxel 1993:415)—possible evidence of socialist domestication. Of course there were also many villagers whose experiences with the Communist Party or the socialist state rendered them rabidly anticommunist and ready to embrace any alternative, but not as many as one might think.

By investigating the arrangements that made it possible for Bulgarian villagers to domesticate socialism, we get a better understanding of the socialist system and its legacy in the transition. The very strategies and connections that villagers developed to survive (and even thrive) made the system increasingly intertwined and interdependent. The paternalistic state's total responsibility for the society forced it to accept many of these arrangements, even when they were in conflict with other state structures or objectives—a situation I call "conflicting complementarity." Such dissonance, however, provoked state redress through escalating reform programs, which in turn induced villagers and others to make new accommodations, further integrating the socialist system and provoking more radical reforms. By the time of the transition, the systemic connections had become so extensive and intricate that attempts to alter parts of the system had widespread and unexpected consequences. Even elements of socialist development that seemed preadapted to capitalism, such as industrialization and agricultural "modernization," were difficult to sustain without the complex network of relations in which they were previously embedded. The extent of the collapse tempered early enthusiasm for the transition, but attempts to continue socialist arrangements outside of the previous system eventually deepened the economic crisis. These dynamics can be seen most clearly in agriculture. While the Communist Party achieved a shift of economic gravity in favor of industry, the local integration of the socialist system continued to privilege agriculture beyond its macroeconomic significance. The centrality of agriculture, then, made it an early target of transition, and the resulting destruction negatively affected rural perceptions of transition. Subsequent efforts to maintain socialist agricultural institutions, however, eventually diminished their economic viability.

Since this argument revolves closely around life in the Bulgarian countryside, it is not necessarily transferable to other countries. Thus, the term "domestication" acquires further significance in that village practice transformed socialism into a particularly Bulgarian, or domestic, product. In remaking socialism, Bulgarians made it their own. Indeed, the very idea of domesticated socialism seems absurd for Ceauşescu's Romania. As that case disturbingly verifies, the potential impact of everyday practice is always shaped and constrained by the broader structures of domination and control within which people operate and maneuver. Thus, explaining *why* Bulgarian villagers were able to ameliorate the system would require a complementary ethnography of the socialist state itself, preferably in a comparative context. Fortunately for all involved, this is no longer possible. Domestication also depends critically on how villagers interpret their own circumstances, and these views are colored, in turn, by their historical consciousness and by their ideas about their own place in the world. In the history of socialism, then, domestication may be an exceptional outcome. If not, there are certainly extreme differences of degree in regard to both objective conditions and popular perceptions. I will leave such comparisons for another time (or someone else) and focus here on the Bulgarian experience I know well. The remainder of this introduction provides the necessary background to my descriptions. In the next section I explicate the theoretical components of my argument in more detail, making it, I hope, both more complex and more comprehensible. I then provide some basic information about Bulgaria, my fieldsite, and my research.

Socialism, Reform, and Agriculture

Given Marx's insistence on the primacy of economic factors, it is fitting to begin an inquiry into socialism with the economy, and here the dominant theme of both popular impression and scholarly analysis is shortage. For casual observers, long lines of frustrated consumers told the story; for scholars, Hungarian economist János Kornai provided a more extended depiction (1980). He suggested that "soft budget constraints," that is, the socialist state's commitment to support production units whether or not they were profitable, led to chronic investment hunger and the hoarding of resources, which in turn generated shortages throughout the economy. In other words, if enterprises do not have to show a profit, and if performance is judged on output alone, then they had better suck up all the labor and materials they can get. Numerous other factors, such as price controls and ideologically driven centralized planning, exacerbated the problem.

As devastating as shortages were for the macroeconomy, in the village and on the shop floor shortages exhibited positive as well as negative qualities. In Chapter 2 I suggest that shortages may have benefited local farm officials, granting them more discretion in following central plans. Since the state could not provide all the inputs necessary to fulfill production plans, managers often had to decide on allocations within planned parameters. They sometimes used this excuse to violate the plan more radically, planting different crops or not raising unprofitable livestock. Burawoy and Lukács (1992:18–19) make a similar argument about the increased autonomy gained on the shop floor, where pervasive shortage forced workers to improvise. Such flexibility might antagonize or threaten superiors, but it might also be tolerated if the results reflected well on the supervisors. Thus, ethnographic attention to shortage exposes a more essential characteristic of socialism: the problems of the system often had beneficial effects.

Nowhere is this characteristic more evident than in regard to the so-called informal sector, or second economy. Faced with shortages and bureaucratic barriers, socialist citizens pursued alternative means, from barter and nepotism to bribery and theft, to acquire desired goods, services, and influence. This collection of informal activities became another standard attribute of socialism. However, according to Verdery (1991:421), this socialist characteristic ran directly counter to socialism's central imperative: increasing the bureaucracy's capacity to allocate. As she points out, the bureaucracy's drive to control allocation was advanced not only by increasing resources for distribution but also by destroying alternate avenues of allocation, like the second economy. At the same time the second economy was essential for supplying the livelihood of the population, so "there remained a constant tension between suppressing and permitting a certain amount of secondary economic activity" (Verdery 1991: 423). In Chapter 5 I examine in detail the various benefits of informal activities for both individuals and the society. To give only one example, the opportunity for theft on the job secured workers in occupations that were otherwise unattractive. These connections provide compelling evidence that negative aspects of socialism often had benefits and as a result had to be tolerated, even accommodated.

It is this conflict between the drawbacks and benefits of everyday practice that lies at the heart of socialism. Conflict was inevitable because contrary elements were united under an all-encompassing state where they became increasingly intertwined. I characterize this complex dynamic as "conflicting complementarity." By this oxymoron I hope to capture the constant tension generated by socialism's totalizing logic—its holistic integration of political, economic, and social structures. Every aspect of the society was integrated through the state apparatus. Attempting to manage all dimensions of their societies, socialist states left no area outside their purview or, more to the point, beyond their responsibility. Any solution that caused problems elsewhere was just another problem for the state. There was no area of life that could be sacrificed with impunity, no private sector to be blamed or called on to contribute. Consequently, socialist planners and leaders found themselves constantly balancing potentially contradictory demands to achieve some sort of complementarity.

Some became quite adept at the process, which is how these states operated as effectively as they did from the 1960s to 1989. To return to the example of informality, it certainly threatened bureaucratic control, but at the same time it helped fulfill the state's responsibility of provisioning society, indirectly enhancing the bureaucracy's claim to exercise control. Ultimately at odds, however, such arrangements were inherently unstable, requiring continual renegotiation. The adjustments themselves then generated ever more intricate connections. Eventually a single social problem, such as theft, could become elemental to numerous state processes, not only keeping people in undesirable jobs but ensuring that villagers had the resources to raise livestock for the state and helping to recycle wasted state resources.

As the connections thickened, state control grew ever more tenuous and indeterminate. Ironically, then, the attempt of the socialist state to control everything did not lead to total state control as old models of totalitarianism implied (Friedrich and Brzezinski 1956, Arendt 1966) but to an uncontrollable system more in keeping with models of chaos theory (Gleick 1987). Not only were there too many components to manage, but

they were increasingly linked to each other in multiple, incompletely un-
derstood ways. Planning thus became more and more ineffectual: the socialist state retained total responsibility but could actually control less and
less—an ominous combination. Centralized control continued to shape
socialist developments, but in unplanned and ultimately uncontrollable
ways, culminating in the transition itself. As connections between socialist
practices and among individuals became increasingly complex, the actions of everyday people, like the proverbial flapping of butterfly wings,
had ramifications throughout the system, eventually observable on the
macro level. Until the transition, however, the state's total responsibility
for society forced officials to keep trying to control these forces and developments, and each attempt established more connections and adapta-
tions. Thus, in their attempt to build communism they unwittingly constructed the very social complexity that rendered central planning and
control impossible.

Socialist states were driven to keep trying, not only by the desire of state
leaders to maintain legitimacy and power but by the international context
within which they existed—that is, a socialist bloc in which the Soviet
Union often limited the space of member states to maneuver. East European leaders had to negotiate between local practice and Soviet hegemony. As the Hungarian Revolution and the Prague Spring demonstrated, substantially changing the system (redefining the objectives) was
not an option. This forced leaders and citizens to find solutions to socialist problems *within* certain socialist parameters, which generated ever
more systemic connections, with their attendant conflicts, and kept some
of the most effective solutions in the informal sector. These developments, however, could provoke minor shifts and alterations in the parameters themselves through the process of "reform."

Perhaps no topic of east European political economy has received as
much scholarly attention as reform. My purpose here is not to review this
research, a task done by others (e.g., Johnson 1989), but rather to see
how the reform process put a particular stamp on the socialist system,
with consequences that outlasted the eclipse of reform by the transition.
Despite constant failures, the reform dynamic provided a conduit between village practice and state planning that was essential to the process
of domestication. Of course reform was not the only link, and in this
sense there were reforms without reform programs. For example, the declining authority of village administrators and party leaders was hardly
programmatic. Still, even these outcomes were often linked to other official reform projects.

The era of reform in eastern Europe began in the late 1950s. Up to that point, economic development had followed the Stalinist model of rapid expansion of industrial capacity through massive investment in heavy industry, subsidized by agricultural resources extracted via collectivization. This strategy proved effective for a "'catch up' type" of economic development (Höhmann 1982:1), but by the late 1950s it was producing diminishing returns. Since the communist objective was more ideologically important than the means to achieve it, new strategies were required to continue economic development and to maintain popular confidence in utopian possibilities. Reform emerged to answer this call.

Once reform was initiated, however, it was both unattainable and unstoppable. Most analyses focus on the former. The most common explanation for why reforms failed is that they were obstructed by functionaries of the system whose power and privileges were threatened by proposed changes. If reform managed to gain the upper hand anyway, as in Hungary in 1956 or Czechoslovakia in 1968, the same pressures emerged on an international scale, with the beneficiaries of global socialism applying the brakes. At the same time, the failure of reform had a broader basis that harks back to the conflicting complementarity of socialist society and the objectives of socialist ideology. As policymakers oversaw every dimension of society, their reform programs for one sector invariably affected other sectors as well. More often than not, these secondary effects were ideologically undesirable (Lowenthal 1970) or in conflict with other objectives and necessities, notably, centralized political control (Burks 1973).

This very dynamic is also why reform was unstoppable. The failure of reforms not only called for new initiatives, but the secondary effects of reform programs also required reform treatments. In other words, the unintended consequences of reforms provided the motivation for subsequent reforms. Some analysts have presented this dynamic as an alternation between reform initiatives and reversals—advance and retreat. In an insightful version of this perspective, Laky (1980) lays out what he calls the "hidden mechanisms of recentralization," which inevitably countered decentralizing reforms. While enlightening, this perspective is also somewhat distorting since, as Lewin (1988:1–2) points out, the "freeze" following the "thaw" never completely returned society to its pre-reform arrangements. So, what may appear as merely oscillation can still be seen as an ongoing progression of reforms. Thus, the famous "treadmill" metaphor of socialist economic reform, suggested by Schroeder (1982, 1991) and taken up by several other scholars (e.g., Jackson 1988, Ruble 1991), is dangerously misleading. The perpetual cycle of reforms did not keep these economies and polities in the exact same place, as the image of a treadmill suggests. The process itself had effects on the macro and the micro level. Thus, we must see reform as both a solution and a problem, or as Korbonski (1975, 1989) puts it, as cause and effect of social, political, and economic change.

This interaction fueled the perpetual reform process that characterized most socialist societies and established reform as an essential component of the system. In fact, Baylis (1971) suggests that reform itself became an element of communist ideology (see also Taras 1984). Continual reform, in turn, provided the inspiration for economic experimentation, which sustained socialist economic momentum from the 1960s to the transition. As "reform" became increasingly synonymous with "change," the institutional centrality of reform eased the way for changes not connected to reform programs (McIntyre 1988b). However, after recurrent disappointments, people became skeptical of reform promises. As Tamás Krausz put it: "In Hungary we have had reforms for 20 years now—permanent reform you might say. So when Hungarians hear the word 'reform' it doesn't mean anything to them" (Hockenos 1990).[1] The need for ever more extreme programs to break through escalating popular fatigue and skepticism contributed to the transition.

From this perspective, the transition was not a completely novel idea but the result of the snowballing of reforms under way in eastern Europe for three decades. With reform operating almost like a positive feedback system, a radical program was overdetermined. When the Soviet Union itself took the lead with perestroika, the progression was not only tolerated but actually encouraged and hastened. What distinguished this last stage, however, was that it cut some of the connections officially binding and integrating all dimensions of society, thereby terminating some limits to the reform process that had developed under socialism. It did not, however, terminate the political, economic, and social foci of prior reforms—they reemerged as objectives of transition.

Not surprisingly, the transition bears the marks of its reform heritage. First, given that the starting point in 1989 was already a significantly reformed variant of socialism, only extreme changes could qualify as truly transitional. Decentralizing, privatizing, and democratizing reforms were all under way in rural Bulgaria before 1989. Local multicandidate, secret-

---

1. This dovetails with what Habermas (1986) calls the "exhaustion of utopian energies" in western Europe and Zukin's (1992) description of utopian exhaustion in the urban United States. Although the sources of each are different, their confluence may have been mutually reinforcing in the global context.

by 1988 – already experimenting with capitalist economic ideas

ballot elections were held in 1988, and the experimental leasing of large
tracts of cooperative land to private farmers began the same year. Village
leaders had become increasingly dependent on local producers and as a
result had already lost much of the political control stereotypically attributed to communist authoritarianism. So, it was radically reformed socialism that provided the standard against which to measure capitalist democracy, and this accounts in part for the extremism that dominated the early
discourse on transition. At the same time, some of the negative consequences of this type of restructuring were also evident in the village by
1988, notably new shortages of products, increasing labor shortages, im-
pending signs of inequality, and increasing fear of theft. Having had a
taste of these results, villagers thought twice about plunging headlong
into more radical reforms.

Such hesitancy is particularly significant because the development of
democratic capitalism ideally hinges on individual initiative. In this regard
another limitation inherited from reform was made explicit in the commentary that began this introduction: an exhaustion with change. People
I spoke with were tired of living vicariously in the future through the
political rhetoric of change. They certainly did not want stasis, but they
wanted change that focused on their immediate lives, not a new millen-
nium. For those Bulgarians who believed that they had seized the day in
1989, the ensuing transition rhetoric with its recycled ideas of sacrifice for
the future irritated rather than inspired.

While reform dynamics led to the transition, the intricate interrelations
they produced within a system of conflicting complementarity ironically
made it impossible to simply transfer socialist achievements into a capitalist context. Since so many aspects of the socialist system were intertwined,
any attempt to get rid of a particular practice or institution had devastating impacts on the others. More often than not the results were unexpected, for the complete network of connections was impossible to fully
chart.[2] One could not simply privatize a factory and expect it to keep
producing, much less improve, when, as we will see in Chapter 4, the
plant itself was more valuable for its support of local agricultural production than for its own products, or when its supply of raw materials was
assured only by the informal social relations of its manager. As a result of
such interdependencies many socialist enterprises simply collapsed after

2. Furthermore, the totalizing state structure within which these connections developed and adjusted was itself a target of transition, ensuring more severe consequences.

because of previous informal running the privatization of factories was hugely negative, Not positive

1989, while others survived as the private property of previous managers and political leaders who used these same connections to gain ownership—a process referred to variously as political capitalism, spontaneous privatization, or *nomenklatura* buyouts (Frydman et al. 1993, Staniszkis 1991, Stark 1990). Some of these survivors continued to depend on state subsidies or state-owned suppliers. The long-term limitations of these arrangements were painfully evident by 1996.

Such industrial developments are central to the transition, but agriculture provides perhaps a clearer illustration of socialist dynamics and their legacy in the transition. Socialism reproduced many changes typical of capitalist agricultural development, notably what can be glossed as a disengagement from agriculture. By this I refer to the global trend whereby ever fewer individuals proportionately depend on the agricultural enterprise for their primary support. For many who remain involved to some degree in agricultural production, either as wage workers or part-time subsistence gardeners, there is a parallel disengagement from agricultural identities. Such developments were nearly axiomatic to the definitive socialist agricultural objective—collectivization, which replaced peasants with machines and decreased the productive control of remaining farmworkers. In the context of simultaneous industrialization, these changes severely threatened the value of agriculture. Devaluation proceeded from the ideological equating of development with industrialization, the valorization of the proletariat, and the extraction of resources from agriculture to underwrite industrialization—all unconvincingly camouflaged by transparent propaganda stressing worker-peasant alliance and interdependence. This devaluation provoked a disengagement from agriculture, evident in rural out-migration, daily commuting to urban workplaces, and the subsequent industrial development of the countryside itself. As a result farming slipped to secondary importance in most of the collectivized countries of eastern Europe. For example, by the eve of transition in Bulgaria, agriculture accounted for only 11.2 percent of net material product, consumed just 8.3 percent of fixed investment, and employed barely 18 percent of the country's workforce (*Statisticheski Godishnik* 1993:57, 86, 100, 257).

The operation of socialism as a system of conflicting complementarity, however, kept agriculture and villagers more economically and politically significant than such statistics might suggest in a capitalist context. Since various agricultural products were exported to Western countries for hard currencies, they contributed far more to the economy than either their numbers or their value in socialist currencies implied. Begg and Meurs (n.d.) point out that Bulgarian agriculture accounted for nearly 27 percent of exports to nonsocialist countries in 1989, the proceeds of which financed important hard-currency imports. This situation had ramifications for individual villages. For example, the export value of these products ensured that managers of state industries would sacrifice their workers for agricultural brigades whenever needed.

Also apparent in the villages was the well-known importance of so-called subsistence plots, which literally kept the national economy running by providing subsistence for rural workers under conditions of low wages, shortages, and poor distribution. This resource was essential for villagers, and their easy access to it allowed the state to continue privileging cities in the allocation of wage funds and scarce consumer goods. The plots were also important for the country as a whole, since villagers not only supplied their immediate families but urban relatives, town markets, and even state procurement agencies. Urban migration actually intensified this importance, increasing the significance of agriculture rather than diminishing it. Thus, as we will see in Chapter 4, agricultural concerns in a partially industrialized Bulgarian village continued to structure nonagricultural developments, even so far as to derail industrial reform programs. Elsewhere (Creed 1995a) I referred to this as the "domestication of industry." Obviously, such a process was a major component in the more general domestication of socialism, and as such it also underlines the centrality of agriculture to the larger process. In a crystalline illustration of conflicting complementarity, tensions between industry and agriculture ironically verified their continued interaction, which had been an objective of reform policies.

The importance of agriculture granted it influence throughout the society, which kept farming from disappearing altogether—as happened in some capitalist cases of agricultural disengagement (see Douglass 1975, Greenwood 1976)—and granted villagers significant clout in resisting state policies or demands, especially those that might affect agricultural activity. The intricate interactions between agriculture and the rest of society prevented some types of agricultural labor from being thoroughly commoditized,[3] which helped maintain a cultural association among agri-

3. The contrast with Lampland's (1995) findings bears comment. I believe the extensive reforms in Hungary, which allowed more private entrepreneurial agriculture (Szelényi 1988), encouraged the commodification of agricultural labor in rural Hungary to a slightly greater degree than in other collectivized countries, although the process was clearly evident throughout the region.

culture, the cooperative farm, and the village, even as the latter became economically diversified. Through rural economic diversification, however, villagers developed new identities not linked exclusively to farming, even as they continued the part-time agricultural involvements essential to the socialist system. Thus, the apparent decline in full-time "farmers" did not reflect a decline in the importance of agriculture. Just as there were formal and informal economies, the official socialist emphasis on industry was shadowed by the real significance of agriculture.[4] This value made it a powerful tool for villagers in the work of domestication.

The role of agriculture had major consequences for the transition. Most important, agriculture's significance and meaning for socialism made it an early target of transition enthusiasm (just as it was the early target of communist attention after World War II and the continual focus of socialist reform programs afterward). For example, as I show in Chapter 6, the first nonsocialist government in Bulgaria targeted the cooperative farm system for complete liquidation. This attempt reverberated throughout the whole society, not only threatening agriculture but its entire milieu, including rural industries and attendant village identities. These threats provoked rural outrage and even urban consternation, which often translated into support for the Socialist Party. Socialist leaders then overreacted by restraining economic reforms generally, which, over time, also threatened the operation of cooperative farms. Both political groups recognized the importance of agriculture to the socialist system and attended to it for that reason, albeit with opposite intentions. But they failed to appreciate the full density of the connections and interactions developed during decades of conflicting complementarity. In the following pages I hope to convey some of that complexity as it evolved in Bulgaria.

Why Bulgaria? Scholarly and Historical Background

My desire to contribute to an ethnographic model of socialism immediately suggested Bulgaria because it had a reputation as one of the most loyal Soviet satellites and hence one of the most orthodox socialist countries. Indeed, colleagues in the United State (and to my later surprise, Bulgarian villagers themselves) sometimes referred to Bulgaria sarcasti-

---

4. I am indebted to Katherine Verdery for this phrasing.

cally as the sixteenth Soviet republic. I surmised that a robust challenge to existing understandings of socialism would have to come from an ortho-dox case rather than one that could be explained away as an exception. Cumulative research has since corrected the stereotype of Bulgarian or-thodoxy (Stillman and Bass 1955, McIntyre 1988a, Crampton 1988), but its socialist idiosyncrasies remain less extreme than those of other coun-tries in the region. In addition, Bulgaria was among the least studied of socialist countries, especially in regard to ethnographic research. By the mid-1980s only a couple Western ethnographers had worked in socialist Bulgaria.[5] Of course, these two characteristics were related: an aspect of socialist orthodoxy was its closed door to outsiders, especially Westerners. In this way, the difficulty of getting ethnographic access to Bulgaria was part of its attraction.

Bulgaria was also attractive because I intended to focus on collectiviza-tion and agrarian reform. As a classic policy of the communist state, di-rectly affecting the bulk of the population, collectivization offered a use-ful window into how socialism actually worked. This conclusion, of course, reflected the insights of ethnographers working on collectivized agricul-ture elsewhere in eastern Europe (e.g., Bell 1984, Kideckel 1982, Verdery 1983) and continues to be supported (Lampland 1995, Vasary 1987). In this respect as well, Bulgaria was a perfect choice: as I show in Chapter 2 Bulgaria pursued a policy of agricultural concentration unmatched out-side the Soviet Union.

My attraction was confirmed by Bulgaria's checkered past, which prom-ised an interesting agrarian background from which to examine and plot socialist developments. In regard to the issues at hand, we can start with the Ottoman period, which lasted from the late fourteenth to the late nineteenth centuries, and was still prominent in the historical conscious-ness of villagers in the late 1980s. Upon conquest, the Sultan claimed rights to all Bulgarian land, much of which he allotted to the support of warriors, higher officials, royalty, and religious and educational organiza-tions. These organizations or individuals received tribute from the Bulgar-ian peasants, who continued to farm the land much like small owners.

5. These included Canadian anthropologist Eleanor Smollett (1980) and American folk-lorist-anthropologist Carol Silverman (1983). American sociologist Roger Whitaker (1979) had conducted a follow-up to Irwin Sanders's (1949) well-known interwar village study, in-cluding a comparison with another village as well, but it was based primarily on survey data. American ethnomusicologist Donna Buchanan (1991) and Australian anthropologist Deema Kaneff (1992) began fieldwork while I was in the field.

Historians debate the extent to which these arrangements gave way to more extractive types of holdings known as *chifliks* (cf. Crampton 1981: 173 and Jelavich 1983:95). But overall the occupation seems to have maintained what amounted to a rather egalitarian system of peasant smallholdings (Crampton 1981:176, Lampe and Jackson 1982:152, Todorov 1977:319).

Ottoman domination left many other marks on Bulgarian society and culture (Todorova 1996). The most obvious is a sizable Turkish minority (approximately 10 percent of the current population), with associated ethnic tensions (Bates 1994, Creed 1990), and a smaller population of "Pomaks," descendants of Bulgarians who converted to Islam during the Ottoman era (Silverman 1984). More generally, "500 years of Turkish servitude" is likely to be invoked by Bulgarians as an explanation for anything from the level of economic development to the lack of a significant underground communist opposition. In the early 1990s antisocialist supporters used it to explain continued popular support for the Socialist Party. Many times the excuse was offered in jest, but it often seemed to include both jest and seriousness in proportions difficult to determine.

Ottoman control lasted until the Russians drove the Turks out of Bulgaria in the Russo-Turkish war of 1877–78—an event that contributed to Bulgarians' benign (by east European standards) attitude toward Russia and the Soviet Union. Following the liberation, a large independent Bulgaria was established by the Treaty of San Stefano. West European powers, fearful of Russian influence in the Balkans, would have none of this treaty and called an international conference in Berlin to trim down the borders of the new Bulgarian state. Irredentist desires for the San Stefano borders would eventually drive Bulgarian involvement in two Balkan conflicts and two world wars.

After liberation, the country imported royalty from western Europe and set up a constitutional monarchy, but by the 1930s political developments replicated the regional trend toward dictatorship. Perhaps the most distinctive element of Bulgaria's interwar politics, and one of the most interesting from the point of agricultural change, was the election of Agrarian governments in 1919 and 1920, albeit with some subterfuge on the part of the Agrarian leader and prime minister, Alexander Stamboliiski. His programs included the concept of "labor property," according to which land should belong to whoever worked it, and he instigated limited land reforms toward this end. Stamboliiski competed for mass support, however, with the Bulgarian Communist Party, founded in 1891, eight years earlier than the Agrarian Party. The communists were fairly successful in mobilizing rural support, despite ideological conflicts at high levels over the appropriate role of the peasantry in a putatively proletarian party. For example, in the municipal election of December 1919, the Communist Party won control of 65 village councils. Stamboliiski dissolved them and scheduled new elections for 1921, in which the Communist Party emerged with control of 104 village councils (Rothschild 1959:107). The party attempted to expand this rural base without changing its national-level rhetoric by appealing individually to village Agrarian Union cells to transfer their allegiance to the Communist Party (Rothschild 1959:110). This ensured extensive communist agitation in the villages, despite the limited concern for farmers in the communist platform and its dismissal of Stamboliiski's reforms as bourgeois half-measures.

In the end it was not the communists but the right wing of the Bulgarian political spectrum that ended Stamboliiski's programs with a coup in 1923. As there was no love lost between the Agrarians and the communists, the latter made no attempt to intervene. The Comintern in Moscow was less than pleased about this passivity and made its feelings known to the Bulgarian Communist Party. The party quickly changed its mind and launched an attack on the Rightist government, which became known as the September Uprising. The uprising gained widespread support only in a few areas of the country and was suppressed within a week. Following the failed uprising, the Communist Party was outlawed and went underground. A legally constituted Worker's Party was created in 1927 and operated as a parallel communist front. According to Oren (1971:109), the drop in party membership in the 1930s should be attributed to this repression and disorganization rather than a decline in the appeal of communism. Even with this decline, Oren contends, the "overwhelming majority" of party members in the 1930s remained peasants, and there was continual illegal communist agitation in the countryside.

After a doomed attempt to maintain neutrality, Bulgaria ended up on the Axis side in World War II, becoming a client state of Germany. Although never really occupied, the country was "liberated" a second time by Russian troops (this time as part of the Soviet army) on September 9, 1944. The event brought postwar Bulgarian politics decidedly into the Soviet orbit for the next forty-five years. The "9th of September" was designated as the principal national holiday and became synonymous with the beginning of the communist era.

The country's experience with communist political economy followed the broad outlines previously discussed—extensive industrialization followed by reform. The latter commenced in the early 1960s. According to Feiwel (1979:72), the first reform blueprint included the familiar objectives of reducing top-down planning and increasing the role of the profit motive. The Prague Spring in 1968 redirected the reform agenda of the 1970s from general structural change toward specific alterations of particular sectors and enterprises (see Feiwel 1977, 1982). Still, as previously noted, villagers saw the late 1960s and early 1970s as a turning point. The combined impact of agricultural mechanization, rural industrialization, and expanded subsistence possibilities (each to be described in the following chapters) made this a watershed period in domestication. By the end of the 1970s a New Economic Mechanism (NEM) was put forward, reestablishing radical systemic alteration as an objective (Crampton 1988). Never living up to expectations, the NEM gave way to a newer mechanism in 1986 (Jackson 1988), this being subsequently recast as *pre-ustroystvo*, the Bulgarian equivalent of perestroika (Pitassio 1989).[6] This restructuring was in turn the segue to transition.

Perestroika began at the top of Bulgarian society, where it was forced on political leaders by Soviet decisions, but it soon generated popular momentum. The Soviet press had always been readily available in Bulgaria, and this continued even after it became more open. This had two converging effects: it stimulated oppositional ideas and removed the sense of relative advantage Bulgarians had felt vis-à-vis the Soviet Union. As one professor and opposition leader put it, "No matter how bad things were in the past, we always consoled ourselves with the knowledge that we were much better off than Soviet citizens. By 1987 this was no longer true." This realization had a psychologically depressing effect that was paradoxically invigorating regarding resistance. Local opposition and dissent started to coalesce in late 1987. By January 1988 the Independent Society for the Defense of Human Rights had formed in delayed response to the horrors of the assimilation campaign against the Turkish minority (see Bates 1994, 1995). In March 1988 concern over chlorine gas coming across the Danube from Romania to the Bulgarian town of Ruse mobilized a small group called the Committee for the Ecological Defense of

6. The Bulgarian Communist Party sometimes condensed the reform dynamic previously described into a single effort, combining decentralizing reforms with centralizing ones. For example, plans to devolve some decision making to the county level in 1987 and 1988 were combined with a reduction in the number of counties, from twenty-eight *okruga* to seven *oblasti*. So while the new counties ended up with more autonomy and responsibility, they were fewer in number than before and thus more easily coordinated at the national level. Similar combinations were evident in agricultural reform policies.

Ruse. A year later it merged with members of the Club for Glasnost and Perestroika, a discussion group founded in November 1988 by well-placed intellectuals, to form Eco-Glasnost (Mitsuda and Pashev 1995). An independent trade union, *Podkrepa*, was founded in February 1989. These groups and others, both new and revived from the interwar period, became important fomenters of opposition during 1989.

Such developments may have helped Todor Zhivkov, a longtime communist leader unaccustomed to dissent, see the writing on the wall, but the collapse of "the wall" and parallel events elsewhere in eastern Europe probably had a greater impact. He was also under pressure to step down from members of his own party who hoped to ensure their political future by playing a role in his ouster. Zhivkov resigned on November 10, 1989, and that date became the symbolic marker of the democratic revolution. Within two months the parliament abolished the leading role of the Communist Party. The ease with which the communists relinquished control not only reflects international circumstances but also the degree to which their domestic power had been undercut at all levels.

Communist and opposition representatives subsequently negotiated arrangements for a transitional government, including a 400-seat parliament with half the seats allotted proportionally to parties receiving at least 4 percent of the popular vote and the other half reserved for candidates getting clear majorities. The first election was set for June 10, 1990, with runoffs on June 17. The communists, renamed the Bulgarian Socialist Party (BSP), received 47.15 percent of the vote, which translated into a 52.7 percent majority in parliament. Only three other parties passed the 4 percent threshold. The Bulgarian National Agrarian Union received 8 percent of the popular vote but only 4 percent of parliament, since its candidates failed to win any majority seats. The Movement for Rights and Freedoms (MRF), which was basically the party of the Turkish minority, got 5.75 percent of the seats. The rest of the seats were occupied by representatives of the Union of Democratic Forces (UDF), which was actually an umbrella organization of various antisocialist parties, making it the primary opposition. The UDF embarked on a strategy of noncooperation, which gained them the concession of a UDF president (Zhelyu Zhelev), and eventually provoked the resignation of the socialist government in November 1990. President Zhelev asked Dimitur Popov, an independent judge, to form a quasi–coalition government, which survived the difficulties of extensive food and fuel shortages in early 1991 to pass the long-awaited land law, approve a new constitution, and change the structure of parliament, eliminating the majority seats and increasing the number of proportional seats to 240.

New elections were then held in October 1991, and despite having lost a few separatist elements, the Union of Democratic Forces won the elections with 34.4 percent of the popular vote. It ruled in unofficial coalition with the Movement for Rights and Freedoms, which was the only other party besides the BSP to surpass the 4 percent threshold, giving the MRF the balance of power. During the first half of 1992 the UDF government passed significant legislation, including the passage of laws for the restitution of property and the amendment of the land law to initiate decollectivization. But the UDF's unity was based primarily on anticommunism and was damaged by the process of policy making, which exposed the differences between UDF constituencies. So the UDF continued to fracture internally. At the same time, the alliance with the MRF began to unravel as economic programs, such as amendments to the land law, adversely affected the Turkish population.

In October 1992, the UDF government failed a confidence vote, provoking a political crisis that lasted two months. New elections were avoided when Lyuben Berov, an economic historian and former advisor to President Zhelev, put together a government with a MRF mandate and BSP support. This government managed fairly well under the circumstances, but the bipolar parliament and increasing dissension in the UDF, including conflict with its most popular figure, President Zhelev, made the government increasingly unstable. Elections were eventually set for December 1994. The BSP (now in coalition with a branch of the Agrarian Party and a green party) was returned to power with 43.5 percent of the popular vote, which translated into approximately 52 percent of the seats in parliament. The UDF obtained nearly 29 percent of the seats for its 24.23 percent of the vote. The remaining seats were divided between the MRF and two new parliamentary groups: the Bulgarian Business Bloc and the People's Union (a coalition of another Agrarian party and the Democratic Party).

Whether the new government, headed by Zhan Videnov, saw the election results as a popular rejection of transition or whether the government was simply determined to protect partisan and personal interests is debatable, but it made almost no progress toward economic reform and seemed to promote economic corruption. By the middle of 1996 revived inflation and plummeting currency values (provoked in part by low foreign reserves and high debt) again eroded confidence in the government and threatened to unseat the socialists.

A clear sign of trouble came in November 1996 when the Socialist can-
didate for president lost by a landslide to his UDF opponent, Petur
Stoyanov. This inspired the UDF to increase protest action and shook up
the BSP, leading to Videnov's resignation in December. The UDF then
joined other antisocialist groups in a coalition known as the United Democratic Forces (in distinction to the Union of Democratic Forces). As the
semantic similarity suggests, the Union remained the dominant partner.
The coalition's objective was to stop the BSP from forming another government in order to force new elections. By early 1997, daily demonstrations organized by the coalition rocked the entire country. Nourished by
near hyperinflation, as well as fuel and grain shortages, these demonstrations eventually developed into strike actions and street barricades, which
in February 1997 forced the BSP to relent.

New elections were held the following April. The United Democratic
Forces won a decisive victory, securing approximately 52 percent of the
vote. The BSP received only 22 percent, but its more centrist offshoot,
known as the Euroleft, acquired an additional 5.6 percent. The MRF con-
tended in a new coalition called the Union for National Salvation, which
picked up 7.6 percent of the vote. The Business Bloc, with nearly 5 percent, was the only other party to pass the 4 percent threshold. While this
result is certainly understandable, it continues the pendulum effect that
has come to characterize postsocialist politics in Bulgaria.

Notes on Location and Method

I arrived in Bulgaria for my first period of fieldwork in January of 1987,
during the last major reform drive leading to the transition. I intended to
spend a few weeks talking with scholars and interviewing officials about
the rural situation while I located a village fieldsite. As a foreigner I
needed official permission and dispensation to even live in a village, especially with a Bulgarian family, so I was dependent on the intercession of
my affiliate institution, the Institute of Sociology. After nearly three
months of consultations with various specialists and scholars in Sofia I
began to think that (as many American colleagues had predicted) I would
never get to the countryside.

Just at that point the Institute informed me that arrangements had
been made for me to live in the village of Zamfirovo in the northwest of

the country, about two and a half hours across the Balkan mountains from Sofia, off the main road between the small town of Berkovitza and the county capital, Mihailovgrad.[7] I questioned their choice, which they said had been made in consultation with the National Agro-Industrial Union, but queries as to why this particular village were always answered in vague generalities about it being a good size or a good location, which could have been said of numerous other villages as well. They assured me that it met the criteria I had requested, and I was too relieved at having finally received the requisite permission to push the issue further. I was subsequently told that the Ministry of the Interior (the police) had been involved, which was no surprise, and that the lack of a Turkish minority in the area was a consideration. I later heard that someone involved in the decision had personal connections in the village, but I am still not certain who made the final decision and why.

My fear that Zamfirovo was a model village chosen to give me a good impression was dismissed on arrival. Located in the Balkan foothills, with poor-quality land and limited water supplies, its agricultural situation could hardly be called ideal. Zamfirovo was also fairly isolated, and there was even a Turk interned there for refusing to change his name in the recent assimilation campaign—an extreme irony if the choice of Zamfirovo was intended to keep me away from the Turkish minority. In these respects the choice of Zamfirovo surprised me. I was less surprised by the village's numerous nonagricultural enterprises, since that was an issue in my research project and I had asked for a village that was economically viable rather than "disappearing," as some friends referred to the many tiny villages populated only by retirees. Given the rich diversity of the Bulgarian countryside, there can be no "typical" Bulgarian village. Nevertheless, after twenty months living in Zamfirovo and traveling elsewhere in the country, I came to see my new home as somewhat exceptional in the number of nonagricultural opportunities for employment but otherwise not radically different from other large Bulgarian villages. Zamfirovo's most distinctive feature was not physical, fiscal, or demographic but the somewhat greater commitment of its residents to socialist politics. It shared this characteristic with other villages in the county, and this may have been a factor in my placement there. Local residents attributed their socialist leanings to the particular history of the area.

7. Given the officiousness of my stay, any attempt to disguise the name and location of the village would be futile, but I have altered identifying characteristics of individuals in order to protect their privacy.

Not much is known of the early history of Zamfirovo. The ruined walls
of a late-Roman fortress remain atop one of the surrounding hills, but
their exact date has not been ascertained. According to one historical
report the village has existed at least since the eleventh or twelfth century.
It is mentioned in Turkish documents from the early seventeenth century
as "Gushaniche," a version of "Gushantsi," its name prior to the 9th of
September. At some point in Turkish times there were two Ottoman over-
lords controlling most of the land, and during the Russo-Turkish war,
Russian forces passed through the village.

After the 9th of September the name of the village was changed to
Zamfirovo in honor of its favorite son and early communist activist, Zamfir Popov. Under his leadership in 1918–19, the village Communist Party
increased tenfold to eighty members, and he was elected as a representative to government councils at both local and district levels. After the
Communist Party's about-face on the anti-Agrarian coup in 1923, Zamfir
Popov organized a revolutionary committee and led a brigade of 200 men
against the forces of the new government, contributing to the region's
fame as one of the few areas mobilized for the uprising. Thanks to this
history, Zamfirovo not only got a new name after the 9th of September
but acquired glory and a new identity as a politically active village. This
was the history recited by villagers to account for the area's commitment
to socialist politics. However, as the first multiparty elections in 1991 revealed, this commitment was not restricted to the northwest part of the
country.

Local socialist politics certainly played a role in the village's response to
the transition, although this political history is difficult to characterize.
Prior to 1944 village leaders were primarily lawyers dispatched from Sofia
or nearby cities. In the early years after the 9th of September, village
leaders were selected from local residents who had past claims to leftist
politics: perhaps having been members of the Communist Party or having
been involved even marginally in the resistance. Subsequently, in the
1950s, they were replaced by villagers selected by higher organs for their
leadership potential and sent to party training schools. Of course, some of
these promising politicians were selected on the basis of personal connections to higher-level officials. Several had social relations with a local resident who had attained national importance based on his resistance activity as a communist during the war.

This cohort of leaders maintained control of the village until the 1980s,
but, as we will see in succeeding chapters, the actual power associated

with their positions gradually eroded beneath them. This erosion was an important contribution to the perception of domestication and helps explain continued local support for socialism. Most Zamfirovo villagers detested the petty privileges and nepotism of local communist leaders, but by the mid-1980s they were no longer intimidated by them. The officials empowered to send people to work camps in the 1950s could not force residents to fix the potholes in front of their houses in the 1980s. So while urban opposition leaders swore that the electoral support for the Socialist Party in the 1990 elections was a reflection of the powerful hold of communist leaders in the villages, it was just the opposite in Zamfirovo. Villagers clung to the socialist system in part because local communist leaders no longer controlled their lives to the degree they did in the past. With this displacement of power, and the comcomitant improvement of rural economic conditions, the very meaning of socialism shifted.

I believe the domestication of socialism in Zamfirovo, concurrent with the continuing difficulty of life there, helps explain the ambivalent and sometimes contradictory legacy of socialism. I also believe this insight would apply to much of rural Bulgaria, but I do not suggest that Zamfirovo is representative of the country. Indeed, one of the important points of this study is that socialism and the transition were varied experiences. Furthermore, my conclusions about Zamfirovo were colored by my own personal experiences there. During the socialist period I was warmly received and helped by most people I met, but some individuals were understandably suspicious, so I desisted approaching them. I never attempted to talk with the interned Turk, and did not pursue anything beyond casual interaction with the village Roma (Gypsies). Neither were the subjects of my research, and since I knew my activities were monitored, I did not want to raise undue suspicion. Conversely, other individuals were solicitous of my friendship, and their views may color my insights more than others. Similarly, the officiousness of my presence meant that I was necessarily associated with village officials, which probably alienated some other villagers. The most disgruntled, however, seemed attracted to me for that very reason and supplied me with constant criticisms and information to counter official testimony. Given these potential distortions, it was essential to have personal experiences and observations from which to evaluate contrary reports.

My reception changed with the transition, but this did not make things universally easier for field research. In some ways, my official status under the socialist system made it easier to get information from village and county bureaucrats who no longer felt compelled to deal with me after the transition. But some of those who had been hesitant to speak with me before became quite conversant. They admitted that they had been afraid of being questioned by the police if they spoke with me or that I might get them into trouble with something I wrote. On the other hand, a prior friend who became disenchanted with the results of the transition decided my presence in 1988 had something to do with it and swore off further communication. A few villagers who previously thought I was a spy for the United States concluded that my return in 1992 meant I had become a spy for the Socialist Party, joining the few villagers (and, to my amazement, some Sofia intellectuals) who thought I was a communist all along—why else would I have been allowed to live in the village? Others persisted in their belief that I was an agent for the CIA. In sum, the impact of the transition on field research was both liberating and limiting, but most villagers continued to treat me as they had before, with hospitality and forthrightness.

Data collection for the project consisted of numerous techniques, all familiar to anthropologists. I was lucky to live with a retired couple whose village and family connections provided an essential entrée into local life. As the husband had been a local leader in the past, the household was a hotbed of political debate, and I was able to follow political developments by default. In the early months of my stay, the bulk of my data was drawn from observations and casual conversations, conducted while working on agricultural brigades and attending ritual events such as weddings and christenings. People were especially forthcoming with invitations to major rituals, for they were organized as quasi-public displays. However, it was farm labor that provided the most open admission into the village community.

One experience stands out as a turning point. Villagers took turns as the goat herder for their neighborhoods, and one spring morning in 1987 my next-door neighbor was on duty when his elderly mother died. I volunteered to find him and relieve him of the herd so he could attend to funeral preparations. He was very grateful but clearly concerned about leaving the goats in my charge. Against my better judgment I convinced him he should. After a harrowing day, I managed to return all the goats back to their homes and never told anyone how hellish it was or how worried I had been about losing them (I must have counted them a hundred times). This convinced many villagers of my engagement with the community and that I could actually do something besides give myself "a headache with all those books," as one acquaintance described my primary occupation.

This experience was supplemented by numerous days on collective farm brigades (harvesting everything from cabbages to quinces), gathering hay, and stacking endless bales of straw. These events were extremely fecund, forcing interaction with villagers for extended periods in contexts that naturally stimulated conversation on the very issues of my research. To judge from people's comments, these shared experiences were also extremely important in removing the exotic aura that had kept some villagers at a distance. The effect of these activities on my reception in the village gave me my first hints about the broader cultural significance of agriculture, even in the wake of its declining significance as an occupation.

After I began to feel more integrated into the village, I sought out contexts for both formal and informal interviews. I talked repeatedly with village officials and directors of local enterprises, especially those in charge of the cooperative farm. I collected statistics from the village town hall, where I spent time going over old household registers, census data, and cooperative farm records. From Zamfirovo's approximately 700 households, I conducted a random survey of fifty and interviewed members of several others as well. I questioned members of different generations, getting a profile of economic activity over time. I asked the members of five households, each with a distinctive composition, to keep a written record of their finances and activities. The best data, however, came from participation in the life and work of several households where I was a frequent guest. I often helped them with their agricultural chores and was treated like a member of the family. These households had relatives in nearby towns and in Sofia, where I was welcomed as well, gaining insight into the nature of rural-urban relations.

As in the experience that opened this introduction, one of the major contexts of interaction was mealtime, especially dinner. This was the time when villagers relaxed and talked, and although the men were more relaxed than the women, who were busy cooking and serving, the latter joined in as well. Ready to eat, drink, and relax, they were, however, impatient with anything that impeded their progress or violated the anticipated sociability, such as lengthy questionnaires or formal recorded interviews. I soon gave up such attempts, integrating my questions into dinner conversation and forgoing the tape recorder. Any conversation I found useful, whether at dinner or at some other interaction, I tried to reconstruct in writing immediately afterward. The narratives I relate are such reconstructions and therefore not precise, but I have only quoted when I was confident in my recollection and when I wrote it down quickly. The importance of mealtimes for my research was increased by the Bulgarian custom of feeding those who help you with your work. Thus, any time I worked on a private plot, I was obliged to have the next meal with the proprietors. This field technique was revealing, but not without costs: I gained over 15 pounds and lost a lot of work time recovering from excess food and drink.

I traveled one day a week by bus to the county capital, Mihailovgrad (renamed Montana in the early 1990s), to work in the archives, which housed several useful village documents dating back to World War I. I also developed friendly relationships with archive workers. This not only expanded my network of informants but increased my access to archival documents. Halfway through my stay the original access procedure, in which the staff brought me documents they deemed to be relevant to my research, broke down; I was simply handed the archive lists and allowed to see any document I wanted. I worked at the county statistical offices on two occasions, collecting local demographic statistics. I also made four short research trips to the north-central, south-central, and southeastern parts of the country, primarily for comparative purposes.

I left Bulgaria in November 1988, exactly one year before the transition, and did not return until the summer of 1992, just as the process of decollectivization was getting under way. In that year I spent nearly two months in the village and returned for slightly shorter stays during the summers of 1993, 1994, and 1995, and the winter of 1997. This proved to be an extremely useful way to follow the process of decollectivization, which was rather prolonged and was still somewhat unresolved in 1997. Again, for comparative purposes I made short trips to south-central Bulgaria in 1992 and 1997 and brief visits to the northeast and the southwest in 1995. On each return I began by interviewing the major officials involved in decollectivization at the village and district levels. I then charted the attitudes and economic activities of the households that were focal in my prior research. After that I settled into more casual participant observation of the transition. The new situation also allowed me to expand my understanding of the socialist period, especially regarding more sensitive topics, such as original resistance to collectivization. Still, it was the firsthand experience with socialism that made it possible to appreciate its basic structure and legacy.

Plan of the Study

I went to Bulgaria to examine changing agrarian systems as an entrée into the experience of socialism. I quickly discovered, however, that any such undertaking would have to go beyond agriculture to resolve the paradox of agricultural disengagement in Zamfirovo—that is, the continued importance of agriculture for village and household economies at the same time that individuals were dissociating themselves from agricultural occupations and identities. Pursuing this paradox eventually revealed the nature of socialism as a system of conflicting complementarity, which in turn helped explain how villagers could subtly domesticate the socialist system. Their obscure power became more conspicuous in the transition, as villagers mobilized to defend socialist agricultural arrangements. In a way, then, this book is about how villagers in Zamfirovo went from resisting collectivization in the 1950s to defending their cooperative farm in the 1990s. I am also interested in what this change of heart tells us generally about socialism, the transition, and the transforming power of everyday life.

Chapter 1 examines collectivization in relation to prior agricultural arrangements, suggesting that it actually continued the dismantling of truly cooperative relations under way in Bulgaria before World War II. Nonetheless, the event epitomized the early nature of socialism and reinforced the association between socialism and cooperative farms. Chapter 2 follows the changes in agricultural production between the completion of collectivization and 1989. These changes, including mechanization and increasing scale, were crucial to improving rural life. They also demonstrate the escalation of socialist reform, especially the increasing integration between cooperative farms and household subsistence production. This connection, itself a product of conflicting complementarity, provided an important conduit for villagers to influence the state.

Chapter 3 introduces population decline into the picture. This development had two components: fertility restrictions under way since the early part of the century, and the massive out-migration of villagers in the 1960s. Their combined impact provoked both liberating and constraining reforms. Rural-to-urban migration was restricted, but remaining villagers acquired more economic maneuverability from the shortage of rural producers. By the late 1960s their productive contributions were no longer restricted to farming. Chapter 4 takes up this growth of nonagricultural enterprises in the village. While rural industrialization was part of state reform programs, local initiatives were required to actualize reform possibilities, illustrating another type of local influence. The ensuing conflicts between nonagricultural and agricultural activities eased work conditions in both sectors.

Villagers used workplace flexibility to expand their informal activities, the increasing importance of which forced the state to grant informal operators even more concessions. Chapter 5 analyzes these activities with special attention to their contribution to the state sector. Since the informal sector relied on agricultural produce, informal proliferation both before and after 1989 further expanded the importance of agriculture. Chapter 6 follows this importance into the mid-1990s, when agriculture became the target of decollectivization. It examines the unfolding of this process in Zamfirovo as well as concomitant changes in industry and informality, all of which eventually provoked organized resistance from villagers in defense of the cooperative farm.

The Conclusion suggests that closer attention to the particulars of village discontent in the mid-1990s—notably, concern over increasing inequality and probable repeasantization—could be used to break through socialist-capitalist opposition. It entertains the possibility that villagers were using aspects of domesticated socialism to domesticate the capitalist transition as well. Their appeal to the Socialist Party to help in this effort backfired. Still, the resulting crisis of confidence may open possibilities for political innovations, from new platforms to new political behaviors, that better represent rural interests.

There is a loose historical logic to the organization of these chapters: collectivization and subsequent agricultural reforms prompted the outmigration of the 1960s, which in turn inspired attempts to keep villagers in the countryside through local industrialization. The latter created a diversified economic milieu for the village, which stimulated expansive informal arrangements, further integrating the various economic sectors. It was agriculture's central role in this integration that made it an early target of the transition and that explains why the attempt to transform met with resistance. A chronological view, however, is distorting. The forces examined were overlapping in time as well as space, and their interaction rather than the order in which they occurred reveals the nature of socialism and transition.

Given the complexity of the interaction, I do not pretend to have discovered all the factors involved. Worse yet, I have not even been able to analyze all those I know to be important. Paramount among these is gender. Having spent a lot of time with both women and men, I am aware of the gendered differences around several of the topics covered here, from agricultural labor to fertility control. I point out a few of these differences in this analysis, but we need additional studies of rural Bulgaria focused centrally on gender itself. I have also avoided the issue of differentiation for reasons I discuss in the Conclusion. While I do not think it was central to either village socialism or the early transition, it will be increasingly so in the future. Furthermore, the lack of extensive class divisions does not mean that lesser differences were insignificant. However, given that many resources came from informal activities, it was virtually impossible to get the *reliable* data needed for such a fine-tuned inquiry. Both the extent and cultural significance of class differences deserve more rigorous investigation. Finally, the book would benefit from more attention to national and international developments, especially given its consideration of villagers' influence on a state that was itself constrained by the Soviet Union. I recognize the importance of these arenas where powerful officials pushed their own interests, sometimes against those of the villagers. I believe I capture this dynamic in the idea of conflicting complementarity, but given prior attention to state and party actions in the literature, I felt it was more useful to privilege the village experience in the interaction.

A village focus runs somewhat counter to recent anthropological interest in globalization and diaspora processes that challenge the association of cultural experience with particular place/times (Kearney 1995, Marcus 1995). In part, my discussion of agricultural disengagement and rural-to-urban migration reveals similar processes in Bulgaria. Nevertheless, it is important to recognize that not all people have participated equally in postmodern displacements. We need to problematize the locality and investigate its significance rather than either dismiss it or assume its centrality a priori. In the early 1990s the world of Bulgarian villagers had not been rocked by global population movements to the same degree as, for example, that of rural Poles. While socialism provoked urban migration, it also helped keep Bulgarians "in place," limiting exodus first from the country itself and then, by the 1970s, from the countryside as well. From the other direction, however, Western cultural influences had already diffused throughout Bulgaria by the 1980s, and this increased significantly after 1989 (Smollett 1993). Still, in the 1980s and early 1990s the village retained important cultural, political, and economic significance for both rural residents and the country as a whole. This significance will certainly change as the forces of transition drive more international migration, shift village consumption patterns, and reconfigure the very place of Bulgaria in the world. The following analysis will be an essential starting point for understanding these physical and cultural dislocations.

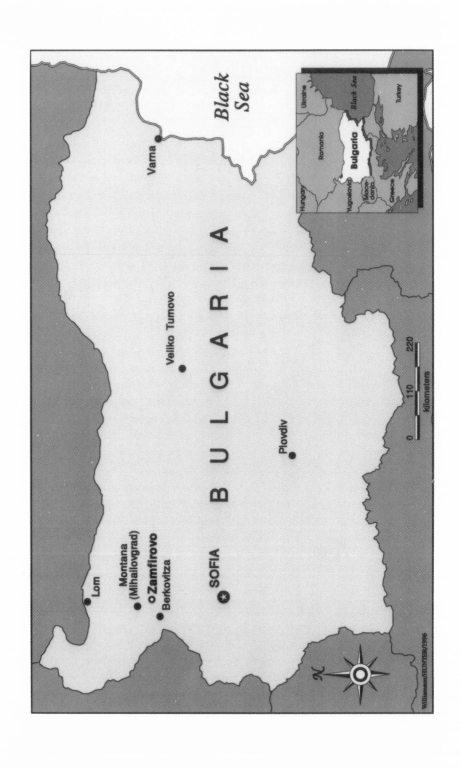

Black Sea

Varna

B U L G A R I A

Veliko Turnovo

Plovdiv

Lom

Montana
(Mihailovgrad)

Zamfirovo

Berkovitza

SOFIA

0   110   220
Kilometers

Williamson/HUNTER/1996

Ukraine

Black Sea

Romania

Bulgaria

Turkey

Hungary

Yugoslavia

Mace-
donia

Greece

RURAL TRANSFORMATIONS

Ask any Bulgarian villager about the changes in his or her village since World War II and you are likely to hear first about collectivization. The prominence of this event in their historical consciousness is due in large part to the dominance of agriculture at the time of communist ascension. Subsequent changes are viewed against this agrarian backdrop, which directs attention to agrarian changes. Of course, the ideological linkage forged between communism and collectivization by the Soviet Union further encouraged such a focus. As a result collectivization became a metaphor for the communist transformation of the countryside. This association proved nearly lethal in the anticommunist backlash after 1989, as the first antisocialist government targeted cooperative farms for complete eradication. The same centrality, however, makes agriculture a useful entrée to understanding political and economic forces in the local context.

While collectivization is central to most villagers' representation of the past, their evaluations are not uniform. Take, for example, Roumen, a sixty-year-old pensioner who continued to advise the cooperative farm on technical matters throughout the 1980s. He occasionally provided me with transportation around the village on his horse cart, and on one such occasion he began recounting the history of the various plots of land we passed.

> See all those meadows over there? Before collectivization they used to be some of the best vineyards in the village. Some years the

owners harvested two [metric] tons of grapes per decare,[1] and the sweetest you have ever tasted. Now look—deserted land from which the cooperative might collect a little hay, if there is rain. The cooperative cannot grow anything but grass! They talked about planting a new vineyard there, but you see what their other vineyards look like, full of grass and weeds. Even when they plant something else, all they grow is grass. Better to leave it meadows; grass is their specialty. If that land was under private cultivation, oh, then you would see a wonder.

This man considered himself a real farmer and staunchly supported private cultivation. Even though he worked for the cooperative farm he never missed an opportunity to deride it, along with the idea of collectivization generally. His disgust with poor farm performance may have been shared by many villagers, but it was less significant to most of them than the fact that collectivization had eased the onus of agricultural labor. A more common recollection was the one related to me by another retiree over dinner: "You should have seen how hard we had to work before collectivization. There were no machines, everything was done by hand—plowing, sowing, harvesting—with a little help from animals. Even the hand tools were primitive. It was backbreaking and endless. Now it is all done with machines, thank God." In fact, the rationale driving these divergent opinions is completely consistent: the limited input of intensive manual labor is why there was so much grass in cooperative vineyards and why the farm continually opted out of such labor-intensive crops, a solution that shows the telltale signs of conflicting complementarity.

While most villagers concurred over the eventual advantages of collectivization, few denied either the difficulties involved in the process or the privation and hardship of early cooperative cultivation. Indeed, the defense of collectivization quoted above was interrupted by the speaker's wife, who provided a temporal correction to his account of hard work: "not only *before* collectivization, but for some years afterwards." Together the couple's comments reveal the dual meaning of collectivization as both a historical process and a key symbol of communist rural transformation. Collectivization had a history grounded in international, national, and local factors. It extended over several years with various local idio-

1. A decare is the standard unit of measure for land in Bulgaria. It equals 0.1 hectare or 0.247 acres.

syncrasies. In the end it established the basic agrarian structure on which all subsequent agricultural reforms operated and thereby became the essential hallmark of socialist agrarian development. Collectivization continued to shape agricultural policy even after 1989 through both the economic situation it bequeathed and the symbolic meaning it had acquired.

Ironically, while collectivization came to symbolize the antithesis of capitalism, it actually produced many of the characteristics of agrarian capitalism, but in a way that kept agriculture and agriculturalists central. By collectivizing agriculture, the state integrated the countryside intimately into the socialist system, establishing the linkages of conflicting complementarity that villagers used to assert their influence even as agriculture declined in apparent significance. Thus, in an attempt to completely control rural producers, the state provided them with the mechanisms to subsequently manipulate state leaders.[2]

In this chapter I present the basic agricultural changes connected to collectivization in Zamfirovo. I begin with a discussion of the agrarian background from the 1920s to the mid-1950s. I then look at the mechanics of collectivization itself. They exemplify the interaction between state and local processes as Zamfirovo leaders devised their own strategy to fulfill the state's demand: using traditional cultural models of celebration they transformed collectivization into carnival. The festivities helped ameliorate the process, but the event remained undeniably coercive and the aftermath equally bitter. From this starting point the perception of a subsequent domestication becomes more understandable.

Why Collectivize? Agriculture Before 1956

Shanin (1971:263) maintains that collectivization was pursued throughout eastern Europe simply because the Soviet Union had done so. In this view, the Soviet experience established collectivization as an essential ideological component of communism, setting the agricultural agenda for all aspiring communist states. In contrast, Kideckel (1979:35) states that the collectivization of Romania was a response to "the objective circumstances which Romania faced after World War II rather than the product of an

2. Of course, rural producers acquired influence in socialist contexts without collectivization, but given that they continued to control important productive property, that was not surprising. In most of these cases, as in Poland, agriculture continued to predominate economically and demographically (see Hann 1985, Nagengast 1991).

ideological posture." For Bulgaria the reality lies somewhere between these stances. The ideological connection must be acknowledged, especially given the extensive and internationally sanctioned Soviet influence in the region after World War II. In Zamfirovo early enthusiasts for collectivization told me that the Soviet kolkhoz was their inspiration and model, and there was no evidence that any alternate program for agricultural development was even considered. The ideological primacy of the Soviet example, however, should not blind us to other factors linked to collectivization. Clearly, the objective economic situation of Zamfirovo after World War II cried out for collectivization, even if the decision to go through with it involved political and ideological considerations, including the desire to gain control of the peasantry. Each of these factors was important in its own right, but what made collectivization compelling was its efficiency in addressing all such factors simultaneously. This is why collectivization was such a popular strategy for communist leaders.[3]

The relative contribution of these different factors certainly varied from country to country, which probably goes a long way toward accounting for cross-cultural variation in the collectivization experience (see, e.g., Nolan 1976, Pryor 1992, Wädekin 1982:63–82). Furthermore, their relative importance within a single country changed over time in response to the consequences of ongoing economic change, including prior collectivization initiatives. It is essential that we be aware of such local dynamics, not only to better understand the collectivization process but also to account for variation in postcommunist agrarian experiences. For example, rural enthusiasm for decollectivization may be greater where ideological and political factors predominated in the original decision to collectivize or where the experience was more brutal, generating implacable resentment. Conversely, the more difficult the agrarian situation prior to collectivization, the less attractive a return to that arrangement will seem at the local level, at least among those who recall the past negatively. At the same time, committed socialists may continue to insist on cooperative cultivation simply because of its ideological connection to their political philosophy. It is perhaps impossible to completely dissociate such ideological and economic factors in agricultural decision making, but we can make some headway by examining the economic rationale for collectivization and the objective economic situation in the period leading up to the decision.

3. Sokolovsky (1990) makes a related argument about the multivariate dimensions of collectivization but fails to adequately consider economic development objectives apart from the state's attempt to control economic resources.

It is useful to start with the Soviet example, for while collectivization emerged from the Soviet precedent as an ideological requisite of communism, Stalin's decision involved political and economic considerations that may have swayed the communist leaders of postwar eastern Europe as well. From the various development strategies advanced in the Soviet industrialization debate between 1924 and 1928, Stalin reversed his earlier predilections and opted for an extreme industrial variant (see Erlich 1960).[4] It stressed extensive investment in heavy industry, on the rationale that by investing in machinery to make other machines, industrial capacity could be expanded exponentially. The benefits of this approach would eventually far exceed the short-run benefits of agricultural investment or investment in consumer industries. The resources for such investment were to be extracted from agriculture via low purchase prices for agricultural goods combined with high prices for consumer goods. This could be expected to undermine peasant market participation, which is where collectivization entered the picture—collectivization guaranteed continued agricultural production and state access to the products. It also conveniently ensured that labor would follow capital as it severed peasants' ties to the land, freeing them up for work in the expanding industrial sector. They could be replaced in agricultural production by machines, either produced by the industrial sector itself or imported in exchange for other industrial products. At the same time, it curtailed what was perceived as the disproportionate influence over economic policy held by those with ample agricultural resources—although, as previously noted, it ironically did so by establishing the very connections that eventually allowed more villagers to influence the economy.

This package fit the situation in Bulgaria after World War II. First, Bulgaria was a predominantly agrarian society, so agriculture was an obvious source for industrial investment. Prior to 1944 approximately 80 percent of the population was engaged in agriculture, and all the country's foreign exchange earnings came from goods of agricultural origin (Tanov 1986:45). The potential contribution of agriculture, however, was constrained by its smallholding subsistence structure. Crampton (1987:137) puts the average Bulgarian holding in 1926 at 5.73 hectares per family. Of course such averages mask significant village variation. Looking at two villages near Zamfirovo in the 1930s, the average size of landholdings was 35 decares in one and 55 in the other (Petrov 1940:8–9). Since each

---

4. See Pryor (1992:46–52) for a rundown of the various additional considerations that may have influenced Stalin's decision.

village household needed parcels of land in different economic zones, including forest and meadow as well as arable land, and given the desirability of locating cultivated plots in different zones so as to minimize the potential damage of hailstorms, these landholdings were usually divided into several widely dispersed strips. According to Sanders (1949:42), the average 18-acre farm in the village of Dragalevtsy in the 1930s was composed of sixteen such strips, one less than the 1926 national average of seventeen strips per holding (Crampton 1987:137).

The situation in Zamfirovo mirrors these descriptions. Based on a list of land use in 1916 and a list of households from 1917, the average landholding per Zamfirovo household can be approximated at 36 decares. According to land claim documents submitted during decollectivization, the average holding had dropped to 27.8 by the mid-1950s. This number included all land, but it may have been depressed slightly by underreporting at the time of collectivization. There are no data on the number of plots during the early period, but a "historical note" prepared for the local archives reports that before 1944, the arable land in the village was divided into more than 15,000 parcels. Officials involved in decollectivization put this number significantly lower, at 12,300. Using their more precise number and their household count of 763, the average number of parcels can be estimated at sixteen for the early 1950s, and perhaps somewhat fewer in earlier years. Whatever the specific number, the situation was clearly difficult. Villagers recounted elaborate work schedules with different family members sent to work on different parcels because plots were too dispersed to walk from one to another and still get any work done in a day's time. Others reported spending the night in the fields during peak work times for related reasons. At the same time land fragmentation discouraged more permanent residence in the fields. Older villagers recalled that in the first decades of the century, "most village families" had a permanent animal pen in an area where they had significant pasture land. The oldest generation of the family—usually the grandparents—lived there from spring until fall in a meager stick and mud hut, tending the family's livestock and processing the products. The grandfather sometimes stayed there year-round. Fragmentation obviously threatened this arrangement: as parcels of pasture became smaller and more dispersed villagers were less willing to live there. The few households not experiencing these pressures by the 1930s usually had an exceptionally small sibling set in recent generations. For example, one elderly village informant reported having 40 decares of land, including about 6 decares of meadow and 6 decares of forest. The remaining 28 decares were divided into approximately seven parcels. This may not seem excessively fragmented, but his father was from a small sibling set and had inherited land with less than the usual amount of division. This delayed fragmentation, but one can imagine what the land would have looked like after division between the informant and his eight brothers and sisters.

Such a smallholding agrarian structure was not necessarily less productive than larger holdings. In fact, Lampe (1986:86) maintains that holdings under 5 hectares may have been slightly more efficient and productive than those over 10 hectares. Indeed, if larger holdings represented a larger number of scattered plots, then the higher efficiency of smaller holdings is understandable—fewer plots meant less time spent traveling from one to another, allowing more time for productive work.

Regardless of any efficiency benefits, smallholdings certainly limited agricultural options such as mechanization, which is another often cited weakness of interwar Bulgarian agriculture. In Zamfirovo the standard cultivation tools were a hoe and plow. The latter was usually wooden, and while most had metal plowshares, some did not. They were pulled primarily by cows or water buffalo. The numerous households with only one draft animal cooperated with each other for plowing, or plowed with one animal they personally guided. Those with no draft animals borrowed them in exchange for other agricultural work. Harvesting and threshing were done by hand and animal hoof, respectively. There was no irrigation apart from bucket brigades for plots close to water sources.[5] Chemical fertilizers were rarely used, although animal manure was scrupulously collected. It was applied primarily to vegetable gardens, with other plots fertilized according to supply on an alternating basis. The attraction of more mechanized technology was diminished by availability and cost as well as by the abundant labor supply, which was already beyond the absorbing capacity of agriculture for the country as a whole (Rothschild 1974:331, Crampton 1987:137, Wolff 1974:60–61). The last thing poor farmers with excess labor needed was expensive labor-saving technology.

With a growing population and partible inheritance some of these pressures could only get worse. The situation was further complicated by a concomitant increase in household fission. Continuing a process that may have been under way in the nineteenth century (Mosely 1940, Zhivkova

---

5. Irrigation was limited to the south-central rice-growing region, where it was accomplished with earthen canals built during Turkish times. Government plans for improving these facilities in 1906 and 1928 had negligible results (Pasvolsky 1930:202–5).

1993:141–43), large extended family households were dividing into smaller household units. In Zamfirovo the number of households rose from 403 in 1917 to over 700 by World War II, while the population increased only 40 percent during this period. As a result the average household declined from 6.3 members to 4.7. This renders temporal comparisons based on the amount of land per family, like those I cited for Bulgaria and Zamfirovo above, incomplete reflections of changing economic conditions at the local level: with households dividing, land per family could decline even without increasing land pressure. At the same time, though, household fission may have added its own problems to the interwar mix. Since separated households usually divided any plots that were still big enough to divide, fission likely increased the problems of fragmentation, which in turn took more borderland out of production. Furthermore, fission was occurring in a context of continuing population growth, making the situation potentially severe. As Petrov (1940:6) describes it, "On the same plot of land lives two to three times as many people. The forests have disappeared. Trade is dying. Animal husbandry is declining greatly. The land is being divided up into infinite numbers of little parcels, so that a large part of it is lost to borders and paths. The weakening [of agriculture] has set in because with the decline of animal husbandry the amount of animal manure has decreased."

Clearly, many interrelated changes were in motion. The shortage of land and excess labor stimulated a demographic transition, which I will discuss in Chapter 3, but it did not immediately halt population growth. The colonization of the commons and the clearing of the forests provided important stopgap measures. The latter probably occurred to some degree by default—a result of the expanding need for fuel and wood—leaving denuded land for potential cultivation or for use as meadows. The state regulated the use and cutting of private forests, but regulations were apparently less than completely effective. Sanders (1949:19) indicates that Dragalevtsy villagers had evidently reduced their forest holdings by the 1930s, and Zamfirovo residents also talked about an unspecified time "in the past" when the surrounding forests were much more extensive. Friends I helped in the fields often mused that the plot we were working on, or a neighboring one, or one we passed on the way to get there, used to be forest. Bringing woodland under cultivation had ramifications for animal husbandry, since livestock grazed in the forest. Prior to 1944 the private forests of villagers were used as common lands. They were privately owned, but if a forest was mature, other villagers might pasture their animals there. Only young forests in early stages of regrowth were off limits. So, in effect, the deforestation of private holdings represented a decline in communal resources as well.

At the same time, the official common lands of the village were also at risk. Villages relied on common land for the communal pasturage of their livestock, but the general pressure on land generated attacks on these resources from various fronts. According to Stoyanova (cited in Kouzhouharova, Meurs, and Stoyanova, n.d.), communal pastures were diminished in the country as a whole by more than half between 1908 and 1931, falling from 900,000 hectares to 400,000 hectares. Sanders (1949: 56) reports that the shepherds and cattle herders of Dragalevtsy came into conflict over grazing rights and that the local government resolved the issue by eliminating communal pasture altogether. In addition, other communal pastures in the mountains some distance from Dragalevtsy were, for an unexplained reason, "no longer available to the peasants" (Sanders 1949:54). Similar processes were evident in Zamfirovo. A written report on the village from 1926 declares a "desperate need" for more communal pasture, since the commons "is small and much has been taken over by cultivation." To make matters worse, part of the commons was shared with a neighboring village; a legal battle between the two villages over use rights in the mid-1920s probably attests to increasing pressure on this resource. The village also lost access to common pasture in the Balkan mountains above Berkovitza where, until the early 1920s, sheep and goats were taken for summer grazing. According to village elders, the sultan gave the village the right to use this meadow in Ottoman times, but the authorizing document was lost. The Bulgarian state allowed them to continue using the plot on a rental basis, but early in the decade the state took part of it away and raised the rent on the remainder, making it unprofitable.

This occurrence was probably not unusual, for common land became a major target of state policies in the interwar period. Stamboliiski's Agrarian government came to power in 1919–20, promising land reform. Because most land was already in the hands of smallholders, only 82,000 hectares were transferred before the fall of the government in 1923. Of this land, almost a quarter (24.99 percent) came from "village councils," while another 10 percent came from state property (Crampton 1987:89). The former was certainly communal property, such as village commons, and in all likelihood much of the latter had been rented to villages for communal use as described above for Zamfirovo. According to Crampton

(1987:137), this division of communal property "continued apace" in the 1930s and early 1940s.

The decline in pasture land could be offset by increasing the use of fallow for pasture. Thus the high percentage of fallow cited by Crampton (1987:139) was likely a consequence of the very low national percentages of meadow and pasture land he also notes. At the same time the increasing land pressure certainly restricted this strategy; as Lampe (1986:86) points out, much of the expansion in cultivated land in the 1930s occurred at the expense of fallow. The 1926 report on Zamfirovo states that only "the few better off farmers" left their weaker fields fallow for one to two years. The limitations on manure and fallow were particularly detrimental in Zamfirovo because the land was generally of poor quality.

Zamfirovo's limitations provoked residents to seek temporary work elsewhere. A few villagers recounted going abroad to work in agriculture or construction. Many more, including the man whose complaint about the cooperative farm introduced this chapter, spent time working in the Danubian plain. He recounted spending the growing season several years in a row working for a rich man with 600 decares of wheat and corn near the town of Lom. Aided only by horsepower, he and another laborer worked every day for six months in return for room and board and a final payment of 4,000 leva.[6] He contextualized the paltry sum by contrasting it to the 2,000 leva the boss's son received to fritter away at the annual town fair. He sometimes stayed around the Danube for the winter as well, making bricks for even lower wages. He said poverty and the lack of options drove him to such labor, and he complained about being away from the village—a situation he blamed for a variety of problems, from his inability to find a wife to his difficulties completing a village house. This history makes his earlier defense of private agriculture even more poignant. The village schoolmaster's report in 1926 verifies that poorer village families sent one of their men to work as hired hands in the plains to get cash for taxes and material needs. The worker might trade places with other men in the family so that no one had to stay away permanently. The author suggests, however, that this practice had declined by the time of the report: "In older times residents went as hired hands to villages in the plains, but now this is less common."

This apparent decline suggests a slightly different interpretation of the interwar village economy. Clearly the period produced adversity, which is

---

6. The lev (plural, leva) is the Bulgarian currency unit, equivalent to 100 stotinki.

perhaps not surprising given the global depression in the late 1920s and 1930s. Still, on closer examination, comments by the same individuals who complained about interwar difficulties, as well as documents and secondary sources, suggest that there may have been periods of deceleration, respite, and even reversal in the spiraling decline. For example, while talking about the land shortage, many informants also complained about how much they had to work: "We got up before dawn and worked until dark." Although this attests to the difficulty of life, it also suggests that there was work to be done and that underemployment had not reached the point of widespread idleness. The schoolmaster's claim that temporary labor migration had diminished in the 1920s may also support such an interpretation. While it likely reflects a decline in the demand for such labor on the part of landowners, it may also reflect an increase in local possibilities.

The land use statistics in Table 1 suggest that local resources indeed played a role, for the total land under cultivation in Zamfirovo seems to

Table 1.   Zamfirovo Land Use, 1916 and 1931

	Decares	
Crop	1916	1931
Barley	137.0	600.0
Beans	0	55.0
Corn	4177.8	7600.0
Fallow	453.7	—[a]
Flax	5.5	0
Fodder beets	0	5.0
Fruit orchard	0	3.0
Hemp	19.9	48.0
Meadows	3451.8	4630.9
Oats	1241.0	2000.0
Poppy	0	5.0
Potatoes	0	80.0
Rye	6.5	1100.0
Sunflower	0	185.0
Vineyards	658.3	1548.6[b]
Wheat	4384.3	8280.0

SOURCE: Mihailovgrad archives.

[a]Not a category in 1931 document.
[b]Plus 338.4 decares of young vineyard not yet bearing.

have increased significantly between 1916 and 1931. Surprisingly, this expansion outpaced village population growth, so that the amount of land cultivated per capita went from approximately 5.67 decares in 1916 to approximately 8 decares in 1931. Unfortunately, the increase could not be sustained: decollectivization records put the per capita rate for the mid-1950s back at 5.9 decares. Although this shows a significant decline since 1931, it is still higher than 1916 averages. Thus, the previously cited decline in the size of Zamfirovo holdings in the interwar period was solely the result of extensive household fission; cultivated land per villager actually increased. I am skeptical about the extent of the improvement in the 1931 data, which runs counter to general national statistics for the period,[7] but I do believe Zamfirovo residents were able to hold their own during this time. As intimated above, population pressure could be redressed by cultivating commons and forests. Zamfirovo was in a wooded area of the Balkan foothills and thus able to benefit more from clearing forests than either villages in the plains, with less forest, or mountain villages, where steep terrain and rocky soil limited cultivation. Zamfirovo was also off the beaten track and perhaps less susceptible to the enforcement of state forestry regulations.[8]

Deforestation and the cultivation of common lands were simultaneously products and provocateurs of a wider change: the intensification of animal husbandry through increased feeding with cultivated fodders, including grain. This suggestion is consistent with the rise in per capita grain consumption in the second half of the 1920s (Lampe 1986:53) and the dramatic increase by 1931 in Zamfirovo acreage devoted to rye, barley, oats, and corn—grains used primarily as animal feed (Table 1). General land pressure and the fragmentation of holdings threatened old extensive methods for rearing livestock. This provoked farmers to transfer common lands and forests to grain production, which could support more animals than equivalent amounts of pasture. Cultivation, however, required more labor, so farmers had to work much harder—hence the complaints about hard work—but it reduced the need for large extended families to over-

7. Based on the rural population and agricultural land measures from the Statistical Yearbook, agricultural land per villager declined a little over half a decare (from 9.36 to 8.73 decares) between 1926 and 1934 (*Statisticheski Godishnik* 1939:30, 181).

8. The cutting of forests, whether on private, municipal, or state property, was restricted. However, only large state forests were usually monitored by state rangers. Districts appointed their own overseers and private forests had little if any oversight. The potential for violation was extensive, and discussions of the regulations actually suggest as much (see, e.g., Hristov 1941, Mihailov 1941).

see dispersed flocks and herds, and this likely encouraged household fission. At the same time, the cultivation of forests and commons exacerbated the problem it responded to, that of limited pasture. Thus, as cultivation proceeded, it maintained a demand for animal feed, which also ran into competition with household consumption needs for wheat. Here the decline in grain prices in the 1920s—a result of North American competition—was crucial. Faced with a continuing need for animal feed and household wheat in a context of declining grain prices, Zamfirovo farmers bought grain. Villagers consistently reported that the majority of Zamfirovo residents could not support their household economies with their own grain production and actually had to purchase it. A common assessment was that they could grow enough for about half the year and the rest they had to purchase. The above argument suggests that in the economic environment of the 1930s, it behooved them to do just that, at least as long as they could get the money to do so from selling other agricultural products and meat.

We do not have adequate historical data on animal production in Zamfirovo to analyze the fuller economic consequences of these trends. Table 2 shows a clear decline in cattle holding, but other data suggest that sheep more than compensated for these reductions. A brief historical note in the county archives says that in the 1930s nearly every household in the village had seven to eight sheep, while nearly a hundred households had more than thirty. This suggests a clear increase over the number in 1925, but the latter may have been diminished by villagers' ten-

Table 2. Numbers of Selected Livestock in Zamfirovo, 1920–31

		Year	
Livestock	1920	1925	1931
Cows	403[a]	—	329
Goats	—	300[c]	—
Sheep	—	4540[b]	—
Sows	18	—	100
Water buffalo	128	—	117

NOTE: A dash indicates lack of data.
SOURCE: Mihailovgrad archives.

[a]208 households
[b]293 households
[c]67 households

dency to underreport. Without more specific numbers, any conclusion would be speculative. We also do not know the amount of commerce in animal products or rates of consumption. My informants complained about periods of hunger and a generally limited diet consisting primarily of corn mush or white bean soup. Milk from sheep, goats, and cows was made into a homemade cheese, much like feta, which constituted a dietary staple, but meat was a luxury limited to ritual and festive occasions. Additional meat was sold. Several villagers reported the regular sale of lambs and eggs to Berkovitza merchants, as well as the occasional sale of pork and veal in Mihailovgrad (then called Ferdinand). Thus, village consumption was not necessarily improving with intensification, and higher grain consumption cannot automatically be interpreted as an indication of improved living standards. The higher consumption may simply have enabled household economies to maintain their customary access to animal products in the face of increasing population, declining pasture, and deforestation.

At the same time there was a related change, evident in Table 1, that likely did help villagers—the expansion of viticulture. This expansion predated and probably contributed to the national increase in grape exports following the reduction in grain and tobacco exports in the 1920s. We should note, however, that positive assessments of the Bulgarian agrarian economy in the 1920s and 1930s, based on the shift in exports from wheat to tobacco and subsequently grapes, cannot be assumed to reflect improving economic conditions across the country. Areas of tobacco cultivation do not correspond exactly with major grain- or grape-growing regions, so economic transitions at the macro level tell us little about conditions on the ground. In this particular case, however, Zamfirovo was lucky. Its climate and soil, though not ideal, were at least suitable for grape cultivation. The viability of viticulture was demonstrated by limited cultivation immediately after World War I and by state agricultural extension agents who gave courses on viticulture and winemaking in nearby villages. When markets expanded for grapes in the 1920s, residents eagerly planted more, and although the area never achieved a reputation for high quality, villagers managed to reap economic benefits. One older woman said her family had 15 decares of vineyards in the 1930s and it took all fourteen family members a solid week to pick them all. Her father made wine and brandy, which he sold in neighboring villages and towns. During this time, homemade wine and brandy became cultural essentials of village life as well as important sources of income.

The expansion of viticulture reflects the generally increasing commercialization of the village economy. Grape cultivation was underwritten by the sale of spring lambs to merchants in Berkovitza, which provided the cash to buy chemicals needed to protect vines from blight. Fresh grapes as well as wine and brandy were sold or exchanged in other villages and in Berkovitza for staples such as salt and sugar, additional grain, and farm equipment. Additional cash was used for taxes, but there was apparently enough left over for villagers to buy clothing rather than make it, as older villagers reported that most of their clothes in the 1930s were purchased. In the village description from 1926, the school principal wrote that most clothes for men were still made at home, but their dress clothes and almost all women's clothes were store-bought: "In regard to fashion, the village woman is imitating the city woman. She is abandoning the traditional clothes which she could make herself, and which are inexpensive and durable, for foreign things, even though they are often less comfortable and less attractive. Very few of the women's clothes are made at home. They are mostly bought in stores at high prices." Such developments increased the opportunities for village craftsworkers and artisans. In addition, it was in the 1920s and 1930s that villagers began purchasing metal plows, a clear indication of prosperity. The plow, made in Germany, was available in Mihailovgrad (Ferdinand) for 3,000 leva. Villagers remember this clearly because it was a significant event when people first started buying such plows: "It was a big occasion in the village and people would say, 'Oh, what's-his-name got a German plow.' And then they would walk by his house on some pretense to try and get a look at it."

Ironically, commercialization was combined with an increase in subsistence activity. Villagers diversified their subsistence economy to satisfy certain domestic consumption needs so that cash could be used for other things. This can be seen in Zamfirovo in the emergence of sunflower acreage (see Table 1). Planting small amounts of crops such as sunflowers and, in a few cases, even sugar cane limited the need for purchases of oil and sugar, reserving exchange resources for other products. I am not suggesting that life was easy, but farmers were able to adapt to changing local, national, and international forces in order to maintain and at times even to improve their situation. The depression restricted some of these possibilities in 1929 and the early 1930s (see Molloff 1933:60–62), but they were revived by increasing German trade later in the decade. Villagers report that prices for their products increased in the late 1930s and the early war years, supporting Lampe's (1986:85) claim that the purchasing power of the rural population had regained 1929 levels by the end of the 1930s.

During the war there were forced requisitions, but apparently they were not overly exacting. The increasing importance of grapes in the local economy probably helped in this regard, since fruit had higher requisition prices and was less subject to governmental control than grain. Moreover, villagers apparently found ways to circumvent the grain requisitions. As one villager put it, "I do not remember the exact amounts of the requisitions, but they were not that bad, and it did not matter because we hid the goods instead of handing them over." Like the villagers of Dragalevtsy (Sanders 1949:187), they shook their own supply of grain from the sheaves before taking them to official threshing stations. Successfully retained grain could then be sold on the expansive and lucrative black market, itself a product of the system of requisitioning. Prices for black market food were so high that farmers could get significant cash returns without cutting into their subsistence production. Villagers said they could get any price they wanted for goods during the war, and many reported that Germans arrived in Berkovitza with small printing presses and printed as much money as they needed to purchase village products. Sanders (1949:184) says that the prosperity brought to Dragalevtsy by the war was reflected in the number of new modern houses built in the war years and in the number of radios.

This system of exchange obviously had limits, and soon there was less for villagers to sell and nothing for them to buy. "Yes, we could get a lot of money for everything we raised," one villager recalled, "but we didn't have much to sell and there was nothing for us to buy with it." The situation worsened significantly after the war. Requisitions increased in both the number of affected crops and the amounts demanded, while prices paid for agricultural products declined. In addition the program of labor service begun by the Agrarian government in the early 1920s continued, requiring residents to work at least six days per year, usually on village construction projects. Amounts of agricultural quotas were assessed for local districts as a whole on the basis of the category of the local resources. Local councils then distributed the burden to residents according to the size of landholdings and the amount of livestock, usually giving some consideration to the number of household members, much like a progressive income tax in kind. Rates were high. As of April 1950, holdings over 10 hectares owed the state 75 percent of their grain crop (Lampe 1986:148). Dobrin (1973:44) claims that the requisitions were so high that some farmers were forced to purchase produce on the black market in order to fulfill their quotas. Documents from Zamfirovo give the amount of hay required from the village in 1949 at 28,500 kilograms. A document from 1953 puts milk obligations at 160 liters per cow and meat requisitions, which were based on landownership, at levels listed in Table 3. The document points out, however, that these rates represent a 21 percent reduction from previous years.

Like the Transylvanian villagers interviewed by Verdery (1983:35), the residents of Zamfirovo were uncharacteristically reticent about the privations of this early postwar period. Recollections of the past were usually prefaced with the common Bulgarian expression "before the 9th," which referred to the official beginning of the communist era on September 9, 1944. Temporal comparisons in the other direction were usually prefaced with "after collectivization," which was completed for the village in 1956, leaving the intervening dozen years unaccounted for. Persistence paid off, however, and several villagers eventually testified to the difficulties of the postwar period, especially the distress caused by quotas. As one man described it, "From our twenty-five pails of wheat, they took ten to fifteen for the state. We had to keep five to ten for seeds for the following year, which left us five pails for our own use. Nothing! We fared better with animal products because we continued to hide them [the animals] in the forest, but then we had nothing left to feed them, so what could we do?" As this comment suggests, villagers continued the subterfuges perfected during the war to elude extractions. They hid animals in the forest to reduce the amount of milk, wool, and meat they were required to hand over. They even hid wine and brandy to escape the tax assessed on these products. Land could not be concealed, but some people hid the products and claimed that the harvest was insufficient to fulfill the quota. The postwar government, however, was more vigilant than the wartime regime in collecting these obligations, and it became progressively more so with

Table 3. Meat Requisition Rates for 1954 in Zamfirovo

Size of Holding	Meat Requisition
1–10 decares	2.1 kilograms per decare
10–30 decares	2.3 kilograms per decare
30–50 decares	2.6 kilograms per decare
50–70 decares	2.9 kilograms per decare

SOURCE: Mihailovgrad archives.

the consolidation of Communist Party control. Higher administrative levels held village officials responsible for fulfilling requisitions, forcing them to scour the village for clandestine operators and their caches. The officials recounted to me the difficulty of their assignment while villagers complained about unfair officials and burdensome exactions. It was clearly a constant struggle.

Evidence of the struggle is recorded in the minutes of meetings of Zamfirovo's governing bodies during the late 1940s and early 1950s. At the meeting of the local Fatherland Front committee on May 15, 1945, officials reported that the requisition of lambs was stymied by the large number of "hidden lambs," and the committee authorized village leaders to search out and take them. At the same meeting they also discussed difficulties collecting milk requisitions due to the collective pasturing of sheep. They resolved that communal shepherds could not milk sheep for personal consumption until the amount of the required requisition had been collected from each sheep owner. In 1949 difficulties related to requisitions were brought up at five different meetings of the People's Council, and by 1950 it was virtually a regular item on the agenda. The list of products at issue grew. Pork products—lard and meat—became a central concern in 1950. During this period the progress of requisition campaigns of milk, hemp, grain, wool, and hay were also repeatedly recorded in the minutes.

Given such a frustrating and potentially precarious procedure for resource mobilization, it is no wonder that as the state grew more powerful, it became increasingly involved in assuring the production of goods to be requisitioned. Village leaders were charged by higher levels to oversee and assure that private farmers operated to maximize output. There were timetables for sterilizing seed grain, planting, weeding, and harvesting. The minutes of the village council include numerous reports on the progress of these various campaigns. Committees were formed for surveying the harvest—making sure it was completed in the most propitious time frame, with the least waste, and, obviously, with the fulfillment of requisitions. In the spring of 1951 the village council decided that those who had not planted their crops or weeded their fields by the specified deadlines would be "severely punished." Government organs were involved in all phases of private agricultural labor, from plowing to harvesting and requisitioning the products. Furthermore, through requisition demands the government could determine what was planted; quotas placed on particular products forced villagers to produce them.

Another trend clearly evident in these records is the increasing diligence and power of local officials in regard to collecting these quotas. In March 1950, a 500-leva fine was threatened against those who did not fulfill their hemp quotas, and fines of unspecified amounts were subsequently levied against those not handing over their wool. Officials authorized extensive searches of the village for cows and milk. Villagers were told in the fall of 1950 that they had to present the lard requisition immediately upon slaughtering a pig, and officials were charged with keeping track of who killed pigs. One report authorized officials to check all those who had not provided their hay quotas to see if they had any hay. If not, it was decided officials should take more hay from someone who had it. On a related issue, officials suggested that villagers be prohibited from selling eggs at the Berkovitza market in order to ensure their sale to the local cooperative. In January 1951 a fine of 500 leva was levied on those who had not fulfilled their labor obligations for the previous year. These measures make it clear why villagers may have resorted to black market purchases to fulfill requisitions.

Under this array of obligations, villagers were certainly feeling increasing pressure. In the meantime the problems of the prewar period had not disappeared. Population increase had slowed but as of the late 1940s was still a factor. At the same time, communal grazing lands continued to be encroached on, now by the officially favored cooperative and state sectors. In 1945, 3 decares of commons in a neighboring village were given over to a labor cooperative for the raising and grafting of young grapevines. In April 1948 the Zamfirovo village council expropriated the plots of three villagers and compensated them with money and common lands. In 1949 similar arrangements were made in exchange for a section of private forest and for a man's garden plot, which was taken over for use by the school.

Certainly the pressure on land did not abate, and given the increasingly strident requisition program, the limited strategies developed in response to land shortage in the 1920s were no longer viable. Consequently, the second half of the 1940s and the early 1950s saw a decline in economic conditions for villagers. According to Lampe (1986:125), by late 1946 farmers were slaughtering livestock due to lack of food. When the Zamfirovo village council was asked by higher government organs in 1948 to provide a list of families in the village who were "poor and needy," the council responded that "all are poor and needy except for 106 families," and they provided a list of these names instead. By this time there were probably 700 households, so at least 85 percent of the village was considered "poor and needy." Even considering the possibility of exaggeration for political effect, this is a significantly negative appraisal. The difficulty of the period was also verified by the thoroughly negative assessments offered by villagers whose confidence I shared. Several villagers recalled wearing coarse silk shirts in the summer because there were no clothes to buy and silkworms were one of the few products they could raise and process locally for lightweight cloth. This contrasts vividly with the availability of ready-to-wear clothes during the interwar period, as previously noted. One friend described this period as "a battle," and another characterized it with the standard Bulgarian cliché for hard times, saying, "It was worse than Turkish servitude."

Apparently the government was aware of the increasing difficulty. A Zamfirovo document from 1954 reported the national change from a progressive milk quota to a flat rate per cow, citing the disincentive of the old arrangement, which had led people to reduce their cattle holdings and thus had exacerbated the decline of this sector evident in the 1920s. This change accompanied the previously mentioned reduction in requisition rates across the board. Both changes suggest a general governmental sensitivity to the deteriorating predicament of agricultural producers.

These difficulties made it increasingly imperative that the country complete collectivization. Collectivization allowed for consolidation of arable land, which made it amenable for an economy of scale sufficient to increase output. Redundant labor could then be siphoned off for the industrial workforce. The remaining agricultural workers, detached from their diversified subsistence base, would depend on the compensation they received from the cooperative farm, the rates of which would ensure the necessary resources for state investment priorities. There were other routes to development that the Bulgarian communist leadership bypassed, no doubt because of an ideological preference for the Soviet model, but at least this model fit the Bulgarian situation. Furthermore, Lampe (1986:124) suggests that the prospect of acquiring Soviet agricultural machinery was a factor fostering the consolidation of Communist Party control in Bulgaria from the onset. In other words, agricultural objectives could shape ideological choices as well as the reverse.

Whether or not agricultural needs actually influenced ideological preferences, it is inaccurate to view collectivization solely as a solution to the above problems. Collectivization had been under way in the village since 1948, and early efforts in this direction contributed to the problems just described. Furthermore, collectivization was part and parcel of the national industrialization drive, which sapped resources from agriculture via low purchase prices and requisitions, contributing to the deteriorating conditions of village life after World War II. Thus, we must see this period as part and parcel of the collectivization-industrialization program. As it proceeded, additional agricultural resources, both labor and capital, became increasingly essential for industrial expansion, pushing collectivization to completion. At the same time, the experiences of the late 1940s and early 1950s shaped the response of villagers to the more relentless pushes that ensued.

Collectivization: Coercion and Carnival

The collectivization drive began in 1945 as a preemptive strike by Bulgarian communist leaders and their Soviet benefactors attempting to secure a position in the postwar power vacuum. Communist control, however, proved to be a prerequisite for collectivization rather than a result, and limited progress was made until the consolidation of communist power in 1947. Between 1945 and 1947 the cooperative share of arable land rose to only 3.8 percent (Brown 1970:198). Perhaps more significant than the quantity, however, is the fact that cooperatives were organized entirely through voluntary means, amid official party pronouncements against any form of compulsion. During this time Zamfirovo residents frequently discussed cooperativism and the possibility of starting a cooperative farm. No action was taken, however, because of the poor performance of cooperatives elsewhere, one of which was in a neighboring village. It had no machines so the work was no easier than private production and the income was less. Such examples did little to convert village curiosity into enthusiasm.

The situation changed for Zamfirovo with the national consolidation of Communist Party control in 1947. Early in 1948, at the suggestion of higher party organs, the local party committee decided to form a cooperative farm. As in many other villages (see Zhivkova 1989:165) they looked first to existing cooperative institutions. In Zamfirovo a cooperative "Savings and Loan Society" had been founded in 1911, but it had few assets and, according to local reports, did not begin effective operation until 1932. In that year it changed its title to "Credit Cooperative" and attracted an increasing membership. This reflects a nationwide increase during the 1930s in all aspects of the cooperative system—the number, membership, and assets of cooperatives all expanded. The motivation for this included the improved local fortunes previously described as well as national initiatives like the increase in bank loans to cooperatives and the channeling of increased state agricultural investments through the cooperative network (Lampe 1986:83).

Much has been made of this cooperative network as a forerunner of subsequent socialist relations in the countryside (e.g., Kolev and Olovanski 1977). It is certainly true that cooperativism has a long and distinguished history in Bulgaria, beginning as early as 1890 and including cooperation in production and marketing as well as in providing credit (see Billaut 1988; Siulemezov 1986). Indeed, some of the interwar improvements, including small technological advances, can be traced to cooperative initiatives. Still, we must be careful how we interpret this background in regard to collectivization. Danilov (1989), for example, sees cooperativism in the Soviet case not as a predecessor of collectivization but as an alternative Stalin rejected. This distinction was evident even earlier in Bulgaria in the opposition between Stamboliiski's Agrarian platform, which stressed increasing cooperation between private peasant proprietors, and the communist platform of wholesale nationalization. Focusing on such opposition, Oren (1973:114) suggests that the degree of cooperativism actually made collectivization "all the more unpopular." Nevertheless, when the communists came to power, they drew heavily on cooperative arrangements, and the relationship between these two forms became intricately intertwined. Among the cooperative elements of the early farms were the following: villagers retained title to the land they contributed; they could contribute only part of their land; and they were allowed to withdraw, mortgage, or sell their contribution. Most important, the collective paid them rent for their land so that people who contributed more holdings received more income. In Zamfirovo the early cooperative allocated 40 percent of the farm's profits to the payment of rent, with the remaining 60 percent divided according to labor contribution.

As we will see, all these arrangements were gradually eliminated. Thus, the collectivization process can be characterized as the cooperativization of agriculture followed by, and combined with, the de facto (although never de jure) nationalization of cooperatives. Villagers joined cooperatives that were gradually stripped of their cooperative elements. Ludzhev (1989) characterizes the early stages in this process as the "restructuring" of the cooperative movement. Given this progression, Stillman's (1958: 67–68) dismissal of the cooperative movement as insignificant to collectivization is clearly indefensible, but finding socialist predilections in cooperative traditions is also suspect. The two were in a complex and changing relationship.

Cooperatives provided a base of operations for collectivization. Progress during the period between 1944 and 1950 was focused on reinforcing and expanding this foundation. New cooperatives were established and existing ones induced to expand and diversify. In Zamfirovo the credit cooperative took on additional commercial and production activities and changed its name to "Commerce Cooperative" in 1950. In 1947 a new Labor-Production Cooperative was formed with various village craftsworkers. Village party leaders tried to tap these organizations in 1948 when they received directions to organize a "Labor Cooperative Agricultural Economy," commonly referred to by the acronym TKZS (pronounced *tay-kay-zay-say*). In the spring of that year local party leaders approached a villager who had been a strong advocate of these earlier cooperative efforts and convinced him to help organize an agricultural variant. They conveyed to him a list of about six people to serve as an initiating committee, which he convened the following day. They elected him president of the new committee and divided up the village into sections, with each committee member taking responsibility for drumming up cooperative support in one zone. They reported to each other on their progress at weekly Sunday meetings.

According to the president, the campaign got off to a slow start. He blamed several committee members for limited enthusiasm and particularly faulted the party organization for not exerting pressure on party members to join. This suggests that local party leaders were either hedging against an anticommunist backlash resulting from any cooperative campaign or, alternatively, attempting to minimize resistance from noncommunists by keeping a respectable distance from the process. This changed later, but in the meantime, the president and one other committee member ended up canvassing the whole village themselves. They were often met with insults, taunts, and even threats. Even members of the existing cooperatives were uninterested. A common response was that it was "too early" to form a cooperative farm and that the village was "not ready." There is merit in this argument, as the village lacked the farm machinery and other technological advances that make an economy of scale most efficient.

Apparently, the party picked the right man to head the committee: undaunted by failure, he redoubled his efforts, devoting himself full-time to mobilizing support for the TKZS. By October the committee had convinced approximately thirty families to join. Deciding in consultation with village and party leaders that this was sufficient, they convened a meeting on October 14 to officially enroll the founding members, elect leaders, and begin planning the work of the farm. On that night twenty-seven families signed the original document and elected the president of the initiating committee as the cooperative president. Six more families joined two months later. Despite limited interest in joining the cooperative, the hall outside the room where they convened was packed with villagers determined to know exactly what the members were up to. Many no doubt sensed the ominous implications.

The general belief, shared by both Bulgarian villagers and outside observers, is that these early joiners were the poorest farmers. One villager characterized the founders of the farm as "men with only one goat to their name. They were followed into the cooperative by those with one cow, and only later by those with two cows." Another villager made the same point in joke form when he asked me, "What do big frogs say?" I admitted my ignorance of frog communication and he responded, "k-u-lak, k-u-lak," drawing out the word to make it sound almost amphibian. "What does the tiny frog say?" he then inquired. I shrugged and he delivered the punch line in rapid syncopation, "Tay-Kay-Zay-Say, Tay-Kay-Zay-Say." I laughed and pretended not to notice the disapproving glare his wife gave him.

Data challenge this stereotype. A description of the TKZS from the archives characterizes the founders as "poor and paltry" but gives the amount of land they contributed as 1,085 decares. Even discounting the 74 decares that may have come from other village holdings, the average contribution works out to nearly 32 decares per member. Although indisputably a small holding, this amount is larger than the 27.8-decare village average at that time. Also, we must bear in mind that members were not required to contribute all their land at this point; in all likelihood many withheld some holdings for private cultivation. The inventory of property contributed by early members shows that none gave vineyards, which certainly they had. So, the landholdings of early members were even greater than the total for the new cooperative. By 1953, when membership had passed the 200 mark, the annual farm report verifies that the majority of members brought in less than 30 decares each, but thirty-two members

contributed between 31 and 50 decares, and eleven members gave between 51 and 100 decares. One member actually contributed over 100
decares. Clearly, limited land was not the only motivation driving cooperative membership.

Political commitment was a factor for some. One member said he
joined because "once the people's power had been established, it was
expected that we would move toward cooperative production." For others
their social connection to people in the initiating committee was instrumental; at least three of the founders were either relatives or neighbors of
the president. Conversely, other people refused to join because they were
at odds with someone else supporting the cooperative. Still others who
were previously on good terms came to loggerheads because of their different attitudes toward the initiative.

The potential role of social and economic relations within households
and families is even more fascinating. While several of the founders were
reputed to be from poor families, many had married into families that
were significantly better off, improving their economic prospects. Dependence on the wife's property, however, also meant dependence on the
wife's parents. In some cases this included moving in with her family in
order to inherit her family's property. This culturally undesirable and demeaning arrangement placed the in-marrying male in a subordinate relationship to his in-laws. The cooperative offered a way out.

The tension between in-laws is a significant theme in Bulgarian folklore, reinforced by everyday gossip. The possibility that such a motivation
underlaid cooperative membership was suggested by a large extended-
family household in the village in which two married sons lived together
with their wives, children, parents, and grandmother in clearly cramped
quarters. It was customary for the youngest son to bring his wife to live
with his parents. Older sons could do so as well, but in this case it was
seen as an inconvenience because of the limited space and facilities. A
friend of the family told me that the wife of one of the sons was an only
child whose parents had a big house but refused to let the young couple
live with them because of the potential for conflict with the son-in-law.
The friend attested to the wisdom of this decision by pointing out that
you can have many hens in a chicken coop but only one rooster. I began
to explore this issue and soon discovered that several early cooperative
joiners had been dependent on their in-laws in various ways. Cooperative
membership was a godsend for these men. Not only did it allow them to

escape an unhappy subordination, but as the national preference for cooperative membership became more pronounced, it actually allowed
them to invert the relationship.

While a father and his sons were able to negotiate the multiple rooster
problem more easily than in-laws, sometimes they had problems. Adult
sons often resented continued parental control. Upon marriage their
wives entered the household, increasing their potential support and
bringing new sources of conflict. Still, with limited employment options
outside of farming, children were dependent on their parents for the
land they needed to survive. As a result there were numerous adult men
living less than happily with their parents. Again, collectivization provided
a way out. The importance of this consideration is supported by the multiple cases of family division recounted during descriptions of collectivization. Almost invariably a son wished to join the cooperative but his father
did not. In one household, two brothers wanted to join while a third and
their father refused. They eventually divided the property into three parts.
The two sons left home, joined the cooperative, and built adjoining
houses on a plot they received in the village. The oldest son stayed with
the parents and received the old homestead, which should have gone to
the youngest. Another young man was actually one of the original instiga-
tors of the cooperative, but he could not convince his father to join or
hand over any land so he could join: "'Why should I give you our land,'
he would say, 'only for you to pass it on to strangers. We need it ourselves.' He really made me mad." After the cooperative was formally inaugurated in October, the fighting got so bad that the father relented and
divided the land. The son was able to join in the small second cohort of
joiners in December, but he had been denied the distinction of charter
membership, which he continued to hold against his father forty years
later.

The desire to escape unhappy household arrangements continued to
attract members, but as production actually got under way, new considerations emerged. Members contributed disparate fragmented parcels. In order to consolidate them into larger blocks amenable to collective cultivation, the cooperative was legally empowered to expropriate private land
bordering or separating cooperative plots, compensating the owners with
equivalent land elsewhere. The exchange was very complicated, time consuming, and the source of endless conflicts between the commission responsible for coordinating the exchange and the private holders involved.
Very few people were satisfied with the exchanges. They complained

about the quality of the land they received, the lack of consideration for location, and especially the lack of compensation for resources that were on their land at the time of the exchange, such as hay in meadows, wood in forests, and fruit trees on cultivated lands.

Some took their complaints to the county level but apparently got little satisfaction. Others went straight to the top, writing directly to Chervenkov, the leader of the Communist Party at the time. Responding to a deluge of complaints from all over the country, the Central Committee in Sofia deployed county representatives to deal with them. A party leader from the town of Lom came to Zamfirovo for this purpose, bringing with him 500 complaints that had been registered against the Zamfirovo TKZS. The president of the TKZS defended the cooperative against the charges, most of which he told me were minor. While many plaintiffs received additional compensation, most still got less than they thought they deserved. Perhaps sensing their disadvantaged position in these negotiations, a few individuals decided to join the cooperative rather than accept or contest the land offered in such exchanges.

Once land had been consolidated into large blocks, the cooperative requested the plowing services of the machine tractor station in the town of Boychinovtsi. At this time there were relatively few such stations. They were equipped primarily with the limited number of tractors supplied by the Soviet Union after the war to advance the communist cause. It is not surprising then that the tractors never made it to the village. Instead, the cooperative engaged the services of the village's one private tractor owner simply to outline the cooperative plots. With much ceremony, including political speeches and a band, the new era of cultivation began. The president himself rode with the tractor driver, and while cooperative members sang and danced in the field, many of the aggrieved met the tractor with curses and threats. After defining the plots, the excitement was over for a while: the rest of the plowing and most of the other work was done laboriously by hand with only animal traction.

With cultivation under way, the performance of the cooperative provided another consideration for would-be members. The Zamfirovo cooperative did well. Although it lacked the technology of an economy of scale and continued to operate in much the same way as before, it produced more per decare than private growers in the first harvest of 1949. The president attributed this to the fact that most of the members were supporters of the party and devotees of the Soviet model, so "they followed direction closely and were diligent workers." Political commitment may indeed have been a factor, but state supports, including a major loan for construction needs, clearly helped the farm and sustained political enthusiasm. Regardless of the cause, the farm's success inspired fourteen new members to join soon after the harvest and may have been a factor in later campaigns, since the farm continued to perform well and eventually acquired a tractor. At an area conference in 1951 the farm was commended for its exemplary organization and performance.

By 1950, however, such considerations were less significant than the increasing pressures coming from the national level. Various mechanisms of compulsion were put in place in the last years of the 1940s, including the nationalization of forests, the forced sale of large agricultural machinery to the state, and the installation of rationing priorities that privileged cooperative members in the allocation of scarce commodities. By 1950 the increasingly strong state apparatus was enforcing these regulations more severely, in tandem with a stepped-up propaganda campaign. In the early part of that year alone, the county in which Zamfirovo is located reported 600 village meetings and demonstrations involving over 50,000 participants; villagers reported constant visits by initiating committees (Kouzhouharova, Meurs, and Stoyanova, n.d.). This was the beginning of the real push to collectivize. In a nutshell the strategy was to make private cultivation as difficult as possible while making cooperative cultivation more appealing, both economically and emotionally.

To ensure that its message and initiatives were heeded, the party dispatched representatives to villages throughout the country. In Zamfirovo the state came in the form of an agricultural expert who also took an active part in the campaign to increase cooperative membership. This mirrors the account given to Langazov (1984:54) by the first president of the TKZS in the village of Pushevo, who recalled the arrival of a district representative to promote collectivization. At the same time, villages had to send local representatives to attend a one-year course for cooperative farm presidents organized by the state. Zamfirovo sent a younger man who had not been among the original founders. On his return in 1951 he assumed the presidency of the farm. The replacement of the local founder with a party-trained administrator symbolizes the nationalization of cooperativism that was well under way by this time. The local party organization also became more active in the drive. The secretary met weekly with cooperative leaders to discuss the progress of expansion, and party members were told to join the cooperative or risk being expelled. This threat coincided with a national purging of ranks as the party became secure enough to transform itself from a mass movement into a vanguard organization. Lack of support for collectivization or any hesitation in joining the TKZS became grounds for culling. A few such cases were recorded in the minutes of the Zamfirovo village council. These examples were probably enough to bring any outstanding party members into the cooperative, although many (some estimated more than 100) were still forced out of the party for other reasons.

The eventual expropriation of large farm machinery affected very few villagers, but the TKZS's access to it may have made cooperative cultivation more appealing. In contrast, the exclusionary rationing system was acutely felt. Almost all products available in village stores could only be acquired with ration slips that were reserved for cooperative members. As already described, villagers had long since stopped producing many of these items, so they were vulnerable to such tactics. As one villager put it, "Of course, you did not *have* to join the cooperative, unless you wanted shoes on your feet and a shirt on your back." Alternate ways of meeting these needs were checked by a concomitant assault on private craftsworkers, who were forced into trade cooperatives. Permission of the village council was required to practice privately and, based on the disposition of several requests recounted in the minutes, it was never given. Those who continued to operate privately eventually had their tools expropriated and given to the cooperative.

Just as villagers were being denied access to products they did not produce, they were being required to hand over more and more of what they did produce through the expanding requisition program. Of course, the system of delivery quotas itself was intended to encourage cooperative membership as well as to provide resources for the state, hence the lower requisition rates for cooperatives. We should also note that the inability of private farmers to meet the higher delivery quotas was exacerbated by the establishment and expansion of the cooperative itself. Among other things, the exchange of land to create cooperative blocks occurred at great expense to village common lands. The minutes from a meeting of the TKZS land exchange commission on January 10, 1949, states that the land of private farmers incorporated into cooperative blocks would be compensated with equivalent land "from communal or cooperative holdings." Of the fourteen exchanges that were recorded, thirteen of them were made with common lands, amounting to 44 decares; only one plot, measuring 2.5 decares, was compensated with TKZS property. Furthermore, the minutes point out that the new cooperative farm directly an-

nexed an additional 30 decares of communal pasture. The president of
the farm admitted to me that the acquisition of village common lands was
a major contribution to the cooperative's success. Such actions further
damaged the economy of private producers, diminishing their ability to
fulfill the increasing requisition quotas. This actually complemented state
policy, for the quotas were at least partially intended to make life difficult
for the private producer. As previously mentioned, villagers were required
to deliver products they did not even raise. In some cases this forced
production, but in others it forced villagers into cooperatives. For example, because fruit trees took years to bring into production, the requisition of apples in villages with no orchards gave private farmers little
choice: they could try to buy apples or join the cooperative. As the farm
president put it, "They [the state] demanded milk from oxen; it was a
political question." One can see why the cooperative, with its lower delivery quotas and rationing advantages, seemed to be the only choice. This
assessment is reflected in the considerable expansion of the cooperative
in 1950–51 (see Table 4), achieved without physical coercion or violent
resistance.

Those farmers still determined to make a go of it on their own resented
the cooperative campaigners and felt threatened by their project, yet their
opposition was rarely more than verbal. The founding president of the
cooperative recalled only one situation where he was physically threatened. The individual involved had proven particularly resistant to the

Table 4. Number of Zamfirovo
Cooperative Joiners, 1948–56

Year	New Members
1948	33
1949	14
1950	58
1951	69
1952	26
1953	4
1954	29
1955	1
1956	600[a]

SOURCE: Zamfirovo cooperative farm.

[a]Approximate

proselytizing of various initiating committee members, so they decided to go en masse to make a stronger impression. A group of fifteen assembled and headed to his house, where they found him on the balcony, splitting wood for kindling. As two of the group entered the yard, he began cursing and threatening them, insisting they get off his property, then pelting them with firewood when they did not comply. They took cover behind a cart in the yard, whereupon he hurled the hatchet as well. According to the president, it whizzed right by his head, lodging in the side of the cart. At this point the rest of the group subdued the man, intending to take him to the police, but the president decided to let him go. Apparently, this incident was the pinnacle of forceful resistance in Zamfirovo, although the president recounted many episodes of verbal abuse and threats.

Elsewhere, the amount of coercion and resistance was more extensive. In other villages, residents who refused to join reported being beaten and even forced at gunpoint to relent. The most overt manifestations of resistance were riots and revolts. Brisby (1960:40) claims that "widespread discontent led to riots in several parts of the country," but other accounts list only three specific examples of such unrest. Jones and Jankoff (1957:304) report that huge segments of the rural population in the Vidin region and around the town of Kula, both in the northwestern tip of the country, revolted in March 1950. Details are not given, but they claim that "repression by the armed forces was bloody." Brown (1970:202) mentions the Kula incident, along with rioting in Teteven, northeast of Sofia, as responses to governmental pressures. It was officially admitted that even members of the communist youth organization participated in the Teteven revolt, which consisted primarily of plundering the equipment and animals of the cooperative farm.

The plundering of animals, crops, and equipment was a general strategy of resistance evident in other areas of the country as well. Dobrin (1973:45) writes that "there was mass slaughtering of livestock and damage to durable cultures. In the few days prior to their scheduled collectivization many peasants cut down all their fruit trees. In some houses when the collectivization group arrived to pick up the inventory and livestock there were real battles with the peasant families, in many cases with loss of human life." Drawing on published newspaper articles from 1950 to 1951, Jones and Jankoff (1957:304) relate three stories of peasants damaging farm machinery, sixteen accounts of arson, and one report of a massive slaughter of cattle in Stara Zagora. They maintain that such accounts "appear[ed] constantly in the Party press." Similarly, Brisby (1960:44) traces the serious meat shortages of the mid-1950s to the "wholesale slaughter of animals which was the peasants' desperate answer to collectivization."

Further evidence of resistance was the continuing attempt by peasants to leave the cooperatives. Langazov (1984:51–52) reports that 113 people left the cooperative in the village of Pushevo in late summer 1951 as a result of "subjective mistakes" made at the beginning of the harvest. This probably had to do with the right of people who entered the cooperative after the 1951 sowing to harvest their own fields privately, a conflict that developed in Zamfirovo as well. According to Brown (1970:202), it was officially admitted that 4 to 5 percent of cooperative members wished to leave the farms. Indeed, Chervenkov admitted in 1951 that such withdrawals were a sign of "strong hesitation on the part of peasants who were still not convinced of the righteousness of the cooperative idea" (Jones and Jankoff 1957:304). Such hesitation, along with other types of resistance, no doubt induced the government to moderate its drive for collectivization and later to reduce the amounts of requisitions. Zhivkova (1989: 168) says the cooperative in the village of Dobrodan received a "directive 'from above' to halt work on the formation of the TKZS." Zamfirovo officials whom I interviewed did not recall this particular communication among the numerous others they received in regard to collectivization, but they said the intensity of the pressure subsided a bit and is perhaps reflected in lower numbers of cooperative joiners between 1952 and 1955 (see Table 4).

Because collectivization depended heavily on local villagers, the effect of governmental directives and the potential for resistance varied from village to village. Early progress, for example, depended on locals who were committed to agricultural cooperativism or communist ideals. Where such actors were missing, little if any progress was made. Although a new factor was added with the arrival of government representatives to stimulate cooperative expansion, the role of these individuals was generally less significant than that of the local leadership. Once the government began insisting on cooperative expansion, however, local leaders and party members became motivated by a wider set of circumstances, for they were now judged on the progress of the campaign. As Rev (1987:339–40) noted for Hungary, this accounts for some of the "excesses," as ambitious local leaders responded to the expectations of their superiors, even to the detriment of local concerns. Thus, as Giurova (1989) points out, even the excesses of local authorities, which the central government sometimes castigated, were in part a result of the centralized top-down governmental structure itself.

This is not to argue that the national government was completely separated from, or unresponsive to, local difficulties. Its attention was especially evident in the tempering of the collectivization drive by 1952 and the accompanying censure of excesses. In one of the areas of rioting the entire local party leadership was dismissed. This may have been a case of scapegoating, but it was still a response to local discontent. Similarly, the increase in private livestock limits in 1953–54 (from five sheep to ten and from one pig to two) showed national sensitivity to one of the major discontents of cooperative villagers. In this sense the Bulgarian case clearly conforms to Kideckel's (1982) model of collectivization as a multilevel adaptive process between national and local forces. While the two major periods of cooperative expansion in Zamfirovo corresponded closely with national-level pushes for cooperative membership, first in 1950 and then again in 1956, the nature of the process at the local level was determined primarily by local factors. Furthermore, between these major pushes, the dynamism of the village cooperative, with its alternating phases of expansion and consolidation, reflected mainly local patterns of political commitment and farm success.

The respite, of sorts, between 1952 and 1956 proved to be a major tactical success for the government. By the time the national push was revived full force in 1956, those who had previously resisted surely saw the writing on the wall. More important, their harrowing struggle to make a go of private agriculture in the intervening years likely eroded much of their commitment to this form of production. At the same time villagers were starting to see industrial employment as a future option, so landownership and inheritance were less essential. Consequently, when collectivization was mandated again in 1956, it was accomplished with limited resistance in little more than two years, making Bulgaria the second country in the world to fully collectivize its agriculture.

In Zamfirovo three months sufficed. After receiving instructions from the county Central Committee to bring all outstanding farmers into the cooperative, the president of the village council and the party secretary again dutifully canvassed the village, but they only converted about fifty new families, leaving over 500 still to be convinced. Clearly a radical new approach was needed; their strategy combined carnival with elements of psychological terrorism. The 200 politically active or cooperative members in the village were divided into commissions of at least three members, including an Agrarian Party member and an unaffiliated villager as well as a Communist Party representative. Each commission was responsible for agitating in a different area of the village. After they had presented their arguments to each private proprietor in their area, they assembled with all the other commissions for a mass attack. In two large groups, augmented by teenagers taken out of school, and backed up by a musical band, they began canvassing the village, going from house to house playing music, shouting, singing, dancing, and presenting household proprietors with declarations of cooperative membership to sign. As one participant described it, "The people were so shocked by the music and crowds that they hardly knew what was happening. They were frightened and joined because of the noise and excitement and crowd pressure." One of those visited described the process more harshly as "an attack on the people, almost like a war. We did not know what was going on. We were frightened half to death and signed up. No one really threatened us directly, but we were overwhelmed and felt threatened."

At least as important as the threat was its carnivalesque packaging, which denied the coercive dimension and rendered standard resistance seemingly meaningless or inappropriate. Furthermore, the structure of the event followed that of customary community rituals such as Christmas caroling or dancing on Saint Lazar's Day. On these ritual occasions groups of dancers or singers traversed the village bringing good luck and other advantages to the households they visited, usually in exchange for food or money. This ritual form gave the solicitation a very different cultural meaning from that of the prior visits by cooperative agitators. As such it called for the appropriate ritualistic response: joining in and supplying the required contribution. To refuse such ritual participation was tantamount to abdicating one's place in the village community. The entourage also evoked aspects of the wedding ritual in its size and intensity, which added more positive cultural values. As one woman recalled, "It did not seem so bad when you saw all the people celebrating, singing, and the band playing. It seemed like the thing to do, and we wanted to join the festivities." Those who signed were entreated to join the celebration, making the throng progressively more intimidating. Those who refused to sign up were sent to the town hall to meet with the president of the village council. He informed them of their new requisition obligations under a new schedule increasing private delivery quotas. These rates were exorbitant and, as the council president admitted to me, further exaggerated by him for greater effect. "When they heard these figures," he reported, "they usually signed up without any further hesitation."

The Zamfirovo campaign was so successful that a group of villagers was invited to the village of Giganitsa to help with the campaign there. "We all rode to Giganitsa in a big truck along with the band and, aided by the local activists, we completed collectivization there as well." Not every village collectivization effort had such luck. For example, villagers around Belogradchik slaughtered some of their animals rather than hand them over to the cooperative, and cooperative members disbanded in support of the anticollectivization forces. Many tried to run away to Yugoslavia, risking capture and imprisonment. Zamfirovo informants interpreted the absence of such developments in their village as testimony to the good character of the villagers and the ingenuity of their tactics. While clearly self-serving, this interpretation underscores that no village experience could be universal.

The outcome everywhere relied heavily on village social relations. After reaching a critical mass, the cooperative had a snowballing effect due to the dense network of relations between villagers. As more and more villagers joined, it became increasingly acceptable to some of their friends and relatives. It also became increasingly difficult to function outside the cooperative. As one Zamfirovo man put it, "There was no one to help you slaughter your pig or help in the harvest because they were joining the cooperative. What could one do?" Some cooperative members refused to participate in such labor exchanges with private holders for political reasons, but for most it was a matter of simple economics. Having given over most of their land and animals to the cooperative, they no longer needed much help to farm the small plot they received for private use, so why should they continue to help other villagers? Thus, as collectivization progressed, many were pulled into it by ties of interdependence among villagers. For those still adamant, the sight of a hundred or more villagers descending on their house—people to whom they were connected in multiple ways and with whom they had to interact daily—must have been daunting. In some cases their own children were among the throng, adding a very intimate connection.

We can see the same considerations in the profile of resistance from villages where the outcome was the opposite of developments in Zamfirovo: instead of everyone joining, everyone left the cooperative. In both scenarios the pressure of village social relations and ties of interdependence are revealed. I do not mean to minimize internal village conflict, which was often rife and at times a factor obstructing cooperative membership as previously suggested. The idea of collectivization itself caused even more divisiveness and conflict between supporters and detractors. After a significant number of villagers were involved in the cooperative, however, such conflicts could be neutralized by positive relations with other cooperative members.

Given the various considerations and pressures, we can appreciate that even for supporters of the cooperative idea, the decision to join was rarely clear-cut or simple. Most people had attachments they were hesitant to sever. For some the connections were to the land itself, but they were most movingly expressed to me in terms of animals. When the cooperative representatives came to collect the animals of new members, the scene could be heart-wrenching: "The women were crying and wailing like a funeral, and some of the men were so sullen that they could not speak at all. It was terrible. Baba Penka accompanied her animals all the way to the cooperative shed, wailing the whole time."

The requirement to hand over animals was apparently not part of the original cooperative charter, for few animals were included in the inventory of early joiners. It became mandatory later as the state extended control over agriculture, chipping away at the cooperative features of farm organization (see Ludzhev 1989, Migev 1990). Already in 1950, the amount of production returned to members as rent on their contributed land was reduced, and members were required to contribute all their property to the farm; the farm then allocated them a small plot for personal subsistence cultivation, often from the land they had contributed if at all possible. The sale of contributed property was also restricted. These controls continued apace until, by the time collectivization was complete in 1958, the farms were operating more like state farms than cooperative organizations. Land was never nationalized, so it technically remained the property of cooperative members—a fact that would figure in postsocialist agricultural decisions—but in reality villagers lost all control. Such cooperatives have been referred to by others (Keliyan 1991, Pryor 1992) as pseudocooperatives. Having acknowledged them as such I will stick with the simpler designation. The transition to state control was symbolized definitively in 1958 by the elimination of all vestiges of rent payments to original landowners. Such state control, however, may have been less of an adjustment than one might think. As previously discussed, the state had been increasing its surveillance and involvement in private agricultural production since the mid-1940s, even setting and enforcing work schedules. Thus, the control of agricultural activity by the state was hardly novel.

Overall, what is clearly discernible in the collectivization process is a continuing attack on prior cooperative arrangements. This included an assault on communal property, in the form of common pasture; a negation of cooperative labor exchanges, which became unnecessary; and the jural elimination of cooperative elements from the newly created farms. Thus, collectivization, which began as an expansion of preexisting cooperative structures and arrangements, progressed by undermining these earlier forms, actually accelerating processes under way in prewar Bulgaria. In this way, socialist governments used collectivization to accomplish in eastern Europe what capitalism had achieved much earlier in western Europe through the enclosure acts and related attacks on cooperative arrangements.

Some argue that the socialist strategy was even more extreme, leading to the so-called individualization or atomization of socialist life (Kideckel 1993, Rev 1987). Kideckel suggests that collectivized agriculture paradoxically individuated village households by transferring responsibilities that previously motivated village collective action to state custody and management. Village families thus became the primary unit of articulation with the state, and the state became increasingly dependent on household producers. Their machinations for survival ended up influencing the state in ways the state could neither ignore nor fully control. In Zamfirovo some of these survival ploys involved networks beyond the family, although most coordinated in some way with household activities. These strategies, in turn, provoked reform programs in agriculture and, ironically, sometimes provided models for such reforms.

AGRICULTURAL REFORMATIONS

Life in the village did not improve immediately following collectivization. Villagers recounted circumstances from the late 1950s and early 1960s that must have provoked second thoughts, even on the part of cooperative supporters.

> It was terrible. I remember nearly collapsing in the fields one day during the wheat harvest. We worked all day in unbearable heat, doing everything by hand just like before, except now the blocks of land were endless, not a few decares like before. . . . The work was hard and the pay very low—only 80 stotinki a day and any pay in kind was deducted from that. People were worse off. Even the poorest people who joined the cooperative with little land felt worse off. I remember one summer somebody came to the fields to sell beer and sodas and even though we were dying of thirst no one could afford to buy them. If they did that today, nobody would do any work until they had drunk all the beer, regardless of the cost. But then nobody had money. With wages so low and the labor so hard people tried to get out of the cooperative. Anybody who had any other skill tried to find a job doing that instead, and brigade leaders would have to beg, coerce, or shame them into helping during peak periods. But I had no choice, so I worked in the fields. I remember thinking to myself many times that I simply could not go on like this for the rest of my life.

When I heard this description in 1988, the situation was very different from that being described. By then the only villagers working permanently as field hands for the cooperative were about forty retirees, and the work environment had changed so radically that one of them had even become nostalgic about the past.

> It was hard work, but agriculture is always hard. There is a Bulgarian proverb, you know: "The land wants a hoe, not a prayer."[1] We worked hard, but look at what we achieved. Now almost everything is done with machines. How do you think those machines got here? On our backs, through our hard work, that was the only way to get them. And it was not all horrible; there were also happy times. We went to the fields in large groups; we would talk and sing and laugh while we worked. Everybody was there, and how we used to celebrate after the harvests! . . . Now there are just a few of us working in the fields; it was harder before, but it was more fun. Of course I was younger then too. Do you think that makes a difference?

How could anyone who lived through the misery described in the first account end up with the nostalgic attitudes of the second? Certainly, different individual experiences account for some interpretative variation, but many villagers *combined* misery and nostalgia in their personal histories of the period, recounting harrowing details with a wistfulness that was hard to comprehend. The explanation lies in the intervening thirty years of reform and domestication, which affected everybody's evaluation of the past and, in turn, their ideas about the future.

The collectivization experience established a general approach to agriculture that characterized the Bulgarian state throughout the socialist era. Leaders were quick to embrace extreme reform measures but just as quick to reverse or scale down programs in response to early failures and difficulties. Cutting back on reform measures, however, did not imply an abandonment of grandiose objectives—it simply meant the state had adopted a practical approach to achieving them. The targets of these agrarian reforms can be grouped into several categories: the size of farm units, the level of technology, the crop base of the farms, the organization

1. This typically anticlerical proverb sounds better in Bulgarian, as the words for prayer (*molitva*) and hoe (*motika*) sound similar.

of production, and the role of the private plots of villagers.[2] As will be clear in what follows, these areas are not discrete categories but overlapping dimensions of agricultural change. Not all of them were the direct object of reform programs, but they were all affected by reforms in some way. This chapter looks at each of these concerns from the perspective of villagers. It is not intended as an analysis of the Zamfirovo cooperative farm nor of Bulgarian national agricultural policy, though it necessarily deals with both. Instead, the objective is to characterize the changing relationship between Zamfirovo villagers and agriculture from the late 1950s to the transition of 1989. In so doing, we will see how continuing agrarian reforms following collectivization enhanced local commitment to cooperative agriculture while also contributing to the process of agricultural disengagement.

Examining this apparent paradox provides important insight into the interactive nature of socialism as a system of conflicting complementarity, where even something as deleterious as chronic shortage had local benefits. If even the most negative qualities of socialism also had redeeming features, how could villagers not be ambivalent about the transition, especially since they had already had a bad taste of it? Indeed, as I show in this chapter, villagers were already under pressure to take back cooperative land for household cultivation in 1988. In these areas the promises and threats of transition were not novel but instead an intensification of prior reforms, which in some cases villagers had successfully resisted under socialism. The resistance itself testifies to previous reform successes that villagers wanted to defend.

By 1987 the average monthly wage in the village was slightly over 200 leva.[3] Most households had two such incomes, plus a pension or two from resident grandparents and numerous other sources of income that will be discussed here and in Chapter 5. Basic food staples were cheap: bread, 40 stotinki; yogurt, 23 stotinki a pint; feta cheese, 3 leva a kilogram; sunflower oil, 1.2 leva a liter; and sugar, 1 lev a kilogram.[4] Since villagers were able to produce most of their own subsistence needs, they expended very

2. Similar concerns were evident in various socialist agricultural systems (see, e.g., Dunn and Dunn 1988, Humphrey 1983, Karcz 1973, Kideckel 1979, Potter and Potter 1990, Pryor 1992, Salzmann and Scheufler 1986, Swain 1985).

3. The official exchange rate for the lev was set by the state at approximately 1 dollar, but the black market rate hovered around 4 to 5 leva per dollar in 1987–88.

4. These are general estimates based on a variety of types and qualities that affected prices. They sound fantastical in light of 1997 figures: bread, 500 leva; yogurt, 350 leva; feta, 3,500 leva; sunflower oil, 750 leva; and sugar, 1,000 leva.

little cash on food. Basic clothing was also cheap, although more stylish clothes could be expensive. One three-generation family of six estimated that they spent less than 500 leva a year on food and clothing. Nonbasics could be quite expensive; televisions and refrigerators cost between 300 and 400 leva, but all village families had both. Many village households also had a Lada (a Soviet-made car), which cost upward of 10,000 leva and required years on a waiting list. Villagers reported saving between 1,000 and 2,000 leva a year for such purposes. Village life in 1987 was decidedly not cushy or affluent, but it was a far cry from the situation at the time of collectivization, when a woman recalled carrying several kilograms of produce on her shoulders all the way to the Berkovitza market during the "hottest days of the summer" and then sharing a small, 6-ounce soda with two friends because they could not afford one apiece. Clearly, not all improvements were a direct result of agricultural reforms, but they were connected. When we see these changes from a local perspective, we can better appreciate the ambivalence that developed around the transition. The rest of this chapter endeavors to convey this experience.

The Economy of Scale

Attempting to capitalize on the momentum of collectivization, the state quickly began consolidating the new cooperatives. Within a year of completing collectivization in Zamfirovo, the local farm was merged with that of Berkovitza, a town some 17 kilometers away. As in similar cases throughout the country, poor performance was the official reason given for such incorporation. The tardiness of the farm in introducing strawberry cultivation, the decline in care of vineyards, and the weak organization of the farm were cited in one document as reasons for the consolidation. In fact, it had more to do with state policy than local difficulties, as the state was convinced that socialist agriculture required large units of production. The limits of this dictum were soon apparent, and the farms were separated again in the beginning of 1958. At this point local difficulties did provide the catalyst, specifically the declining performance of the first year.

Similar scenarios were found throughout the country (Atanasov 1990) and elsewhere in eastern Europe (Bell 1984:139, Kideckel 1979:144,

Lampland 1995:192–98, Vasary 1987:89–90). In the case of Bulgaria, Achagu (1985) suggests that the mountainous and hilly terrain where nearly 30 percent of the arable land was located made consolidation more difficult and less viable. The recurrent complaint about this period from villagers, however, concerned the mismanagement of the larger cooperatives after they were consolidated. Given that adjacent villages often had histories of bad relations and antipathies for any number of reasons, including the disagreements over rights to communal lands recounted in the preceding chapter, such conflict was not surprising. As a Bulgarian rural sociologist put it, "villagers prefer smaller cooperatives corresponding to their village's land, and they want to control the disposition of their own products." They gained concessions in this regard but not a complete reversal. Before the end of the year, the separated Zamfirovo farm was augmented by the smaller farms of the neighboring villages of Purlichovo and Rashovitsa, creating a large-scale cooperative farm (approximately 3,000 hectares) that was more locally focused and administered. While some residents of the smaller villages continued to resent their lack of autonomy, they had no history of conflict or animosity with Zamfirovo, and the arrangement proved to be an optimal and viable compromise throughout the 1960s. In other cases of consolidation, the resentment was more significant and even resulted in violence.

Bulgarian planners, however, did not abandon their prior goals, and by the mid-1970s they had again reduced Zamfirovo to a constituent element within a monumental agricultural unit centered at Berkovitza. This time their modus vivendi was the famous agro-industrial system, which represents the pinnacle of agricultural concentration in Bulgaria. The basis of this system was the amalgamation of the country's approximately 800 separate cooperative and state farms into roughly 150 large "agro-industrial complexes" (APKs). The exact number of constituent farms and resulting APKs varied over time, as more farms were integrated and the size of units altered, first increasing then decreasing the concentration (see Table 5). The constituent farms (TKZSs) were renamed "complex brigades" to reflect their new position as mere work groups within the larger agricultural complex. In the beginning this increased the size of the average Bulgarian agricultural unit nearly nine times, to 25,000 arable hectares per complex (Entwistle 1972:246). Even after the number of complexes was increased, arable land still averaged 15,000 hectares, and Bulgaria could still lay claim to having "one of the most concentrated agricultures in the world" (Grozev 1981:291).

Table 5. Number of APKs and TKZSs in Bulgaria, 1972–82

Year	APKs	TKZSs
1972	170	679
1973	160	535
1974	153	462
1975	152	281
1976	146	89
1977	143	78
1978	170	47
1979	268	34
1980	283	19
1981	281	19
1982	296	0

SOURCE: *Statisticheski Godishnik,* 1977:268; 1982:298; 1983:284.

The motivations for such concentration were varied (see Wiedemann 1980). The communist ideological commitment to large-scale production continued to be a factor. The declining performance of agriculture in the late 1960s also spurred the eagerness for change. Increasing agricultural production was essential for both improving consumer satisfaction and providing crucial export products. Given limited investment resources, the advances scored in the past through increasing concentration, both in agriculture and industry, provided a proven model. Inspiration may also have come from elsewhere in eastern Europe, as the Soviet Union and Czechoslovakia were embarking on programs of consolidation around the same time (see Salzmann and Scheufler 1986:114), though it is difficult to say who influenced whom in this regard. Perhaps even the capitalist trend toward agribusiness was a model, as there were certainly parallels in the two systems. Bulgarian leaders denied the latter and insisted that concentration was necessary first and foremost to facilitate the application of the "scientific and technological revolution" to agriculture.

While concentration was already evident in the model statute on cooperative farms issued in 1967, it probably gained momentum from the renewed emphasis on central planning and control that emerged in the wake of the Prague Spring in 1968. The plenum of 1968 decided that localities lacked the comprehensive view of the economy necessary for efficient planning, especially in the circumstances of scientific and technological advancement—hence the attraction of large complexes reporting directly to Sofia rather than to county ministries. Experimental agro-industrial units were formed the following year and the national-level program was officially sanctioned by the Central Committee of the Communist Party at the April plenum in 1970.

It is important to point out that the primary objective of the agro-industrial system was not, as is often assumed, the vertical integration of agricultural and industrial sectors but rather horizontal integration between farming units. There were approximately ten industrial-agricultural complexes that attempted to coordinate agricultural production with associated industrial processing. However, for the vastly more numerous agro-industrial complexes, the use of the word "industrial" referred simply to the practice of agriculture on an industrial basis. In this sense the relationship between the agro-industrial system and the utilization of science and technology is clearer, since industrial agriculture typically involves both a large scale of operation and extensive mechanization.

In situ the system appears much less formulaic. Some areas of the country were more amenable to an economy of scale, and APKs provided the foundation for a highly specialized industrial agriculture. The prime example is the Dobrudzha in the northeast of the country, where massive grain fields were established. The area around Zamfirovo, like much of the country, is predominantly foothills with a varied crop base. If this terrain was a barrier to cooperative consolidation following collectivization, as Achagu (1985) suggests, then the same can be said of agro-industrial consolidation. There was much less to be gained here from industrial-style organization, and consequently the APK was much less effective (see Boyd 1990).

The deficiencies of the APK system in the area of Zamfirovo became evident only as the system evolved. According to official reports, these complexes were in place by 1972, but Zamfirovo residents and farmworkers dated their entry into the system to 1974. This two-year difference reflects a change in the role of agro-industrial functioning, probably beginning in 1974, toward greater central control. Increasingly, the offices of the APK acted less like a coordinating center and more like a direct administrator, steadily usurping the local farms' decision-making responsibilities. That this trajectory was part of the original plan is verified by Ivanov's (1972:66) statement from 1971: "Conditions for a higher degree of integration [of APKs] and their ultimate transformation into single production units will be created gradually." This process began impinging on Zamfirovo administrators in 1974 and peaked in 1976 when, as one farmworker put it, "Everything went to Berkovitza for administering and organizing. All management and record keeping, as well as all our funds, were transferred there. The APK used up all the funds [several thousand leva] in one year, and there was nothing left. They got all the papers and everything in such a mess that they had to give it all back to the village to keep track of it in 1977. Without the money of course."

The unsuccessful attempt to eliminate the constituent farms as administrative entities reveals the importance of local forces in the larger agricultural system. Following this failure, the agro-industrial system, despite continued emphasis in the national media and scholarly literature, was in retreat. Starting in 1977 the complexes were reduced in size. The Berkovitza complex lost three farms, leaving it with six constituent units including Zamfirovo. The APK was further challenged by the introduction of the New Economic Mechanism (NEM) in 1979, which advocated decentralized decision making, a reduction in the number of plan indicators, and increasing emphasis on contractual arrangements between enterprises. These reforms, which, as Boyd (1990:72) points out, "show many similarities to those implemented by Mikhail Gorbachev in his economy-wide perestroika," challenged the power and role of the APK. Thus, one villager claimed that since 1977, the APK consisted of "over thirty officials who do not do anything. They have a specialist for every type of agricultural activity, but they really do not do anything."

When Bulgaria began its own official version of perestroika, these officials were targeted. In 1988 the staff in Berkovitza was cut to twelve people, and their authority was further reduced. Instead of being pleased, Zamfirovo officials were disappointed that the APK had not been eradicated altogether, as had apparently happened elsewhere. Rumors circulated that it had survived only because the director in Berkovitza had family connections with agricultural leaders in Sofia. Villagers got their wish in 1989, for while the cooperative farm continued to function after the collapse of communist control and even after the legal means for reclaiming cooperative land were established, the APK basically disintegrated. Again, however, it was a process that can be traced to the late 1970s.

Villagers resented the APK as an extraneous drain on village resources: "Why should we hand over money to Berkovitza every year? For what?" The farm had to pay the APK 1,000 leva annually for its administrative services. The APK also required the farm to grow crops and raise animals that were unprofitable. This was partly an aspect of the centralized planning system, but it was reinforced by reforms in the late 1970s aimed at achieving regional self-sufficiency in basic agricultural products. These reforms were intended to reduce energy use and transport costs by having every county provision itself in agricultural staples. This increased the need for farms to produce products they might not otherwise grow, and in so doing, contradicted prior reforms that had increased enterprise autonomy in decision making and heightened productive specialization. The contradiction typified the process of conflicting complementarity. The degree of conflict, however, varied by county; since the area around Mihailovgrad had a very mixed agricultural profile rather than a singular specialization, there was less conflict.

By 1987 I heard little reference to the goal of regional self-sufficiency. Still, the APK continued to dictate particular products. Pork is a good example. In the early 1980s, following the decentralization of the NEM, the farm stopped raising pigs, which, given state purchasing prices, had become unprofitable. Apparently, many other villages did the same, and after a shortage of pork developed in 1985, the APK required the village to recommence pig farming. Workers also complained that second-crop autumn strawberries, which they sold to the APK at low prices, showed up at exorbitant prices in the market: "It is stupid. We sell them to the APK for stotinki when we could get leva for them at the markets in town." Another villager summed it up: "The APK's role is to take from the farms." Significantly, this discontent with the APK helped stimulate reform sentiment in the village toward defense of the cooperative farm rather than its destruction.

Yet the same commitment to the cooperative allowed some villagers to see benefits in the APK, particularly its role in guaranteeing the inputs for village production. For example, through a local machine tractor station (MTS) located in the village, the APK provided and maintained the machinery for the farm. Farm machines remained at the village station and were run primarily by villagers, but the unit itself was administered by Berkovitza, with the cooperative farm contracting the services. The farm could have managed its own machinery, but assuring replacement parts would have been difficult. The APK also advanced other basic inputs such as fertilizer, seed, and fuel. In an economy of shortage, this was a significant contribution, and several people involved in the farm insisted that the cooperative could not have managed alone. Only in the 1980s did this role become less essential, as reforms stressed contractual arrangements between firms, and farms became more responsible for finding their own inputs and markets.

While the APK became progressively less essential, the trade relations between enterprises that had originally been linked through the APK remained important, limiting the actual affect of enterprise autonomy. Because they were mutually interdependent in numerous ways, enterprises tended to perpetuate the same connections established under APK auspices. Thus, at a cooperative farm meeting in 1988, a man complained that the farm was not getting a good price for plums from the state purchasing organization in Mihailovgrad, and the cooperative should find a better deal. This was unlikely to happen, however, because there were many other relations between the farm and this organization, of which plums were only a part. Such connections formed the foundation of the barter arrangements that emerged in the crisis of the 1990s as a basic means of economic exchange. As in the Soviet Union (Humphrey 1991), barter became a common way of exchanging goods. While this was a consequence of the dislocations of the 1990s, it grew out of contract and exchange networks enhanced by reforms of the 1980s.

Mechanization and Labor Supply

The increasing size of agricultural units was closely connected to changing technology. As the informant quoted at the beginning of the chapter vividly pointed out, the early cooperatives often had very little, if any, mechanized technology (see also Zhivkova 1989:165). The units were larger and people worked them in larger groups, but they were doing the same work in the same way—and for less compensation.

In the 1960s the level of mechanization in the farm increased, and the nature of agriculture began to change dramatically. This was especially evident in the expanding stocks of the MTS, but it was also noticeable in the construction of irrigation facilities and the mechanization of dairy facilities. Since 1963 the farm had constructed three reservoirs with irrigation pumps. By 1975 irrigated land accounted for 2,500 decares, devoted primarily to strawberries and corn. Farm administrators still complained that the amount of irrigated land was insufficient and a major limitation for the farm. At the same time, it was clear that this complaint worked to some advantage—it was used to justify devoting more corn acreage to fresh silage, reducing the amount grown for grain. The silage went to cooperative animals, which improved performance in this difficult sector and had greater multiplier effects for the village economy than simply selling corn. For its part, livestock production, especially dairying, was also significantly mechanized. All cattle sheds had mechanized milking machines. One had a system for transporting the milk directly from the cow to a central collection point, though most required workers to collect the milk at each cow and empty it into milk containers. Most were constructed so that food could be delivered directly from trucks that drove down the center of the shed, spreading feed into troughs on either side. This allowed drivers to deliver freshly cut silage, for example, during the day when the milkers were not present.

The increasing reliance on technology was especially pronounced in regard to farm machinery. Whereas the early cooperative had no machines and only limited access to those in neighboring towns, the village got its own state MTS in the 1960s. By 1987 the Zamfirovo station operated thirty-three tractors with attachments for every conceivable agricultural activity, five wheat combines, two silage combines, and a hay bailer. The machines were Soviet made with the exception of three items—two grain combines and one silage combine—made in East Germany. The MTS employed over fifty workers, earning an average of 300 leva a month. The workers still complained, however, about technological limitations. Much of the equipment was old and prone to breakdown. Other specialized machinery was not available. For example, a brigade leader insisted at a meeting of the cooperative farm in 1987 that the plows were inappropriate for viticulture.

Interestingly, mechanization was driven at different times by two seemingly opposite forces. In the 1960s infusions of farm machinery were part of the socialist industrialization strategy. Mechanized agriculture produced a greater surplus for industrial investment while freeing excess village farmworkers for industrial work. By the 1970s, however, the process had gone too far, and rural areas were experiencing labor shortages. The focus on mechanization continued subsequently as a necessary replacement for dwindling agricultural labor.

Most Zamfirovo villagers working full-time for the cooperative farm in 1988 were either administrators, technicians, or machine operators. This farm, with over 30,000 decares of cultivated land, had only two brigades of less than twenty workers each devoted to field labor. This was a major change from the early days of the cooperative, when nearly the whole village was engaged in agricultural labor. As in Romania (Moskoff 1978, Cernea 1978), the few full-time field hands were predominantly women, but what is more significant, they were all, including several men, beyond retirement age. Full-time manual farm labor in much of Bulgaria had been relegated to older people who were retired and wished to continue working or who had not worked long enough to qualify for state pensions. The superior status of industrial work and the elastic, labor-absorbing capacity of socialist industry sapped workers from agriculture. Older villagers who did not learn other skills or trades were the only ones left for agricultural work. Others ended up in the same predicament after retiring from nonagricultural jobs because their pensions were inadequate and they lacked alternate sources of support.

The resulting age profile of agriculture did much to further diminish the social status of agricultural labor in the village. Full-time manual field labor came to be seen as an obsolete occupation, an idea that was both symbolized and reinforced by the age of the brigade workers. In fact, villagers commonly referred to the two brigades of the cooperative farm as "the grannies." This reality suggests that the much discussed feminization of agriculture (Cernea 1978) may have been, at least in Bulgaria, partly a demographic and social derivative of the "gerontocratization" of agriculture. Since women live longer and retire five years earlier than men in Bulgaria, they predominate in a geriatric agriculture. The reliance on retirees had negative consequences. They were not able to perform all types of strenuous labor, and since many worked at their own discretion, the brigades, already small to start with, rarely had a full workforce.

The shortage of agricultural labor was a recurrent constraint for the Zamfirovo cooperative. Large areas of vineyards were not pruned, significantly diminishing the output. Some crops, such as walnuts and tomatoes, were not completely or regularly harvested. In 1987 the crop from a small pear orchard was gathered from the ground after the pears fell because there was no one in the brigades able to climb the trees and pick them. Consequently, the crop had to be used for preserves rather than sold more lucratively as fresh fruit. Any extensive manual work, such as the grape harvest, depended on temporary brigades supplied by nonagricultural enterprises in the village or neighboring towns, occasionally augmented by national youth brigades. Even mechanized labor was often in short supply. When the man who plowed the vineyards for the cooperative died, the vineyards were not plowed, "because there was no one to drive the tractor." Similar stories with more disastrous consequences were reported in the news media from other areas of the country. These reports were often sensationalized for political effect, but my experience in Zamfirovo confirms the deleterious consequences of the agricultural labor shortage.

Crop Profile

Just as the labor shortage drove mechanization, the two together altered the profile of farm products. In 1987 the Zamfirovo farm raised primarily corn, wheat, alfalfa, grapes, and strawberries and tended orchards of plums, quinces, walnuts, and pears. Other crops, including cabbage, tomatoes, fodder beets, beans, cucumbers, and watermelons, were grown on a much smaller scale and primarily for village consumption. Livestock, for the most part sheep and dairy cattle, was as important as the major crops, accounting for approximately the same percentage of farm output as agriculture. The village thus conformed roughly to the pattern described for the county as a whole by Gergov (1984:65), namely, "grain growing, livestock raising and pig producing."

This profile, however, was constantly evolving. Cousens (1967) points to significant changes already evident nationally by the late 1960s, notably the increase of fodder crops, particularly corn, at the expense of wheat. Zamfirovo had clearly been increasing the amount of land in corn production, much of which, as previously mentioned, was cut green for silage. However, as labor became increasingly scarce and machinery more available, local farm managers also increased the area devoted to wheat as well, since it could be plowed, planted, and harvested by machines. Actually, the acreages of wheat and corn were interdependent, the fields being rotated between these crops on a regular basis. Some wheat was also designated for use in a mixed concentrated animal feed produced at the farm's feed plant.

By 1987, then, both of these mechanized crops were expanding at the expense of labor-intensive ones, such as vegetables and fruits, even to the point of eliminating some of the latter. The pear orchard that could not be harvested correctly in 1987 was chopped down for firewood in 1988. A large expanse of vineyard along the road leading into the village was also slated for destruction. When I inquired about the obvious neglect of the vineyard, I was always told that it was old, that there was no one to take care of it, and that they were going to cut it down soon and use the land for grain. I also heard debates among farm administrators and villagers about the rationality of keeping the walnut and quince orchard, given the lack of labor for harvesting the nuts. Were the walnut trees not interplanted with quinces, which were more easily and quickly harvested, they might have met the same fate as the pear trees and the vineyard. In some of these cases the trees or vines at issue were indeed old, with diminishing productivity, but there was no talk of replacing them with young plants, only mechanized wheat and corn. Farm administrators often rationalized their declining interest in vegetable crops as a response to limited water supplies, but as described above, large irrigated plots that could have been used for vegetables were used for corn production instead. Clearly farm officials preferred to produce the corn, which was not labor intensive and which they used primarily for fodder.

The increase in grain and fodder cultivation underwrote the significant expansion of village livestock production over the last three decades. In 1987 the farm had 620 cows giving milk and over 1,000 young cattle to be sold, fattened for veal, or raised for eventual dairy production. Adult sheep numbered 2,465, with about as many lambs per year. The number of pigs averaged about 20 for the year. While the expansion of fodder acreage was important in this development, another crucial factor was the concomitant increase in irrigation. Irrigation reduced the yearly fluctuation of corn production, previously so dependent on precipitation rates, increasing both the quality and security of silage. So even as farm administrators avoided growing *grain* corn by citing irrigation limitations, they were actually cutting *irrigated* corn for cattle silage. Thus, while Ofer (1980:311) attributes increases in the relative share of animal products and feed crops to national economic policy, these increases were also a consequence of changes occurring on local farms.

All these changes were reflected in the diet of Bulgarians, for meat consumption increased significantly after 1960. In fact, one Zamfirovo grandmother drew on meat consumption to epitomize the changes in her lifetime: "When I was younger, even after my son was born, we rarely had meat, except for holidays or special occasions. Now if my son does not see meat on his plate at every meal, he complains." Similarly, people no longer consumed much corn meal, a prewar staple, although it still disappeared quickly from store shelves because it was so cheap that villagers used it to feed household livestock.

While the productive profile described above was a response to technological and labor supplies, other political and economic factors played their part. As Swain (1981:240) notes for Hungary, profitability was a concern. Administrators sought to use their scarce labor resources on products for which the price set by the state was relatively high. In most cases, high prices were restricted to those products exported to Western countries for hard currency. In this way, international trade, although centrally controlled, affected local farm decisions in Zamfirovo. This was clearly the case in regard to strawberry production, much of which was exported. After the strawberries were picked, workers from the Commerce Cooperative washed and packed them into barrels, which were loaded directly onto large refrigerated transport trailers from Holland. The hard currency value of this crop allowed higher payments to the growers, which further stimulated the expansion of strawberry cultivation. Other local crops were also exported, but since they went primarily to east European countries, their prices remained low and did not stimulate expansion.

The disposition of the product affected farm decisions in other ways. Most staple crops and all animal products were monopolized by the state. All wheat and grain corn, as well as all meat, milk, and wool, had to be sold to state purchasing organizations. For other crops, the farm had more options, and while prices were state controlled, the prices for products often varied according to their disposition, allowing room for profit-minded decision making, such as the use of irrigated land for silage. When possible, Zamfirovo farm administrators also privileged products over which the farm had more control. This explains a paradox of local viticulture. During the same period that farm administrators spoke to me of reducing their vineyards for labor reasons, I overheard farm managers making plans for a new vineyard. The new vineyard, however, was for dessert grapes rather than wine grapes. The latter had to be sold to the state winery (Vinprom), whereas dessert grapes could be sold by the farm as it decided—hence the different attitude toward identical production processes.

The impact of the above considerations was ultimately constrained by the important role of central planning. Most crops and animals raised were dictated by the APK, which received its directives from the National Agro-Industrial Union (NAPS) and passed them on to the various constituent farms. In fact, the area's specialization in grain and animal production was nationally dictated. Ideally, these planners considered local possibilities and resources, and even historical agrarian traditions (see Gergov 1984:15), in distributing the assignments. In the absence of market mechanisms, central planning guaranteed the production of necessary items.

We have already mentioned the example of pig production. The Zamfirovo farm did not want to raise pigs because it had difficulty finding
people to take on the job, and those the farm did find always posted poor
results. However, the APK periodically required them to raise a small
number of pigs to satisfy national needs. To compensate local farms for
the losses incurred producing required products, NAPS paid the farm a
subsidy. Thus, while Zamfirovo farm administrators claimed that livestock
production was unprofitable, and indeed farm records showed annual
losses of 166,000 leva in 1987 and 115,000 leva in 1980, they received a
substantial subsidy from NAPS for this production. In 1980 it amounted
to over 250,000 leva just for animal products. This is a significant amount
of money and helps account for the preferences given an apparently "unprofitable" area of farm production. The subsidies, however, were still a
relatively small percentage of the nearly 2 million leva produced by the
Zamfirovo livestock sector annually.

While central planning was a dominant force in cooperative farm decisions, it was not a static one. For example, the previously mentioned attempt at regional self-sufficiency strengthened the hand of the APK,
which became responsible for ensuring production of area subsistence
needs, in addition to allocating the national plan among its constituent
farms. But as the goal of county self-sufficiency waned in national planning, the APK lost leverage, ending up with less control than it had previously had. Similarly, reform programs usually focused directly on the loci
of decision making, generating variation in the impact of central planning as reform fortunes rose and fell. Reforms did not have to succeed in
order to affect the local farm. Local administrators often responded to
reforms as they were instituted, only to find out later, after land was already committed, that reform promises were not being actualized. Conversely, farm administrators with higher-level contacts were sometimes
able to capitalize on reform programs stymied elsewhere by middle-level
obstructionism.

The Organization of Production

All of the changes discussed above overlap significantly with changes in
what we might call the organization of production—including the locus
of decision making, the organization of labor, and the system of remu-

neration. These had been in an ongoing state of experimentation since the installation of the NEM in the late 1970s and early 1980s. With many ups and downs along the way (see Crampton 1988), the general trends were as follows: (1) decentralizing decision making even to the point of instituting "self-management"; (2) making enterprises more responsible for the acquisition of resources and disposition of products; and (3) tying wages more closely to worker production and enterprise profitability. By 1987 and 1988 such reforms had spiraled to the point of trying to force people to take back cooperative land for what amounted to private culti- vation. Foreshadowing one of the leitmotifs of the 1990s, this illustrates how aspects of transition were set in motion by socialist reform processes. The transition was in many ways a radical shift, but its local interpretation and progress were affected by such continuities with the past.

As a precursor of democratization, however, the idea of worker self- management was fairly superfluous in the Zamfirovo cooperative farm, given that most of the agricultural work was done either by machines driven by APK employees or by temporary brigades from other enter- prises. Field laborers amounted to a handful of retirees, and the rest of the agricultural employees were technicians or administrators. Clearly the benefits to be gained from worker input were limited. Also, the continu- ing role of centralized planning limited the decisions over which self-man- aged enterprises had control, so self-management, like prior decentraliz- ing reforms, was more operative in the implementation of policy than in its formulation. Nevertheless, as previously described, the farm did benefit from periodic increases in its latitude of decision making, especially those in 1987 and 1988, which allowed administrators to redirect small amounts of land and resources into more profitable ventures. Increasing control over product dispensation provided similar possibilities for greater profits, but as I recounted above, farm employees complained that managers did not always capitalize on these opportunities.

Changes were more readily evident in the area of labor remuneration. In the first wave of reforms in the mid-1960s, continuing the general trend away from true cooperativism, local farmworkers began to be paid on the "norm" system. Instead of receiving a portion of cooperative profit based on the number of labor days provided to the farm, they were paid according to personal production. In this sense the norm system was a euphemism for piecework, typical of the machinations devised by socialist governments to blunt the ideological contradictions of the wage relation (see Salzmann and Scheufler 1986:51–58 for an extreme example). Daily wage rates were established for every type of agricultural work. Workers were paid on the basis of a day's work, but they received a full "daily wage" only if they fulfilled the norm. The norm was the amount determined by the state that a worker should accomplish in one day. If the norm was not fulfilled, workers were paid on a strict piecework basis—a flat rate per pound of product harvested, per area hoed, and so forth. There was a premium for norm fulfillment, so production even slightly below the norm was less remunerative. Depending on the nature of the work, production might be measured either on an individual basis or for the brigade as a whole, with the total divided equally among the workers.

For some activities the norms seemed reasonable; for others they seemed difficult; for still others, quite impossible. The norm for a day of plum picking was 500 kilograms, for which workers were paid 15 leva. It would have been difficult for an average worker to pick such a quantity, but it could have been done with approximately nine hours of diligent work. However, many of the harvesters were retirees incapable of such diligence. Many could not climb the trees and used long sticks to knock plums to the ground. Clearly they could not fulfill the norm in this manner. Similarly, the norm for grape harvesting, only 250 kilograms, was possible in theory but impossible in practice, as my own experience showed. When one of the brigades in which I participated arrived at the vineyard, the brigade members and I had to first load our van with empty crates at the weighing station because there were no crates near the area being harvested. After one hour of picking, we had filled all these crates, and since the van had left, we had to walk back to the weighing station (ten to fifteen minutes away) to bring back more empties. Unable to carry many crates at one time, we ended up making three such trips in the course of the day, each brigade member losing about an hour of work time. Furthermore, by 4:00 P.M. we had filled all the crates at the weighing station and had to quit picking altogether. We also had to separate the grapes according to quality, which took additional time. Finally, the condition of the vineyards was an impediment. The vines had not been hoed or tied, which diminished the density of the crop and forced us to search among the weeds for the grapes, taking care not to slice our hands on the many thorns. Under these conditions the norm was not possible. We ended up getting about 5 leva each for the day's work—2 leva less than the norm.

Hay raking could also be problematic. The amount of hay was usually not enough in the marginal areas where it was gathered by hand to allow workers to fulfill the norm. Such difficulties led to limited enthusiasm and

even poorer job performance. After gathering with other farmworkers for
what we were told was a day of plum harvesting, we were switched to hay
collecting. Since everyone had brought buckets instead of pitchforks, we
had to drive by each worker's house to get the equipment. By the time we
got to the field, it was approximately 9:30, and everyone immediately sat
down for a break. When I inquired about starting work, I was told that
there was no way to fulfill the norm therefore no need to knock ourselves
out. In contrast, the norm for stacking up machine-baled straw or hay was
very reasonable. In half a day of very hard and hot work, workers earned
15 leva, and they worked diligently, although this particular brigade was a
temporary one made up of office workers rather than field laborers.

Dairying was much more remunerative. Milkers could earn nearly 400
leva a month, depending on milk output. In a typical dairy enterprise,
three and a half employees cared for 126 cows. Two workers milked the
cows and filtered the milk—all twice a day, working a split shift. The first
milking started around 4:30 in the morning, and the second around 3:30
in the afternoon. Another worker cleaned the premises, and a technician
was responsible for maintaining equipment—such as the milking machines and automatic water dispensers—in two different farms.

The picture is quite different in the sheep enterprises. Shepherding
paid lower wages and was essentially unmechanized. Some of the folds
were still made of thatch, and the workers at one enterprise reported that
electricity had just been connected there in 1987. The shepherds had to
live at the fold, which was usually far from the village and close to pastures
where the sheep grazed daily from March to November. Sheep were kept
for five years and then sold for slaughter and replaced by lambs. The
sheep were milked for five to six months between lambing in February
and mating in September. All the milking was done by hand. At one enterprise two workers milked 220 sheep in an hour and a half. Until 1987
shepherds were paid according to the amount of milk, wool, and manure
their sheep produced. Wages averaged 300 leva a month. This was good
pay for one individual but not much when a husband and wife did the job
together, as was sometimes the case. While the wage was less than what
dairy workers earned, shepherds received income on the side. In the summer they took in young, privately owned goats, habituating them to going
to pasture. For this they were paid approximately 20 leva per goat per
month, and I counted more than ten kid goats at one sheep farm one
summer. Furthermore, shepherds kept a ram for servicing the flock and
were paid 5 leva for the ram's stud service by villagers with privately

owned sheep. They might also grow a garden near the fold, since they had access to all the manure they could use for that garden and any others they might have. The manure at dairy farms, in contrast, was carted away mechanically and was less accessible.

These perquisites apparently did not offset the negative aspects of shepherding, and the farm had great difficulty getting shepherds. As one villager explained, "People do not want to stay there with the animals all the time and have to go out in bad weather. It pays well but it is unpleasant, and mostly Gypsies do it." The Gypsies were then criticized for their performance in a job few others wanted. Villagers said they were notorious for coming to the village, taking the job, getting an advance on the sheep products, and then leaving. One such shepherd actually abandoned his herd in a distant field, and farm administrators only found out after the sheep had wandered onto the pastures of another village, creating a scandal.

Given the difficulty securing shepherds, it was paradoxical that the farm actually tightened the wage system for shepherds when it did so for dairy workers in 1988, as part of the ongoing reform drive. In the past shepherds provided the labor while the farm supplied animal food and other overhead costs. As of 1988 these costs were to be deducted from the value of the production, and shepherds were to be paid according to profit, rather than output alone. This continued the ongoing reform trend toward increasing enterprise financial accountability and profitability. It was intended to promote efficiency and constrain the original socialist strategy of increasing output primarily by increasing inputs. Such a strategy made economic sense at the beginning of socialist development when there were more underutilized resources, but the very success of this approach used up the resources that made it attractive.

The shepherds were very pessimistic about their new prospects: "I think we will get less money this way. Now we have to pay for everything the farm provides—the food for the sheep and even the transport expenses to bring the food here. And you know all winter long the animals must live off hay and fodder from the farm, which is very expensive. We will have to wait and see." The shepherds were also not certain they would actually have much control over inputs, which were specified by the central plan. This is a typical illustration of the "irresponsibility thesis" of socialism, in which nearly everybody is liable for more than he or she can actually control (see Humphrey 1983:263). This limitation alone could completely contradict the objectives of the reform. Furthermore, shepherds probably had little leeway for cutting expenses. As one shepherd put it, "What can I do about the costs? Starve the sheep?"

The same model was applied to dairy workers, who were told their salaries would be based on the profits of their enterprise rather than gross production. One worker put it this way: "It will be like private production. We are starting to become more like your system. But it is not so easy for us because we are not such a rich country with so much good land, and we cannot grow the food to feed the cows they way they should be fed." Given such limitations, livestock workers might find it more profitable to cut production slightly if doing so significantly reduced input costs. Such a result was surely at odds with farm and national objectives to increase both efficiency *and* production. It would also increase conflicts between sectors of the farm economy—such as that previously described between silage and grain corn—since the reforms made the quality of animal food more significant to workers' salaries. While shepherds could not control that quality, the need to keep good shepherds and to increase production probably provoked the farm director to pay even more attention to livestock foods at the expense of other activities. Each reform generated new conflicts that drove new complementarities. A village administrator, commenting on all these potential conflicts, replied simply, "All this is so new that nobody really knows how the system will work." Time, however, proved to exacerbate rather than resolve the uncertainties.

The reforms in the remuneration system for shepherds were partly connected to the drive, beginning in 1987, to extend the *akord* system of labor payment, which had recorded successes in selected agricultural sectors. This contractual arrangement was similar to the *acord global* in Romania (Kideckel 1979:198) and, to a lesser degree, the Soviet "collective contract" (Laird and Laird 1988). In the Bulgarian version, the farm allotted villagers tracts of land to grow a particular crop. In return the workers agreed to provide the farm with a given amount of the produce at minimal or no cost. The produce exceeding this contractual amount was purchased by the farm at more lucrative rates. The costs of any inputs provided by the farm were then deducted from the value of the produce, and the workers received the balance in cash. Contractors were also allowed to take a small, prescribed amount of the produce for their own personal use at no cost.

The unit contracting land could be either an individual, a family, or simply a group of villagers working together. The vast majority were family groups, and most people referred to the system as the "family *akord*." This reinforced households as productive units in the village vis-à-vis the state, since contracting households could apportion their labor as members saw fit. In Zamfirovo the only contract group larger than a family was the one growing watermelons, in which five families cooperated. Quite successful, this group took over watermelon cultivation from the farm in 1986, starting with 20 decares. Production statistics were not available for that year, but the enterprise was clearly profitable, for the following year the group took on an additional 10 decares. From 30 decares they gathered 60 metric tons of watermelons, which they sold for a total of 20,000 leva. This was enough to merit mention on a Bulgarian television program devoted to agricultural news. The workers paid half of the total to the cooperative farm for seeds, plowing services, fertilizer, taxes, and land use, leaving them with 10,000 leva, or 2,000 leva per family. This is not a bad supplement, given that an average annual salary was only slightly more. Spurred by such success, the group increased its contract yet another 10 decares in 1988, but they actually produced less than the previous year due to poorer weather conditions.

From this example it is already clear that there were deviations from the *akord* arrangements previously outlined. The use of cooperative land for watermelon cultivation could be recompensed in cash because watermelons were sold almost exclusively by the farm to the local population, making the difference between a set payment in kind and the equivalent value in cash moot. This fact also enhanced the income for the workers, since the farm could sell the watermelons directly for 33 stotinki a kilogram, instead of the 25 stotinki specified within the commerce cooperative system. The latter would be essential, however, if the farm grew large quantities of the product, requiring national or international distribution.

Such was the case for strawberries. The village was famous for its strawberry cultivation, which began in the late 1950s and expanded quickly. Strawberries were an extremely profitable endeavor for the farm because of their export value. Cultivation, though, required manual harvesting, so with decreasing labor supplies it was a perfect venue for the introduction of *akord* arrangements. In the first year that such contracts were offered, several villagers, most connected to the cooperative farm, took over small amounts of land, while the farm continued to work the bulk of the strawberry acreage. After villagers saw the money made by the first contractors, interest in the arrangement grew rapidly. Within a couple of years the majority of village families were involved, and all strawberry production operated on an *akord* basis.

The farm supplied the plot of land already planted with strawberry plants, plowed between the rows with a tractor, irrigated the fields when necessary, and provided straw and fertilizer. The contract workers hoed the plot several times, put the straw around the plants, and harvested the crop. On harvest they were required to turn over to the cooperative farm the entire crop excepting 15 kilograms per decare for personal consumption. There was little attempt to monitor the amount for personal consumption, however, and some people took close to the limit each time they picked, which was every two or three days during the harvest period. The remaining yield was weighed at the site and recorded by farm officials. For the first 300 kilograms per decare they received no payment; beyond this amount they were credited 80 stotinki per kilogram. The vines were cut off after the harvest in order to induce a very small second crop in the fall. For this crop there was no production quota—workers were credited for every kilogram delivered, and at a higher rate. After the season was finished, the costs of farm inputs, including the strawberry plants if new, the straw, the water, and the plowing were deducted from their accounts and the balance paid in cash. As in all agricultural endeavors the outcome was variable and somewhat unpredictable, depending especially on weather and the age of the vines, but generally the returns were high. From one decare of strawberries a family could earn between 700 and 1,000 leva. This was a significant addition to the household income, especially given that it required only a couple of months of part-time work and that some families contracted for more than 1 decare.

The successes of the system no doubt inspired expansion. The *akord* system in Zamfirovo began in the early 1980s and was clearly an outgrowth of the NEM. Although already on the wane in Romania in the 1970s (Kideckel 1979:232), when I arrived in Bulgaria in 1987, the *akord* system was elemental to agrarian operations and expanding. Sociologists and agronomists described it to me as the primary solution to shortages of agricultural labor for intensive cultivation. However, when I met with government officials in the National Agro-Industrial Union, they stated unequivocally that the *akord* system was to be installed throughout the farm economy, not just in labor-intensive operations. Clearly, I entered the picture between an official change in policy toward the *akord* system and its dissemination throughout the society.

Subsequently, I witnessed this change as it trickled down to the local level. When I arrived in the village, strawberry cultivation was the only major operation conducted solely on an *akord* basis. Vineyards were available to villagers on that basis, but less than 200 decares had been contracted. Between 1987 and 1988 numerous other activities were put on the *akord* system, including fodder beets, tomatoes, and cucumbers. The previously noted change in payment for livestock workers was presented as part of this package as well. Even drivers at the MTS were assigned particular plots for which they were individually responsible, their income depending on the productivity of these plots. The APK called this an *akord* arrangement, although it hardly followed the ideal system. Elsewhere in the country the same process was evident. In Bulgaria's famous rose valley, for example, the hoeing of rose plants came under *akord* contracts, as a step toward moving the entire operation to such an arrangement.

These developments, however, should not be seen as simply the local consequences of national reform policy. *Akord* arrangements spread because of various factors acting in concert, including increasing international pressure for reform and prior local successes. At the same time, the expansion encountered obstacles at the local level, limiting its achievements and driving the reform process in other directions. Thus, the success of strawberry cultivation in Zamfirovo generated enthusiasm among farm administrators for grape cultivation under *akord*, but the results of the latter were disappointing. People did not take on grape contracts, for the terms were not as lucrative, reflecting the fact that Bulgarian strawberries were in greater demand in Western markets than Bulgarian grapes or even wine. Also, villagers grew grapes on their own personal plots, thus labor demands overlapped and the *akord* allowance for personal consumption was no incentive. The limited interest in grape contracts certainly contributed to farm management's decision to alter the crop profile of the farm, expanding strawberry cultivation and cutting back the cultivation of wine grapes.

The combined promise and disappointment of akord reforms stimulated a more extreme attempt to overcome resistance by offering households large plots of land to use as they saw fit. The management of the Zamfirovo farm concluded a trial contract with a villager in 1988 to work 30 decares of land under a sharecropping arrangement. The farm even sold him a tractor for 6,000 leva. He was guaranteed the necessary inputs from the cooperative farm at cost and was obligated to sell his produce to the cooperative farm at state prices. This was arranged quietly on an experimental basis and was far from constituting private cultivation. Still, it clearly shows that the socialist system was generating some radical experiments and ideas—ones that could even be seen as threatening the bases of a socialist agriculture—before the collapse of communism. Indeed, this same arrangement is similar to the Chinese responsibility system, which was considered by Chan, Madsen, and Unger (1984:267) as a process of decollectivization. Furthermore, discussions with the village party secretary in 1988 revealed that this arrangement was more than experimental. The secretary said it was already considered the next wave of socialist agrarian reform, and he expected cooperative farms across the country to be leasing large tracts of land to village households in the near future.

The attempt at both the local and national levels to expand *akord* arrangements underlines one of the major complications of reform: the recurrent homogenization of programs resulting from centralized decision making. While reforms may have redressed very specific difficulties, all too often they were generalized and applied beyond the sector or area where they were most appropriate. For example, making producers responsible for the costs of their inputs may seem like a legitimate way to rationalize an economic system, but when there is limited worker control over inputs, or a major labor shortage, as in shepherding, such a reform might lead instead to job desertion or other conflicts.

Especially glaring in this regard was the attempt to assign tractor drivers a designated plot of land and pay them according to the harvest. Attempts at tying remuneration to productivity may have been reasonable where worker attention and diligence significantly affected output, and they had been effective in both industrial and agricultural brigades. Combine drivers, however, had limited control over the wheat crop. How much could they vary their effort? Even the directors of the cooperative farm were hard-pressed to explain the rationale of this idea. Perhaps it ensured more timely attention to their particular plot, but it diminished their concern for the rest of the farm and ensured that they spent any extra time working in the private sector of the village rather than for the cooperative farm. Although a potential problem for the cooperative, this result would perhaps improve private production, another perfect example of conflicting complementarity.

Personal Agricultural Production

The issue of private sector production brings us to the final dimension of Zamfirovo's changing agricultural situation. In nearly all collectivized agricultural systems, the cooperative or state farm provided workers a small plot of land to cultivate for household consumption. This sustained the economic viability of disadvantaged agricultural workers in the socialist economy and allowed the state to continue exploiting them. In 1987 the Zamfirovo farm allowed villagers 5 decares of land for such use, including the yard around their house, which they actually owned privately.[5] If their yard was small, as in most cases, then the farm allotted them the full 5 decares from cooperative property. The few villagers with larger yards received enough land to bring their total area to 5 decares. Typically, villagers used 3 decares of this land for corn and wheat production. The remaining 2 decares were divided equally between a vineyard and a vegetable garden.

While these plots were an aspect of cooperative agriculture from the earliest stages of collectivization, their size and role changed significantly. After the beginning of economic reform in the early 1960s, state policy moved fitfully but inexorably toward the expansion of the private sector and its increasing articulation with the state (see Wyzan 1990). The greatest changes began in the early 1970s: plot allowances were increased and private livestock limits eliminated. Perhaps more important, by 1987 most of these private agricultural activities were closely tied to the cooperative farm. This relationship renders the commonly criticized but persistent comparison of private and cooperative sectors in socialist economies fallacious. For the same reason, Bulgarians used the term "personal" rather than "private" to refer to this arena.

The land granted for personal use remained under the control of the cooperative farm. In the early years after collectivization, the Zamfirovo farm often repossessed these plots for its own use, giving individuals different plots in return. Once the farm had established large blocks for mechanized cultivation, however, this occurred much less often, and the security of tenure approached that of private property, even to the point of being inherited. While I was in the field, there was only one exception, involving the repossession of several personal vineyards by the farm in order to plant a cooperative vineyard of dessert grapes. In compensation, the cooperative granted all prior holders a different plot to plant a new vineyard and allowed them to harvest an equivalent section of the cooperative vineyard while their new vines matured. Most were satisfied with this arrangement, although one man gave up viticulture altogether because he claimed the area they offered him was not as good and the

5. Amounts varied according to land quality and topography, but the Zamfirovo limits were about average for the country.

cooperative vineyard was in such poor condition that it was not worth the trouble.

The latter issue has been mentioned previously, and it may have been a legitimate complaint. In fact, a comparison repeatedly pointed out to me by villagers was that between cooperative vineyards in poor condition and personal vineyards impeccably maintained. If such conversations occurred near both cooperative and personal plots, I was likely to be taken to see for myself. The comparison was also brought up by the farm president in a cooperative meeting in 1988. Since viticulture was the activity within the personal economy least integrated with the cooperative farm, the opposition was perhaps merited and instructive. Apart from the land, the farm provided no inputs for personal grape cultivation. Vintners hoed, sprayed, harvested, and pruned their vines by hand. They made their own wine and consumed it themselves or gave it to friends and relatives.

Despite the subsistence nature of personal viticulture, it did spill over into the cooperative sector. Grape must was distilled into brandy at a still operated by the Commerce Cooperative, for which the villagers paid a fee. Villagers also paid a tax on their total wine and brandy production. When the national government announced a massive increase in the wine tax (not coincidentally on the heels of Gorbachev's anti-alcohol initiative in the Soviet Union), there were vehement complaints, including a threat to stop growing grapes. Within two months the legislation was reversed. Not only is this a clear example of how local sentiments, without demonstrations, affected central decision making, it also suggests that viticulture was not simply a subsistence issue. Why else should the national government be so troubled by a threatened reduction in the *personal* production of grapes? As we will see in Chapter 5, grapes and wine from personal plots made their way illicitly into the wider economy, contributing importantly to the provisioning of the society at large.

The connections between the cooperative and personal sectors were much more explicit in grain production. Personal corn and wheat plots were plowed and sown by tractors from the MTS. Corn was subsequently hoed and harvested by hand, but wheat was harvested by MTS combines, and in most areas the straw left behind was baled by a MTS baler. In fact, the only operation in personal wheat production not performed by the cooperative sector was the broadcast application of fertilizer. On farms in the Danubian plain nothing was done by villagers: personal grain plots were no more than allocated segments of the cooperative's grain blocks. Clearly this was not private cultivation.

Villagers used the products from their corn and wheat harvests, including corn stalks and field stubble, to feed their livestock, the fruits of which were sometimes sold back to the cooperative farm. Typically they raised one goat, several sheep, a pig, and several chickens. The goats and sheep were pastured communally in neighborhood groups on cooperative farm land. This arrangement expanded after collectivization because villagers had to work for the farm and were not allowed to keep enough animals to warrant daily trips to pasture.

Prior to collectivization, communal grazing was limited to families with few animals and was usually organized by a single shepherd, who received cash from each owner plus a portion of the milk produced. After collectivization, most families began to participate, taking turns providing the shepherd—one day for each pair of sheep. The arrangement became more important as livestock limits were liberalized. Most households increased their sheep fold and acquired a goat as well. This meant going to pasture one day for each goat owned, three or four times during the grazing season. Shepherds and goatherds were usually men, but women would step in when men were not available. The animals were pastured in cooperative forests and meadows that the farm was not harvesting, either because of their inaccessible location, steep terrain, or poor productivity. Herders were fined if caught on cooperative meadows exploited by the farm, and while conflicts sometimes emerged between the cooperative farm and individuals over these resources, enforcement was not overly strict. This is another example of the interwoven conflicting complementarity that both confounded and sustained socialist agriculture. The farm needed hay from the meadows for its livestock production, but at the same time it allowed villagers to use these resources for their personal livestock holdings, knowing it would later benefit from purchasing livestock products. This balance involved the nonagricultural sectors of the economy as well, since most people had to take off work in order to fulfill their herding responsibilities.

The animals were raised for milk, meat, and wool, as well as for sale. Wool was sheared in the spring and washed at home. Some women still carded and spun their own wool, but most used the facilities provided by the cooperative farm for mechanical carding and spinning, paying a small fee. Older women made socks, sweaters, or tufted spreads from the wool. Milking began in early spring after kids and lambs were partially weaned and continued until mid-fall when the females were impregnated. In the early spring and fall the animals spent only half a day at pasture and were milked by their owners before and after. If there were children in the household, the milk might be given to them, or it might be fed to a small piglet to fatten it quickly. More often it was taken to the village square, where a cooperative farmworker collected it and kept a record of how much each family sold. The milk was then transferred by the state purchasing agency to milk-processing plants. Farm administrators estimated that villagers sold 100,000 liters of milk to the cooperative annually in this way. At fall's end, when the milking had ceased, the farm compensated villagers for their milk with high-quality animal feed. One family with only a single goat got 80 kilograms of wheat, even though a small amount of their milk had been consumed by household members and several liters had been sold to another villager.

From mid-spring to late summer, the animals stayed all day at pasture. Owners took their goats to the neighborhood pen early in the morning after milking. The goatherd then drove them to pasture and brought them back to the pen at lunchtime for milking, keeping all of the milk for his own family or, perhaps, selling it to the farm or another villager. He took the goats back to pasture for the afternoon and returned them at nightfall to their owners, who milked them again. Unlike goats, sheep spent the night at the fold and were not returned to their owners at all during the period of intense pasturage. The shepherd for the day assisted by a family member milked them in the early morning and at night. Entitled to all the milk, he usually transformed it into cheese for household consumption, sometimes mixing it with goat milk purchased informally from the goatherd.

Families slaughtered a kid goat or lamb on special occasions throughout the spring, summer, and fall, including any of the following: May Day, St. George's Day (a celebration in honor of the patron saint of Shepherds, referred to officially as the Day of Shepherds), Easter, the annual village fair, and the 9th of September. Villagers decided when to slaughter according to the number of lambs and kids they had in a given year and their personal preference of holidays. They also reserved animals for special family occasions such as birthdays. Often they sold a kid or lamb to the cooperative and received part of the payment in fodder to help feed their other animals over the winter. Very young animals sold in this way were often exported for hard currency, usually to the Middle East. For accounting purposes the cooperative farm technically acted as an agent for the state meat purchasing agency, which sold the animals abroad, but on occasion the farm delivered the animals directly to foreign representatives in nearby towns.

I attended one such collection in May 1988. The farm posted notices that they would buy kid goats meeting certain weight limits. A dozen villagers showed up on the designated day at the farm livestock scales with their kids in tow. A farm representative weighed them there and recorded the weight beside the name of the owner. He complained that the previous year they had collected twice as many and he could not understand why there were fewer this year. The kids were then loaded onto a truck and taken to Berkovitza, where a representative from the United Arab Emirates looked them over before accepting them. In the past he had refused solid white animals for "religious reasons," and for a period after the Chernobyl disaster he also checked for radiation. Apparently the hazards of both radiation and sacrilege had diminished at the time I was there, for he checked only for general health and size. He accepted all the kids from Zamfirovo, as well as all those in a subsequent truck from another village. The animals were taken by truck to the town of Burgas on the Black Sea, where they were flown to the United Arab Emirates for ritual slaughter on *Bakra eid*. The representative of the United Arab Emirates spoke fluent Bulgarian and told me he collected anywhere from 500,000 to 800,000 kid goats a year in Bulgaria. He also bought them from Greece and Syria. His company paid the Bulgarian state purchasing agency 3 dollars per kilogram for the goats, but the local villagers received only 3 leva per kilogram plus twice the weight of the animal in feed grain.

Villagers sold other animals through the farm to the state purchasing agency on a similar basis, especially pigs and young sheep. These arrangements worked much like the *akord* system in agriculture. Villagers purchased young lambs and piglets from the cooperative farm. Some of the piglets were raised originally by other villagers who sold them to the cooperative farm. The farm also provided fodder if desired. The individual raised the animals for several months and then sold them back to the state meat purchasing agency. Pigs were by far the most common animal raised in this manner. The farm collected pigs twice a month, generally taking in around twenty. Most villagers raised at least one pig for sale, and many raised several. The major risk in this endeavor was the high death rate of piglets—one woman said she lost two at one time, and another said she had lost ten in the last couple of years. If they survived, the pigs brought 33 stotinki a kilogram or 23 stotinki a kilogram plus four times the weight of the pig in fodder. The outcome varied, but for five months of feeding, one could usually clear 100 leva per pig plus 250 kilograms of fodder. There was a consensus that selling pigs without the fodder supplement was unprofitable, and only a few villagers elected complete cash payments. Some villagers questioned the profitability of raising animals for sale even with the fodder payment, and this led to numerous arguments between villagers.

Whether or not they raised a pig for sale, most villagers raised at least one pig for household consumption. It was slaughtered before New Year's Day and provided the meat for the rest of the winter. Every Saturday and Sunday in December I awoke to the screaming of pigs going under the knife. A horrible sound, it pervaded the village like a perpetual echo, first from one direction, then more distantly from another. It was a major event for the household. Family members came from throughout the village to assist, and neighbors were called on to help hold the animal while someone slit its throat. Neighbors were then given shots of brandy on their way out, and the family set about the task of butchering. The animal was skinned and the skin sold to the Commerce Cooperative for 10 leva. The layer of fat was cut off and rendered, the intestines washed out for sausage casing, and the remaining guts used to make a stew. As soon as possible, because the exquisite fresh flavor diminished quickly, a large piece of meat was cut out and given to the women to cook for lunch. Most of the remaining meat was then sliced into cutlets, salted, packed tightly into jars, and sealed over with a layer of rendered fat. It kept this way in cold cellars for several weeks. Along with homemade sausage it provided meat for much of the winter.

The winter diet also consisted of vegetables canned from the garden plots of villagers. The major crop in the gardens and in the Bulgarian diet was peppers, which were eaten and canned in a variety of ways. Tomatoes were a close second, and beans, often interplanted with the corn crop, were third. Cucumbers, lettuce, and squash were also grown for summer consumption. The crop profile of the garden plot changed a little from year to year, as gardeners responded to market supplies. For example, during my first year in the village few villagers grew potatoes in their garden. That year there was a major shortage of potatoes, and the following year almost every household planted them. Cabbage was an important vegetable for villagers, but the cooperative farm grew enough cabbage to provide villagers with their winter needs so they did not have to waste the land of their personal plot growing it.

Villagers worked on their personal plots and with their livestock continually during the agricultural season. Many able-bodied retirees occupied themselves full-time just with their personal sector activities. This was one reason why the farm brigades had few laborers—most retirees able to work spent their time and energy on their own personal plots. Younger people worked in their personal fields after leaving their official job, and all day on weekends. Personal plots were so valuable that after collectivization numerous households attempted to divide in order to get more acreage. With the subsequent economic development of the village and the arrival of better-paying jobs, the demand stabilized somewhat. Furthermore, as we will see in Chapter 5, villagers found easier ways to get more time and resources for their personal economy, generating additional conflicts between personal and cooperative sectors. They were also able to expand the former somewhat through *akord* contracts.

The Agricultural Balancing Act

The paradox of a planned agricultural system that, in apparent need of field laborers, provided potential workers with alternate possibilities for personal agricultural work technically *outside* the cooperative underlines the importance of seeing agriculture holistically as part of a system of conflicting complementarity. We need to look at the numerous factors bearing on agriculture and how the system balanced these factors. Equally important is how this balance evolved over time. As previously suggested, the growth of the personal sector was made possible by reforms, starting in the mid-1960s, which encouraged personal plot production. Subsequent reforms, especially after 1979, focused on capturing more of this personal productive effort for the cooperative sector. Concomitantly, the local cooperative farm tried to minimize its own demand for labor by shifting its crop profile and increasing mechanization. It continued to grow a few basic subsistence products for villagers—such as cabbage—freeing up more of their personal resources for the production of goods integrated with the cooperative sector. The *akord* system, then, was founded on the prospect of tapping even more energy from the personal domain. Success of the *akord* in Zamfirovo strawberry production stimulated the spread of this arrangement to crops such as grapes, fodder beets, tomatoes, and cucumbers. These attempts failed precisely because they could not be integrated into the wider network of interactions. But such failures provoked new variations, including the subleasing of large tracts of land.

This network of connections illustrates well how reforms could inspire

Spiralling reforms grow into transformations

or stimulate other reforms, sometimes escalating into quite radical transformations. Part of the dynamic underlying such an outcome was the conflict between component elements. As Humphrey (1983:266) has pointed
out so well for the Soviet case, the numerous elements of the cooperative
farm often found themselves at odds, especially in regard to labor shortages. During most of the peak agricultural season in Zamfirovo there were
never enough workers to accomplish all the necessary tasks, and some
jobs went undone. The competition between various labor needs was summarized succinctly by one brigade member, a retired woman, while en
route to the fields one day. The van driver asked who was going to pick
strawberries and who would harvest watermelons, whereupon the clearly
exasperated woman asked, "How are we supposed to do everything? Pick
plums, pick strawberries, harvest melons, gather hay, load bales. . . . Stop
already!" As on Buryat farms (Humphrey 1983:304), the sheer amount of
farmwork, which in Zamfirovo was partially a result of labor shortages,
further discouraged workers from coming out to work on the farm, exac-
erbating the problem. Consequently, tomatoes, for example, sometimes
rotted in the field for lack of pickers. Tomatoes became a priority only
when the farm had a delivery contract to fulfill. Brigade workers harvested enough to fill the order and went on to more pressing work. Tomatoes were only grown under duress from the APK, so it was not surprising
that they received low priority.

Here we see another example of how shortage may have actually empowered local farm management. While much of the productive profile
of cooperative farms was dictated by the APK and ultimately by central
agricultural planners, farm-level shortages, especially of labor, allowed local managers to allocate resources according to their own preferences.
This gave them more control over farm production than was apparent in
the formal administrative structure. Thus, shortages, which were often
seen as the bane of socialist economies, may have been instrumental in
resisting the weight of top-down planning, another limitation of socialism.
In a local context we see that these two fatal flaws of the socialist economy
may have actually been integrated in a way that facilitated local action.
From a holistic perspective on the local context, the conflicts become
complementary. This distinguishes my conclusions about labor shortages
on the Bulgarian cooperative farm from Humphrey's insights. While she
sees the resulting conflicts producing a balance or compromise, I also see
a complementarity emerging in which the compromise itself redressed
other problems, facilitating local power.

Transport was another resource that often did not meet farm needs, allowing for local allocation preferences. In peak periods, the breakdown of a single truck caused major problems. Food had to be delivered to the livestock enterprises, so this often took precedence over other types of transport needs, sometimes leaving the limited number of field laborers without anything to do or, as was recounted in my story of the grape-picking brigade, lugging their own empty crates to the fields. In a fitting conclusion to the ill-fated grape brigade, after filling all the available crates, we had to lug them back into the vineyard to hide them from potential thieves during the night because there was no truck available to pick them up. In another case I accompanied a brigade going to load hay bales. When we got to the work site, the truck had not arrived, so we waited. After an hour and a half the van returned to pick us up—it seems we were not going to load hay after all because the trucks were too busy hauling silage.

These examples reveal a potential problem for any reform that increased the productive responsibilities of farmworkers. If such workers depended extensively on unreliable farm transport, to what extent could they really control their own system of production? In my experience, the less responsible the cooperative farm was for a particular activity, the lower the priority it assigned that endeavor. Farm management directed resources first to those areas for which the cooperative farm was directly and completely responsible and only subsequently to those areas where workers bore greater responsibility themselves. Thus, the people growing watermelons on *akord* complained that the TKZS and the APK never did anything for them except take their money, probably because their product was their own responsibility and intended only for local consumption. Giving these farmers more responsibility also increased their "irresponsibility," in the sense discussed previously, since they were less able to command attention from the farm or APK.

Political factors must also be taken into account, for, as Humphrey (1983:266) notes, allocation decisions were often influenced by political considerations. In Zamfirovo people complained that the agronomist for the farm was unduly influenced by political concerns, and this influence adversely affected people's returns on *akord* contracts. One specific case concerned the watering of strawberries. The strawberries in one section were rotting due to overwatering, and contractors claimed that the agronomist watered them whenever the party secretary, who had no agricultural training, expressed concern about the strawberries "looking dry."

The party secretary also had input into decisions about the allocation of labor and other scarce resources. The conflict generated by the secretary's involvement was itself a reflection of agricultural disengagement. When the majority of villagers were working in agriculture, the party secretary for the cooperative farm was the major village political leader. As villagers took up other jobs, political power shifted to an autonomous village party secretary. As this position was not connected to the cooperative farm, villagers filling it often had less knowledge of agriculture and less experience with the farm. Thus, their engagement with agricultural management became more problematic. At the same time, the interests of local farm officials were politically divided by agricultural reforms. Since these officials continued to depend on the goodwill of their superiors for career advancement, they sometimes tried to maintain relations by handing over farm produce to them rather than actualizing reform possibilities for finding more lucrative contracts. In other words, reforms giving farm administrators more leeway in decision making may have been negated by the continuing political influence of their superiors over other dimensions of their life and work.

I have already pointed out several conflicts between the personal sector and the cooperative sector. We need not go over them again, but it is important to include them among the other tensions and potential conflicts that had to be effectively managed by the farm. Indeed, these tensions have been evident since the completion of collectivization. One such conflict was cited in a report on the village's agricultural activity from October 1956, which states that "many of the [farm's] draft animals are used for personal work and this has slowed down the plowing and sowing."

Balancing all these often conflicting demands was an essential part of the socialist agricultural endeavor. This need sustained the official apparatus of socialism until the late 1980s when ideas of perestroika began to cut agricultural units and individuals loose, making the coordinating apparatus less necessary. Radical reforms, however, must also be seen as a response to problems generated by prior solutions. The APK system, for example, was intended to increase agricultural productivity, but the administrative division of these large units by type of farm activity generated conflicts. As Smollett (1980:54) describes for a village in southeastern Bulgaria, the creation of an APK-wide transport section led truck drivers to drive furiously in order to rack up miles for the transport enterprise. In so doing, they damaged the fruits and vegetables grown by the agricultural sector. Such conflicts, like others discussed above, were not necessarily terminal. They provided the basis for new reforms and adjustments. Through perpetual reform, new solutions emerged and unsuccessful ones were superseded or abandoned.

The process was not one-sided but an ongoing negotiation. Not only did the cooperative change through attempts to tap personal sector re- sources, but the personal sector itself changed in response to the coopera- tive farm. Just as the farm increasingly emphasized grain production and animal husbandry, villagers focused their personal economy increasingly on sheep, goat, and pig raising, devoting much of their personal plots to fodder production. Most villagers did not even bother to grind flour from their wheat crop, feeding it instead to their animals and buying the flour they needed for household use. Cows, however, declined drastically in the personal economy of villagers—in marked contrast to their role in the cooperative farm. While several villagers had previously kept a cow as part of their personal livestock holdings, by 1987 few villagers owned one, and while I was in the field, three of the remaining cattle owners also got rid of theirs. This profile reflects the increasing integration of cooperative and personal sectors. Given the mechanized support provided by the farm, a household's need for the draft power of cows virtually disap- peared. The ease of mechanized grain cultivation, however, maintained the viability of raising other animals to fulfill diminishing milk demands.

The increasing attention to grain and livestock production came at the expense of garden plots. The cooperative also helped in this regard by supplying some traditionally important garden products, such as cabbage and watermelon. Conversely, the cooperative sector could rely on the per- sonal sector not only to supplement production but to stave off disasters. In the early 1980s several successive dry years caused a severe shortage of grain, and each village household was required to hand over a peck of corn from its personal production to the cooperative sector. This requisi- tion sustained the cooperative economy. Furthermore, as we will see in Chapters 3 and 5, the extensive out-migration of villagers created net- works for the movement of goods from the village personal sector into the cities, guaranteeing a minimum well-being for the population of the country as a whole.

Given that *akord* arrangements were in effect extensions of personal plot production, it is not surprising that their ultimate success depended on their articulation with the personal economy. Thus, strawberry cultiva- tion was a major success not only because it paid well but also because it fit in well with existing personal plot cultivation. The work on strawberry plots was concentrated in mid-spring before personal plot work intensified. Furthermore, it was concentrated in a short period of time, so it did not overlap with most other activities. The cultivation of grapes, tomatoes, and cucumbers was just the opposite. These crops required continual attention from late winter to early fall and demanded intensive work exactly when villagers were most occupied with their own vineyard and gardens. Once strawberry cultivation became a part of the picture, it also inhibited other types of *akord* arrangements. A major drive to get villagers to raise silkworms failed miserably because sericulture required intensive work around the same time as strawberry cultivation and was not as lucrative. The village government was given several thousand worms to distribute, but officials at the town hall ended up raising them because no one else was willing.

This incident also revealed the extent to which local power over villagers had eroded by 1988. The retired village mayor was appalled when he heard about the officials raising silkworms. "What has happened to political power? When I was mayor I simply went to the villagers and said, 'Here are some silkworms, you have a mulberry tree, you have to raise them.' Now they do not have any power at all. Let them spend their day gathering mulberry leaves if they cannot take charge." This shift explains why compatibility became a significant issue in the outcome of reforms. As administrators became more dependent on village producers through earlier reform programs, they lost much of their ability to force village participation in subsequent reforms. The latter, therefore, had to be increasingly attractive.

Compatibility with the personal sector affected not only *akord* crops but the crops grown entirely by the cooperative farm, especially as restructuring granted farm management greater latitude in planning its overall profile. This is seen in the farm president's plan to expand Zamfirovo's plum orchard. Plum production was strictly a farm activity, but it was viable for the farm because it articulated well with both cooperative and personal involvements (and, the small subsidy paid by the government certainly did not hurt). Labor requirements were minimal except during the harvest, which occurred around late August and early September. Plums were harvested over a period of less than three weeks, with each tree being picked clean in turn. In Zamfirovo no important labor demands, either on the cooperative farm or in personal plot cultivation, competed with the plum harvest, so the farm could accomplish the task easily with brigades. Moreover, as the work was considered rather pleasant by agricultural standards, and since many people relished the possibility of getting plums for themselves, the farm did not have major difficulties raising additional voluntary brigades of villagers for this activity.

Unlike plums, the expansion of strawberry cultivation and other *akord* crops hinged on getting more people to take on *akord* contracts. Most villagers interested in such arrangements were already involved. A few people came from nearby towns to tend strawberries as a supplement to their income, but not enough to underwrite significant growth. Consequently, the farm turned again to the personal economy. Technically, the right to use personal plots was a fringe benefit of working for the cooperative farm, but as villagers gave up farmwork for other jobs in the village (see Chapter 4), they continued to exploit their personal plots. Given the importance of personal plot production for the village and state economy, the requirement of cooperative work was rarely enforced. To the contrary, the personal plot came to be regarded as a right of village residence rather than a benefit of cooperative labor.

At a meeting of the cooperative farm in 1988, tellingly on the heels of a complaint about the villagers' poor response to tomato and cucumber *akord* programs, the farm president announced his intention to revive the old requirement. Personal plots were to be provided only to those people who worked for the cooperative farm, with the important modification that *akord* work would now count as a cooperative contribution. In this way the farm expected to force the small number of villagers not currently working land on *akord* to do so. Notices were sent out informing villagers who did not work for the cooperative farm that they would lose their right to their personal plot if they did not take land on *akord*. The reactions were mixed and the outcome disappointing. A few people acquiesced and took on contracts. Several people were very angry about the threat and contrived counterstrategies. One man said he would take a decare of strawberries but not do anything to it. He expected the plants to bear something without any work on his part and planned to harvest just enough to fulfill the contract, leaving the rest to rot. Most simply ignored the threat. As one villager confidently put it, "Never mind their threats. They say they are going to take back the personal plots? What are they going to do with them? They cannot get anybody to work the land they have now; what will they do with more? This is only an idle threat. People who are weak and intimidated by their threats will be eaten up, and those of us who are not will be left alone." He lived with his wife and two young children in a house they were still completing. With limited household labor and competing construction demands he preferred to get extra income from raising pigs—a choice influenced by the fact that he was good friends with the man responsible for buying village livestock for the state.

The irony of agricultural reforms in the 1980s was not lost on older villagers. It was summed up best by one man's comment: "After the 9th of September they beat people to get them to give up their land; now they are going to beat them to make them take it back." This comment was made in *1987*, raising doubts about current analyses that treat the return of land to prior owners as solely an issue of transition. However, as we will see in Chapter 6, this preparation did not necessarily pave the way for land restitution after 1989. Rather, these reforms kept agriculture at the center of political and economic consciousness and provided new avenues for the domestication of socialism. This helped ensure that agriculture was both a target of transition programs after 1989 and a base for resistance to those very programs.

There are other ingredients in the postsocialist equation as well. Most villagers were no longer employed in agriculture and were not enthusiastic about full-time agricultural work. Even if they were, they lacked enough household labor for an extensive household-based agricultural enterprise. These factors were themselves the outcome of other changes interacting with agricultural developments, specifically industrialization and demographic transitions. In the next two chapters I deepen the analysis of agrarian disengagement and socialist domestication in light of these two changes.

Fig. 1. A view of Zamfirovo from one of the several surrounding hills. The old name of the village, Gushantsi, may have referred to its location, "nestled" among the hills.

Fig. 2. The village square served as the administrative, commercial, and social hub of the village. Much of the activity on this day in 1995 involved the weekly outdoor market, inaugurated as part of the transition.

Fig. 3. Villagers take a break from a wedding banquet in the neighboring restaurant (1987). After the banquet, the festivities often continued on the square, where there was more room for folk dancing. The sweet shop behind these guests became a bank in the early 1990s.

Fig. 4. A parade commemorating the fortieth anniversary of the founding of the village cooperative farm. The "Agemates of Freedom"—villagers born the year of the socialist revolution—usher in charter members of the cooperative farm, just visible in front of the town hall (1988).

Fig. 5. Entrance to the cooperative farmyard (1992). During the 1980s the farmyard served as a transport and storage depot. It also contained two of the farm's livestock enterprises, its textiles workshops, and a feed plant. Farm administration, however, operated out of the town hall.

Fig. 6. Workers from the village machine tractor station planting corn in 1988. During the 1970s and 1980s the farm turned increasingly to crops like corn and wheat because they could be cultivated entirely by machines.

Fig. 7. Like the cooperative farm, most village households relied on the machine tractor station to plow and plant their corn and wheat plots. But a few villagers with horses, such as the two brothers pictured here in 1987, avoided the associated service charge (and extra bribes) by plowing their own "personal" land. By 1997 the rising cost of mechanical services had driven many more villagers back to animal traction.

Fig. 8. Personal corn and wheat plots were essential for feeding household livestock. Here a retired couple and their neighbor shuck the abundant corn harvest of 1988.

Fig. 9. A worker collects strawberries raised by village families through contracts with the cooperative farm (1988). This contract (or *akord*) system allowed the farm to produce labor-intensive crops without its own field hands. In the 1980s most Zamfirovo households maintained strawberry contracts, but they refused similar arrangements with less lucrative crops. The contract system and strawberry production collapsed with the beginning of decollectivization in 1992.

Fig. 10. One of the cooperative farm's two brigades of field hands on a break from the grape harvest in 1987. Nearly all the remaining manual laborers for the farm were elderly, and the vast majority were women. As a result, villagers sometimes referred to the brigades as "the grannies."

Fig. 11. Villagers making brandy at the village distillery (1988). Each
household maintained a personal vineyard sufficient for a year's supply of
homemade wine. Prior to the grape harvest the must of the previous year's
vintage was distilled for brandy.

Fig. 12. Villagers with adjoining personal plots share an impromptu lunch
after a Saturday morning of farming (1987).

Fig. 13. The village factory in 1988. Workers here produced electrical motor parts for a parent plant in Sofia. The sign in the left foreground reads, "Self-management, Democracy, Restructuring!" Clearly, these objectives had a local history prior to 1989, which colored villagers' interpretation of the transition.

Fig. 14. Processing tomatoes in the village cannery (1988). This small enterprise relied primarily on fruits and vegetables grown by the cooperative farm and destined for area consumers. However, it occasionally processed goods from neighboring farms and even exported products abroad. Although privatized in 1994, it was still dormant in 1997.

Fig. 15. Part of the cooperative farm's textile enterprise. These weavers produced traditional tufted wool rugs (used primarily as bedspreads and coverlets) on a made-to-order basis. Weaving was a traditional craft for women, but in the late 1980s few households still had a working loom.

Fig. 16. One of the most attractive jobs for village women in the late 1980s was packaging drugs and other pharmaceutical products. It was organized by the cooperative farm on a subcontracting basis with a large pharmaceutical plant in Sofia. The workshop closed after 1989 as loss of markets, unemployment in Sofia, and high transport costs made subcontracting with the provinces unattractive.

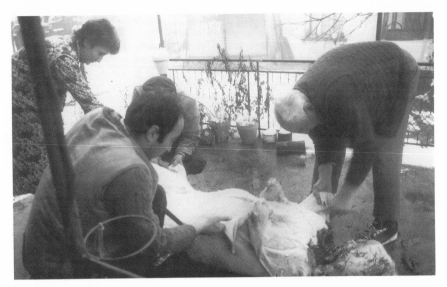

Fig. 17. Relatives and neighbors help butcher a pig (1987). Most households kept at least one pig, which was slaughtered at the end of the year to provide the family's winter meat supply.

Fig. 18. One of the cooperative farm's sheep folds in 1987. The shepherd and his wife lived at the fold most of the time, attending to everything from pasturing and feeding to milking, birthing, and shearing. Not surprisingly, the farm had difficulty keeping good shepherds. The farm's sheep were sold off or returned to cooperative farm members during decollectivization.

Fig. 19. A woman canning beans in 1995. A high degree of self-sufficiency was common under socialism, partly because the supply and quality of food in stores was uncertain. After 1989 such activity became even more essential, as food prices skyrocketed and villagers lost their jobs.

Fig. 20. The village bread bakery with a small line of customers in 1987. Fresh bread was a cultural necessity for every meal, and it was so cheap during the years of socialism that working women stopped baking it (except for special occasions). They continued to buy it despite radical price increases in the 1990s that made the cost of bread a major part of the family food budget.

Fig. 21. The mother of the groom presenting gifts to the newlyweds (1987). As she piled their arms with textiles, the gifts were taken from behind into the house. The groom's mother was followed by other gift-bearing relatives of both the bride and groom, and the presentation continued for well over an hour.

Fig. 22. Proud great-grandparents creatively present their cash gift at a child's christening banquet (1987). Christenings were second only to weddings as festive occasions for conspicuous giving, although both were diminished somewhat by the economic crises of the 1990s.

Fig. 23. Other villagers look on as a custodian cleans up the village square (1995). The building in the background—previously part of the old town hall—was one of the first private bars to open during the transition. By 1995 it had a lot of competition.

Fig. 24. A statue of Zamfir Popov, the early communist activist for whom the village was renamed after World War II. His reign over the village square was still unchallenged in 1997.

3

DEMOGRAPHIC TRANSITIONS

During the socialist era, extensive out-migration became a new fact of life in Zamfirovo, the ramifications of which were amplified by an earlier and continuing fertility decline. Villagers talked about a rural exodus with metaphors as seemingly disruptive as those used for collectivization.

> They were like refugees fleeing a war, carrying their belongings on carts like Gypsies. Everybody seemed to be moving out, and I was afraid nobody would be left in the village. I was too young to leave on my own, but I remember telling my father and mother that we should go. They said we had nowhere to live in town and no work there. . . . The movement eventually stopped, and now [1988] it is the reverse: you cannot leave. I wish we had moved when it was possible. Now we are stuck here. But at least there are a lot of others stuck here too [laughs]. I mean, it's not like living in Rashovitsa [a neighboring hamlet with only a few elderly residents].

The motivations behind this movement were varied. While some villagers insisted that migrants left because they did not want to do the arduous work required by the cooperative farm, most urbanites claimed they left because there was no work for them in the village, and they could not survive. Some were influenced by the popularity of the process itself, as the above quotation suggests. Just as collectivization broke villagers' attachment to the land, migration weakened the network of village social relations, eroding individuals' ties to the community as well. Each departure thus made migration more attractive for those left behind, especially since demographic transitions had already diminished the density of close kin relations.

Together, migration and fertility patterns account for much of the agricultural labor shortage and associated reforms discussed in the previous chapter. As such, these population changes were inextricably bound up with collectivization and its policy counterpart: industrialization. As all these processes unfolded within a system of conflicting complementarity, population dynamics became a policy concern in their own right, provoking reforms and providing more avenues for domesticating socialism. This chapter examines the interconnected roles of migration and fertility decline in the socialist transformation of the village and the village transformation of socialism. I begin with a description of the rural exodus of the late 1950s and 1960s, subsequently placing it in the context of shifting demographic trends since World War I. Then I trace related changes in the structures and relations of village households, eventually focusing on the rural-urban interface generated by extensive migration. Finally, I attend to the responses of the Bulgarian state: a combination of restrictions and enticements that paradoxically ameliorated aspects of socialism for villagers while increasing their discontent.

The data necessary for a thorough analysis of population processes are not available for the village. Official statistics are excessively aggregated and focus primarily on gross population changes. Until the mid-1970s village population records were kept in the form of household registers, but they were less than meticulously maintained. Dates of events such as marriages and deaths are often missing, and while there was usually a notation when individuals moved out of a household, the dates they left and their destination were usually not noted. Consequently, it was difficult to distinguish household fissioning within the village from village out-migration. More contemporary data were further clouded by the socialist distinction between relocating and officially changing residences. Everyone in socialist Bulgaria had an official place of residence. It could be changed for nreasons we will discuss later, but people could also live elsewhere with special permits for long periods, even permanently. These individuals were not counted as having migrated, since they did not officially change their place of residence. Furthermore, official statistics did not differentiate among various segments of the population, such as the Roma and the ethnic Turks, who were thought to have much higher birth rates and greater geographical mobility. These limitations necessitate a somewhat impressionistic approach, with statistical rigor playing a supporting rather than starring role. Luckily, villagers offered plenty of impressions and observations to fill out the picture of population change.

Village Exodus

Past village leaders offered dramatic accounts of the early 1960s, when, "in a few years' time, more than 1,000 people left the village." This number does not appear in official statistics, possibly owing to the difference between relocation and an official change of residence, but statistics do show a sharp increase in out-migration during the early 1960s, especially in 1962 (see Table 6). Regardless of the exact numbers, it was certainly a

Table 6. Zamfirovo Migration, 1950–1988

Years	Individuals Leaving the Village	Individuals Moving into the Village
1950–51	160	42
1952–53	183	86
1954–55	153	39
1956–57	166	14
1958–59	231	24
1960–61	216	41
1962–63	359	38
1964–65	159	29
1966–67	213	50
1968–69	182	16
1970–71	170	14
1972–73	165	11
1974–75	88	25
1976–77	97	16
1978–79	42	4
1980–81	73	19
1982–83	56	27
1984–85	40	10
1986–87	83	6
1988[a]	41	5

SOURCE: Zamfirovo village administration.

[a]Does not include the last quarter of the year (October through December).

shock to the village to lose such a large chunk of its population in a relatively short span of time.

This shock was even greater in the context of what appears to have been a relatively stationary population. One does not want to imply that rural-to-urban migration is a socialist phenomena. As Todorov (1983:314) has shown for the Danubian port of Lom, about 50 kilometers north of Zamfirovo, there was clear evidence of in-migration by villagers in the mid-eighteenth century. This movement probably continued and perhaps increased in the late nineteenth century with the repatriation of Bulgarians to towns freed from Turkish control. Supporting this view, an interesting analysis of early twentieth-century Bulgarian literature suggests that this influx inspired a new literary genre, the trivial novel, which "intended to give moral and practical instruction to the newly-arrived and newly-literate hordes of villagers moving to the cities" (Roth 1989:20). Population statistics for two towns close to Zamfirovo suggest that such a process may have been operative in the area at the turn of the century. Average annual growth in both was much greater between 1892 and 1900 than it was in the five years prior (see Table 7). Such increases, however, did not significantly counter continuing rural population growth. The percentage of urban residents in the population increased only slightly between liber-

Table 7. Population of Zamfirovo and Neighboring Towns, 1887–1986

Year	Mihailovgrad	Berkovitza	Zamfirovo
1887	2,738	4,977	—
1892	2,875	4,998	—
1900	3,794	5,607	—
1905	4,468	5,784	—
1910	5,104	5,932	2,516
1920	6,064	6,078	2,561[a]
1926	7,174	5,961	3,067
1934	7,708	6,081	3,455
1946	9,874	6,876	3,719
1956	15,122	9,227	3,624
1966	28,344	11,917	2,925
1976	42,510	16,438	2,554
1986	52,993	16,842	2,408

NOTE: I found conflicting statistics for Mihailovgrad for the years 1900–1956.

SOURCES: For Years up to 1965: Tsentralno statichesko upravlenie, 1966:9. For 1966: *Statisticheski Sbornik*, 1969:24. For post-1966: unpublished tables of the Mihailovgrad regional statistical bureau.

[a]Data from year 1917.

ation and 1892 and then remained remarkably stable until World War II (see Table 8).

In Zamfirovo, life history informants always responded to queries about past migration with accounts of temporary labor migration, suggesting that the movement of villagers in the interwar and early postwar period was primarily temporary in nature. The degree of permanent migration can be approximated by combining village birth and death statistics with official population statistics for the village. If we assume that migration accounts for the difference between the natural growth indicated by local birth and death records and the net population growth indicated in census statistics, then between 1927 and 1934 migration losses from the village averaged fewer than twenty persons per year.

It is little wonder then that the large number of migrants from the 1950s onward made a lasting impression on villagers. Indeed, I was unaware of even a single village family that had not been affected directly by the process of migration. Most villagers had numerous close relatives living in cities; according to one informant, "over half the village has relatives in Mihailovgrad." The other half probably has relatives in Sofia or Berkovitza. Villagers have moved to other cities as well, but most ended up in one of these three destinations. In fact, it was common to find villagers who had relatives in all three places. An uncanny number had a sibling or child in both Mihailovgrad and Berkovitza, as if the most probable destinations had been divided among family members like some sort of migrant inheritance.

Table 8. Percentage of Bulgarian Population Designated as Urban, 1887–1992

1887	18.8
1892	19.7
1900	19.8
1905	19.6
1910	19.1
1920	19.9
1926	20.6
1934	21.4
1946	24.7
1956	33.6
1965	46.5
1975	58.0
1985	64.8
1992	67.2

SOURCE: *Statisticheski Godishnik 1993*:47.

An extreme example will help illustrate the situation. One woman over eighty years old in 1987 came from a family of ten children, of which four died in childhood or infancy. Of the six siblings surviving to adulthood, two moved to Sofia, one moved to Mihailovgrad, and one moved to Berkovitza. Only she and her youngest brother remained in the village. They each raised two children in the village, but all four of these left as young adults. Recently, her youngest brother died, leaving her sister-in-law alone in the old house. As she says, "They all took off to the cities, here and there, and now she is alone in that house," and one might add, alone in the village as well.

The trend I discovered in Zamfirovo was repeated throughout the country. According to Ruskova (1987:27), 1,299,775 people moved from villages to cities between 1960 and 1975. Totev (1984:119–20) points out that at the peak of the migration process in 1965, 185,000 people migrated in one year, the vast majority going from villages to towns. As one sociologist phrased it in a personal conversation, "Nearly half the population of the country migrated during the last 40 years." By 1985 nearly 65 percent of the population lived in towns or cities (Table 8).

One does not have to go beyond explicit national policy to find the explanations for this process. Indeed the process itself can be treated as part and parcel of the Soviet development strategy, the objective of which was a structural transformation from an agrarian to an industrial economy. The labor and capital necessary for industrialization were to come respectively from the rural population and the devaluation of agricultural production rendered expendable and extractable by the concomitant process of collectivization.

Villagers certainly associated the flight from the village with the process of collectivization. With only symbolic wages from the cooperative farm and restrictions on personal agricultural activity, many villagers said it was nearly impossible to survive in the village. One villager who otherwise did not express negative assessments of collectivization admitted that "it was right after collectivization that masses of people ran away from the village." At the same time, we know that the village experienced economic hardships prior to the completion of collectivization in 1956, and at least one villager cited this as a factor affecting migration: "The years after the war were very difficult and hard. We couldn't get materials to work with. The sewing cooperative, for example, couldn't get cloth or thread or equipment, so we couldn't produce. It was hard, and that is the reason people began leaving the village. By the 1950s people were selling their plots and moving to the cities because life was so hard here and in the cities there were better-paying jobs." This description suggests that collectivization itself was not the sole culprit; the general economic difficulties of the period, including the weakening of village crafts, also played a role. As we saw in Chapter 1, these problems were all part of a singular national strategy. The attack on crafts was intended to undermine local production, making farmers dependent on government provisions that were rationed only to villagers joining the agricultural cooperative. Collectivization, in turn, severed villagers' links to the land and provided the conduit for channeling agricultural profits toward industry.

For many of the villagers who followed the path of state investment to work in industry, factory labor was not the panacea that migration statistics might suggest. Their most vivid memories were of difficulties getting industrial employment and the hardships of the jobs they got: "One had to take all sorts of terrible jobs. When I told people I was moving to Sofia, they told me how hard it was and that I couldn't manage, but I worked at various terrible and difficult jobs for several years and managed to get better ones by and by. Times were very hard then." One village couple who left the village in 1959 recounted a particularly circuitous route. First they moved to the nearby town of Vurshets, where the wife had been offered a job as a store clerk. The job never materialized, so they loaded their belongings onto a horse cart, selling an heirloom wardrobe and other pieces of furniture that would not fit, and set out for Sofia in 1960. Unable to find work there, the husband was forced to take a job as a coal miner in the nearby city of Pernik. After several years he landed a position at the infamous steel plant in Kremikovtsi, on the outskirts of Sofia. Such accounts suggest that the push from the village must have been greater than the attraction of towns and cities.

Clearly, not everybody left, despite being equally exposed to the pressure of collectivization and the promise of industrialization. It is through examination of the social relations in the village that the bases of migration decisions take on a more accurately complex character. Certainly, migration decisions were influenced by the relationship of individuals to the newly ascendant power holders in the village. The new communist administrators came from the village, and when it was time for them to allocate scarce resources, their prior village social relations no doubt exercised influence. Ivan was a casualty of such discrimination. Born in 1945, he lived in Zamfirovo until the age of twenty, when he married his village girlfriend. Both of them wanted to stay in Zamfirovo, but the cooperative farm director would not give him a job:

> I was trained and had experience as a woodworker, but he [the farm director] said they had no use for a woodworker in the TKZS. Mind you, not before he had asked about my family connections and figured out who I was. So I took a course to be a truck driver and heavy equipment operator. I passed it and asked him for a job as a driver. He said they did not have any openings for a driver either, but that if I could wait two or three months he might have a job for a truck loader. When I heard this I decided I had to move away. We moved to Sofia and lived in a small dorm room for almost ten years while we waited to get an apartment.

Who family nv is important

It was impossible to document such influences for even a small percentage of village migrants, but it was clear that the families of village leaders were much less affected by migration and had more members in the village in the late 1980s than most other families.

A more general and pervasive influence was the composition of the household and the domestic cycle. In very few cases did entire families or households leave the village; rather, members of the younger generation usually left while older people remained. Villagers attributed this pattern to the adaptability and energy of youth, but the success of young people in the city depended on their village relatives, who maintained subsistence production and guaranteed food. In this way the ability of young people to leave the village was predicated on their parents staying behind. This created a predominantly young migration stream. Only those individuals with a safety net of able-bodied parents remaining in the village would gamble with urban migration. Middle-aged villagers whose parents had died or who were involved in caring for disabled parents and children were less likely to see migration as a real option. The overall result for the village was the further simplification of households—leading to numerous units consisting of only an older couple—but a continuing, perhaps expanding, domestic cooperation between these households and their urban satellites. This ironic development illustrates well the multidimensional complexity of "householding" described by anthropologists (see, e.g., Sanjek 1982).

Fertility Decline

The ultimate result of massive village out-migration was amplified by the demographic context in which it occurred—that is, a population where fertility had been declining since World War I. As with migration, the local evidence of the fertility decline was dramatic. In the generation of Zamfirovo residents born before 1920, almost everyone was a member of a sibling set of four or more, many having eight and nine siblings. When these people began having children, however, two was the modal number of offspring. Thus, in the local village context a major demographic transition seems to have occurred in the span of one generation. Of course the members of this generation were spread over a rather broad period of time, so that in terms of years the transition was more gradual. A sample of entries from the village household register, for example, reveals several instances of couples having more than two children after the 1920s. Visual evidence of these larger families is missing from the current village profile, partly due to the out-migration just described. Still, these cases notwithstanding, the village fertility shift was dramatically evident within one generation.

The comments of older villagers thus promised to be enlightening—having grown up in a large family context, they chose to restrict their fertility. When asked why, they invariably cited economic problems and the increasing difficulty of providing for children: "Times were really hard and we couldn't support a lot of children." At the same time, the discordant experiences of this transitional generation were reflected in other comments that revealed their ambivalent acceptance of fertility restriction. Older women who had restricted their fertility often recited the Bulgarian aphorism that "a house without children [is like a] graveyard." I vividly recall a virtual lecture given to me by a sixty-seven-year-old mother of one, whom I fortuitously interrupted in the midst of a futile telephone attempt to mobilize her daughter for an unstated activity. Being at that moment her most convenient sounding board, I was exhorted to have several children: "You should have several children, certainly more than one or two. When you only have one, like me, or even two, look what happens. One moves off here and another is busy somewhere else and there is never anybody around—not like it used to be. When I was a kid there were always many people around the house doing something. Listen to what I tell you, you must have several children." Mind you, this same woman would often shake her head in disapproving disbelief when discussing a neighbor who had four children. Such contradictory comments reflect the intermediate position of these older villagers in the fertility transition; the younger generation was not so conflicted.

Zamfirovo's demographic transition followed general trends in the country. As McIntyre (1980:147) points out, "by the 1920s relatively low overall fertility levels had been achieved in what remained a backward agrarian society." According to him, this "achievement" (the semantics of "modernization" creep in even in its objective absence) can be attributed to a combination of "dashed dreams of development and prosperity on the one hand and intensifying rural poverty on the other" (McIntyre 1988a:24). Certainly, the liberation of the country and the selling of Ottoman holdings to Bulgarians created an environment of opportunity, and new owners apparently responded by maintaining high birth rates—according to Lampe (1986:55), the highest in the Balkans during the period 1906–10.

Their optimism was soon tempered, however, by an amazing concatenation of forces and events, including three consecutive wars, a large reparations burden from World War I, the continued operation of partible inheritance, the difficulties of repaying debts incurred to purchase abandoned Ottoman holdings, state extractions, and volatile agricultural prices, especially for grain. As discussed in Chapter 1, these forces created economic crises, making it difficult to provide for children. As a seventy-year-old Zamfirovo mother of two put it in 1987: "My husband's family didn't have much land and he had three brothers to boot. How could we have more children? Oh my God, with our property it was hard to provide for two children." In the context of smallholding agriculture, with high birth rates, declining mortality, and a system of partible inheritance, an impasse in providing for offspring in culturally accepted ways was reached rather quickly. This accounts for the striking change in village fertility in the span of a generation. Fertility decline, in turn, may have contributed to the economic improvements of the 1930s and 1940s discussed in Chapter 1.

There may have been other costs. In a lengthy description of Zamfirovo written in March 1926, the headmaster of the village school wrote, "Unfortunately the peasant woman walks in the steps of city women and tries to imitate them in all things. She no longer wants to bother to have many children. Therefore she resorts to various means, and since she is often ignorant and there are no doctors, she becomes a victim of her own folly. The consequences of this for the future of the nation if measures are not taken will be catastrophic." The author suggests obliquely that abortion was a common (and dangerous) means of fertility control. This would be consistent with the early and near-universal marriage patterns in Bulgaria (Hajnal 1965, Sklar 1974, McIntyre 1980), which precluded fertility regulation through delayed marriage or celibacy. Of course, coitus interruptus, widespread in western Europe, may have been practiced privately, beyond the purview of such social commentary. However, the above comment suggests that it was either not universally practiced or not entirely effective and that women were not averse to controlling fertility with abortion. In fact, legal abortion was widely adopted in Bulgaria after the liberalization of abortion laws in 1956, but with less impact on fertility rates than was the case in other east European countries. McIntyre (1980:165) suggests this may indicate a prior use of illegal abortion.[1]

Whatever the mechanisms of fertility restriction in Bulgaria, they were effective and established a trend that continued well into the socialist era. According to one compilation (Berent 1970:249), the crude birth rate for all of rural Bulgaria dropped from an annual average of 25.1 per 1,000 in the years 1946–49 to 14.2 births per 1,000 in 1967. However, McIntyre (1980:156) suggests that there may have been a slight increase in age-specific fertility since the 1960s. This may be reflected in Zamfirovo, where the number of births per year after the 1960s, especially between 1975 and 1989, remained essentially stable (around 29 to 30). Given a generally declining population and the increasing average age of village residents, this stability in births may actually reflect a slight increase in age-specific fertility. If so, it could reflect any number of factors, but it would certainly correlate with the domestication of socialism since the 1960s.

Household Dynamics

The population trends discussed above obviously impacted household organization and relations. While the historical significance of large communal families, or *zadrugas* (Mosely 1940), is uncertain in Zamfirovo (cf. Todorova 1990), there was a clear decline in Zamfirovo household size during the interwar period. As we saw in Chapter 1, the number of house-

1. The means of fertility regulation have significant connections to gender, family relations, and women's health. These links are important areas for future research in Bulgaria.

holds nearly doubled between 1917 and World War II (and in fact *had* doubled by the early 1950s), while the population increased only about 40 percent during the same period. This shift reflected the decline of the agro-pastoral economy brought on in part by land shortage and the shrinking of common lands, which simultaneously diminished the household's need for multiple laborers and its ability to support them. At the same time the delayed impact of previously high birth rates continued to increase population pressure. Political events in the 1940s and 1950s also probably accelerated the process of simplification, particularly the system of forced requisitions. While some allowances were made for household size, in general, the larger the holding, the higher the rate of requisitions. Thus, household fissioning and concomitant property division could reduce the total requisition burden of the people involved. At the same time, division did not necessarily require that separated households cease to cooperate economically.

As pointed out in Chapter 1, disagreement among family members over the cooperative farm also led to household divisions in the years leading up to collectivization. If members of the household were strongly at odds about joining, household division was the only solution. Such disagreements were commonly recounted in stories about early collectivization, and division was usually the ultimate resolution. I have already suggested that in-marrying sons-in-law were particularly receptive to the idea of collectivization, precisely because of the prospect for household division. By looking closer at the household level, we can also see that the situation prior to collectivization may have increased the number of in-marrying sons-in-law, thereby increasing the degree of support for cooperative agriculture. By the 1940s the generation born during the early fertility decline of the 1920s was entering marriageable age. This likely resulted in a greater number of families with only daughters eligible to marry. At the same time, economic privation and land shortages probably encouraged men of lesser means to join the families of these women. Collectivization subsequently allowed them to escape.

Following collectivization there was another motivation to divide—the expansion of personal plots mentioned in Chapter 2. Since each separate household had the right to a personal plot, division could double the amount of land available for personal use. Not surprisingly, the division of households then became a concern of the state, which attempted to guard against artificial separations. Any household wanting to be recognized as two distinct units had to make a request to the village council, which then decided on its legitimacy. Between 1956 and 1959 there were eighty such requests recorded in the council minutes; of these, thirty-four were granted, and thirty-three were denied on the basis that the individuals concerned were not living separately. One of the affirmative decisions was later reversed when the households were discovered to be living together. The council postponed the remaining thirteen requests while it investigated their legitimacy. Evaluation by the village council ensured against bogus petitions, but some of the households that actually divided may have been motivated to do so by the prospect of getting more personal land. Consequently, the council banned all requests for division in March 1957 because there was no more land to allocate for personal use. The moratorium was supposed to last through October, but no new request was recorded until April of the following year.

The disruptions of the 1950s and 1960s, especially collectivization and migration, led to a period of smaller average household size. This was especially evident in an increase in the number of households consisting only of a wife and husband whose parents had died and whose children had moved away. In the late 1960s and 1970s, however, the context of domestic arrangements was altered yet again by the stabilization of the agricultural system, the restriction of migration, and, as we will see in the next chapter, the availability of nonagricultural work. As possibilities for nonagricultural employment increased, there was less need to migrate, and migration restrictions (to be described below) made it more difficult. Other labor involvements no doubt competed with work in the personal agricultural sector, but the latter continued to be essential due to the economy of shortage and the increasing role of informal activities to be discussed in Chapter 5. The situation led to the revival of three-generation stem families sharing a single household economy. By 1988 this domestic arrangement characterized nearly half of all Zamfirovo households (see Table 9).

Table 9. Sample of Zamfirovo Households by Type, 1988

Type of Household	Incidence
Retired couple, widow, or widower	18
Nuclear family or young couple	4
Three generations	22
Four generations	4
Lateral extension	1
Four generations with lateral extension	1

NOTE: Based on a sample of 50 village households.

The three-generation arrangement was clearly economically strategic. Survival for a village family required extensive work in personal agricultural production, especially growing vegetables and tending animals. Even a few sheep, a goat, and a pig required daily attention and, occasionally, that one spend an entire day as the neighborhood shepherd. Cultural requirements for homemade wine, so central to village life and hospitality, necessitated investment in viticulture. At the same time, people had to be employed full-time in the state sector until retirement in order to qualify for state pensions and to earn needed cash. This situation resulted in an extreme version of what Halperin (1990) calls a "multiple livelihood strategy." Managing all the requirements was difficult, if not impossible, for a nuclear family, but a three-generation household was better equipped to handle it.

These larger households typically consisted of one or two grandparents, usually their son and his wife, and the younger couple's children. The older generation would retire at minimum retirement age and take care of most of the agricultural requirements as well as the children. They might also work part-time periodically for extra money or to acquire access to products gathered by the farm brigades. The younger couple would be employed in village enterprises, certainly not field labor, and would help in agricultural work on the personal plot after work and on weekends. Typically, it was the daughter-in-law who did the cooking and other domestic activities. Children pitched in with various chores and agricultural work, especially during the summer and on weekends, when they were not in school. It was the labor potential of the three-generation household and its efficiency in personal production that inspired state reforms such as *akord* contracts. By tapping domestic units in this way, the state actually reinforced households and became even more invested in accommodating them, opening up new avenues for domestication.

By the mid-1980s the results of this domestication, which included improving economic circumstances, allowed a few village couples to establish separate dwellings on a neolocal, nuclear-family basis, although most continued to cooperate economically with their parents. Some villagers thought this was a good idea, but few actualized it. Of course, there continued to be a large number of couples and widow(er)s living alone (see Table 9)—the combined result of fertility restrictions and migration.

The dissolution of larger households was accompanied by a change in the cultural meaning and value associated with particular household forms (see Halpern and Wagner 1984). Whereas in the past, households with multiple sons and their wives and children symbolized economic stability, this was no longer the case in the 1980s. The three-generation stem family household was considered desirable, but anything larger became synonymous with economic difficulty and was nefariously associated with Roma and Turks—ethnic minorities stigmatized for their large households. At the same time, the cultural bias toward ultimogeniture gained greater force as the basis for forming three-generation living arrangements.

The lack of deeper historical data on household structure in Zamfirovo makes further analysis of long-term change speculative. However, it is clear that the resulting household structures reflected an interaction of demographic and migration decisions with economic forces and cultural ideas about family and household.

The Rural-Urban Interface

Migration and fertility decline caused a drop in the village population and diminished the basis for future population growth. Since most migrants were young people, the percentage of villagers of childbearing (and working) age declined, and in a context of low fertility, this nearly fulfilled the catastrophic prophesy of the Zamfirovo schoolmaster back in 1926. In fact, migration and fertility decline interacted to produce a nationwide calamity—there were not enough people in the villages to expand agricultural production, and there were too many people in towns to be serviced by the existing urban infrastructure.

On the rural end, the demographic developments help account for the difficulties and inefficiencies of the cooperative farm described in Chapter 2. On the urban end, the results were manifested in the housing crisis characteristic of major cities. This crisis resulted from what Ofer (1977) calls "economizing on urbanization" and what Konrád and Szelényi (1976) refer to as the "underurbanization" of eastern Europe. While underurbanization has symptoms similar to capitalist overurbanization, the cause is different. The latter results from urban population growth outstripping industrial growth, whereas underurbanization results from "excessive industrialization at the expense of the infrastructure." They list Bulgaria as one of the worst offenders, with only 2.9 percent of national income going to housing construction compared with 32 percent in "developed capitalist countries" and 17 percent in the Soviet Union (Konrád and

Szelényi 1976:165). The resulting housing problem was severe, especially in the largest cities. One resident of Mihailovgrad, which was certainly not one of the more desirable urban addresses in the country, said, "There is no serious housing problem here. The wait for a new apartment in the building zone is only three years or so." Such shortages, however, exerted a useful negative influence on rural-to-urban migration.

At the same time, industrialization was not the only urban drawing card. Of the young people I met in the village, not one said they wanted to remain in the village after they finished school. Two of the households where I conducted extensive research had teenage members, and through them I was often invited to various gatherings of young people. Whether sitting around a table eating and drinking on some ritual occasion in standard adult form or at a cookout in the woods near one of the village reservoirs, they usually expressed amid their future plans the desire to reside in a large town or city. Not one of a group of approximately fifteen young people with whom I periodically socialized said they preferred to stay in the village, although several acknowledged that they would most likely remain there anyway.

Their attitudes were partially a product of the fact that there was no high school in the village. After the eighth grade young people not only had to go to town to continue their education, but because of limited bus routes, they actually had to live there, returning to the village only on weekends. This pattern of living away from home is understandable for those pursuing specialized education at schools far from the village, but in fact most went to school in one of the nearby towns less than a thirty-minute commute away. Workers commuted on a daily basis to the very same towns and spent more time on the job than students spent in school. For the state it was better to house students, usually in private residences paid for by village parents, than it was to provide transport for students to and from every village. Of course the young people were quite happy with the arrangement, as it relieved them of work back in the village, but it aggravated the rural labor problems, forcing adults to do most of the work in the personal economy and reducing the time and energy they had for the state or cooperative sector. While this may have been good for their children's education, it reflects a major shift from a time when school schedules were modified to fit agricultural cycles.

This "modern" priority is at the crux of agrarian disengagement and the associated distaste for village life. It is part of a larger shift in the attitude toward agriculture from a valued and respected occupation to a secondary involvement that must be organized around more central requirements. The educational setup itself was not so much responsible for this change as it was a reflection of the changing attitudes, but such arrangements no doubt exacerbated the devaluation of agriculture and village life. In the final analysis, these developments are manifestations of the socialist development strategy, which economically and ideologically devalued agriculture, so that agriculture was correctly evaluated by villagers as among the most difficult and undesirable types of work. At the same time there was a persistent identification between agriculture and village living (see Creed 1995b). Indeed, it was the desire to escape agricultural labor and the daily requirements of the rural household economy that provoked people to leave the village and search for alternatives.

This was reflected not only in young people's ambitions but also in the comments of adult villagers. To a person, they maintained that the reason people left the village was because they did not want to work so hard. One night on the 8:30 bus from Mihailovgrad to the village, I was engaged in conversation by an elderly man sitting behind me. He was over seventy and lived alone with his wife in the village. They had a son and a daughter, both living in Mihailovgrad. In the winter he spent weekends with the son and returned on Monday night to the village. His wife "preferred to stay home." He said he still worked occasionally in good weather on the brigades of the cooperative farm. He talked extensively about people leaving the village, invoking the image of deserted village houses to illustrate his point. He recounted several "house histories," all following basically the same trajectory: the children left the village for urban life, their parents died, and the house was left abandoned. His concern with this process was clearly personal, as he concluded by saying that the same thing would probably happen to his own house, a prospect that obviously saddened him. When asked why people left the village, he did not hesitate or equivocate: "They run away from the work. They are lazy and do not want to work hard. That, in a word, is why they leave."

His explanation was repeated by numerous villagers of all stripes. A man of forty living with his parents in the village had harsh words for his brother living in Mihailovgrad: "He does not like to work. He does not want to do any physical labor such as pruning the grape vines, but he loves to drink the wine." Another woman complained about her daughter-in-law in Mihailovgrad: "She does not want to do anything outside her office. She absolutely refuses to do any agricultural work." Perhaps the most analytical observation of urban sloth came from a middle-aged village woman who lived in a household with her husband and her husband's elderly father. Both of her children had left the village. "They go to towns because they do not have to do any work there, and if you do not believe me just look at their fingernails. They have fingernails out to here," she said, indicating more than an inch of growth. "Tell me they do any work." I was more cognizant of fingernails from that point on and did note a correlation between long fingernails and urban residence.

Lest one think this is only the villagers' side of the story, the comments of urban village expatriates were remarkably similar. Granted, they did not describe themselves as lazy, and many insisted they had originally left the village to find work, not escape it. Still, they often admitted that they preferred the town because the work was less arduous. While I was in the village, the bookkeeper for the post office retired and was replaced by a young woman from Berkovitza. She had a grandfather in the village, but her parents moved to town before she was born and she had lived there her whole life. She commuted back and forth to the village to work. When a villager suggested that it would be more convenient to live in the village, she replied indignantly, "I did not go to school and study in order to dig." Although phrased in occupational terms, her comment reveals the desire not only to escape agriculture as a vocation but to escape the whole rural social milieu, of which digging and hoeing were epitomizing symbols. Villagers, in turn, interpreted urban cultural and social activities as signs of laziness: what people did when they did not have work to do.

It is impossible to miss in these revelations the antagonism, bordering on hostility, that existed between urban and rural residents. As the above examples demonstrate, villagers were quick to label urban residents lazy and often pretentious. Urbanites, for their part, often viewed villagers as hicks and the village as backward. Such attitudes were full of ambiguity, as urbanites often had close relatives in a village and, as discussed before, did not hesitate to avail themselves of the rural agricultural bounty. I even came across one attempt to deny the village this contribution in the form of a cartoon in the Mihailovgrad newspaper. The cartoon pictured a man running along a street carrying a gigantic cornucopia overflowing with various food products. In the background were the tall apartment buildings of the city and in the foreground a street sign, pointing in the direction he was traveling and saying "village." The caption read, "Who says the village feeds the town?" The opposition achieved perhaps its most explicit demonstration in postcommunist election results, which divided along rural-urban lines (Creed 1995b).

This conflict was not new—it dates back at least to the interwar period and probably to the beginnings of industrialization in the last quarter of

the 1800s (Creed 1993; see also Bell 1977:155, Crampton 1987:74, Mouzelis 1976, and Todorova 1992). This is not the place to pursue the issue,
but it is important to recognize that the continuing rural-urban opposition had a long history of interaction with political and economic processes. The policies of the communist regime played an important part in
transforming this clear-cut distrust into a conflicting ambiguity. Industrialization, collectivization, and massive rural out-migration led to a shortage
of rural workers and difficulties for the village economy. Those who stayed
in the village were exposed to heavy state demands, and with declining
labor reserves, they perceived those who migrated as increasing the burden of those who remained. Their resentment underlaid subsequent accusations of slothfulness. Since the "deserters" were likely to include kindred, an ambivalent situation arose for people who disliked urbanites and
blamed them for their own exploitation but nevertheless had close relatives who were urban residents. Paradoxically, it was often their urban
relatives—a positive element in their ambivalent attitude toward the
city—who in fact received the brunt of their resentment. It was between
such relations that the mutual social and economic commitments were
strongest, and consequently the breaches most egregious. The distribution of these relations across rural and urban contexts did not eliminate
the expectations; rather, it contributed to the expansion of informal exchanges between rural and urban relatives discussed in Chapter 5. This
led to differential interpretations of who was benefiting more. The evaluation was also influenced by aspects of communist ideology, which associated modernity with urbanism and valorized the working class over and
above the farmer. Many villagers accepted these ideas and at the same
time resented the devaluation they implied for the countryside.

The ambivalence acquires a material manifestation when the physical
conditions of the city are considered. Much of the urban housing stock
could hardly be considered modern. Many houses in Berkovitza did not
have indoor plumbing. New apartment blocks in both Berkovitza and
Mihailovgrad lacked central heating several years after habitation. Telephone lines were also years away from realization, whereas most Zamfirovo households got a telephone in the mid-1980s. Still, infrastructural
investment in the village was hardly satisfactory either. The village was
provided with electricity in 1958, and people recounted wondrous stories
of turning on electric lights for the first time. In the mid-1960s houses got
running water, but in the late 1980s most houses did not have indoor
toilets, although many had indoor showers. As late as 1988 the village

school was still heated by individual woodstoves in each room, and steam heat remained in the planning stages. Many village roads were unpaved, and mud was one of the symbols of rural inferiority. At the same time, baseline economic issues, such as the limited selection of consumer goods in the village, clearly influenced perceptions of "rural" and "urban" and structured the interaction between the two, including the movement of people. As one middle-aged villager stated, "We have to go to Mihailov-grad if we want a cone of ice cream on a hot summer evening. And Berko-vitza is not much better than here. They never have produce like oranges or bananas when Mihailovgrad does. Berkovitza is just like a village."

The nature of rural-urban interaction was complex. Neither the city nor the village was unqualifiably attractive, nor was either entirely undesirable. For certain people in certain times and circumstances, the scales tipped one way or the other. This was the case during the exodus of the 1950s and the 1960s, and it holds for subsequent migration as well. Employment continued to be a factor in this balance, but its role should not be over-emphasized. This fact was brought home to me in a discussion with a retired man in Berkovitza about my own future. When I began complain-ing about the difficulty of finding a job in anthropology and the possi-bility of having to get a job outside of my field, I was dismissed and told that it was the same in Bulgaria, where "people give up training and expe-rience and take on any job just to get into a city."

I was personally aware of one such case, involving a young couple from the village. They had moved to Mihailovgrad, where their living condi-tions were terrible—they lived in a small basement apartment that was inadequate for them and their two children and that often flooded in wet weather. Although trained as a machinist, the husband worked on a five-year contract as a "general worker" for a building firm, which basically meant he did unskilled manual labor. On fulfillment of his contract, he would get an apartment in one of the new high-rise apartment buildings being built around the city. He said he would then hunt for a better-paying job, hopefully one for which he was trained. This issue is well expressed in the memoirs of the Bulgarian dissident Georgi Markov (1984:162):

> A universally applicable law of our social order then, as now, de-creed that a huge number of people should devote their energies to work for which they were not suited. Under this law, which led to the most inexplicable and impossible appointments, colleagues of mine who were specialists in rubber were sent to produce glass,

specialists in glass found themselves in the pharmaceutical industry, while food experts ended up in heavy metallurgy. All this was partly the consequence of an almost hysterical scramble to remain at all costs in Sofia, where with good reason life was considered to be better than in the provinces.[2]

Such a situation reveals the distortion of unidimensional economic explanations suggesting that employment possibilities pulled people to towns. Rather it seems that the privations and difficulties of village life, in concert with the various amenities associated with urban living, drove people to cities, where they took whatever jobs they could get.

A similar critique can be made of the role of education in the migration process. Education was important in migration from Zamfirovo for all the reasons Simić (1973:80) elaborated for Serbia: (1) it creates an increased desire for participation in the world outside the village; (2) skills are acquired that often cannot be practiced in the countryside; and (3) higher education usually requires a period of residence in larger population centers. As described above, the latter was particularly true for Zamfirovo. This view alone, however, is unidirectional, with exposure to higher education seen as creating motivations for migration. In Zamfirovo education was as much a strategy for migration as a cause. Young people certainly did leave the village because they were trained for occupations irrelevant to rural life, but they actively pursued such areas of study in the first place precisely to escape the village, and they often made these decisions before being exposed to higher education. Young people in the village often expressed their career ambitions in terms of occupations that would most likely take them into urban environments, attempting to train for careers that could only be practiced in cities. So while education may have generated migration desires, the desire to migrate generated the interest in higher education.

The role of education in migration has led some to suggest a rural brain drain, in which villages lost their brightest and best and kept only the less capable, thereby deepening rural social and economic problems. Taaffe (1977:162–64) claims such a process was characteristic of Bulgaria, and other scholars (Konrád and Szelényi 1976, Bell 1984, Douglass 1975:

2. This fact is not unique to Bulgaria. The *New York Times* (January 12, 1984) reported that there were hundreds of young specialists, including doctors and dentists, out of work in Yugoslavia's big cities because they did not want to go back to smaller towns and villages where jobs were available. One such graduate of the medical faculty of Belgrade University chose to sell worms to fishermen along the Danube rather than leave Belgrade.

151) have suggested the same for other countries. But looking at the role of social relations diminishes the potential damage of brain drain. Many times it was indeed the most educated that left the village, but their education was sometimes a reflection of advantageous social relations rather than superior intellect. During my stay in the village, two individuals with similar levels of education left their village jobs for positions in the nearby town. One was uniformly acknowledged to be smart, the other universally held to have gotten her education only through social connections.

Young people also candidly admitted that urban residence was a factor in spouse selection. For a village young person who lived in town while going to school, finding a spouse from the city was one way to forestall a return to the village. Urban residence was usually mentioned when young people described the desirable qualities of boyfriends or girlfriends, either actual or potential. This was verified in a somewhat reverse way by a typical piece of village gossip. A village friend I visited frequently lived next door to a family with a nineteen-year-old daughter. Distant relatives in Sofia were trying to matchmake her with their neighbor. As my friend related it, "He is single and has his own apartment in Sofia. All she has to do is take off her shoes and go in." After a contemplative pause, she added, "Although, if he has an apartment in Sofia and no marriage prospects, then there is certainly something wrong with him."

These examples underline the attraction of urban residence (and by extension urban residents). The situation was a spiraling one—as people left the village it became less viable, less attractive, and less deserving of investment, which increased the desire to migrate. This process, in combination with the fertility decline, contributed to the agricultural problems described in the previous chapter, but the increasing need for investment in urban infrastructure and agricultural mechanization to replace farmworkers threatened to undercut industrial development as well. Indeed, declining birth rates jeopardized the labor prospects in all sectors of the economy. The state had to take measures on both demographic and migratory fronts to correct these imbalances.

State Policies

On the demographic front the government attempted to increase fertility by a combination of abortion restrictions and pro-natal financial incentives. Abortion legislation, liberalized in 1956 following Soviet precedent, was restricted between 1967 and 1970 and again in 1972 (McIntyre 1975: 367), but abortion was never completely outlawed. Informants confirmed that the regulations in 1988 remained similar to those described by Berent (1970:280ff.) in 1970: married women with three or more children could obtain legal abortions, whereas married women with less than three children could not. They also said that all unmarried women were able to get legal abortions. As very few villagers had more than two children, either the letter of the law was not observed or alternate forms of birth control were used.

Other legal methods included the pill and condoms. Being legal, however, did not mean that birth control products were always available. For example, following a radio program on AIDS prevention, a listener called in to ask why condoms were not available in drug stores. The medical expert had no answer. Given the problems of availability, I suspect that illegal abortions and possibly coitus interruptus continued to be important means of fertility control, supplemented by more modern techniques when available. As our earlier discussion indicated, Bulgarian villagers had been controlling their fertility for decades, and jural constrictions, short of the kind of interventions found in Romania (see Kligman 1992, n.d.), were likely to be of less consequence than planners intended.

Perhaps in recognition of this fact, the government also began at the same time an elaborate pro-natal campaign based on financial incentives. The system was extensive and changed often, primarily in the amounts of compensation. Incentives included a very liberal system of maternity-leave benefits, a lump sum payment at birth, and a monthly wage supplement. The rate of compensation varied according to the birth order of the pregnancy, as summarized in Table 10. In addition, women could extend their maternity leave for up to four years—they could remain on leave until the child's second birthday with a minimum salary of 120 leva a month and elect to take an additional two years' leave without pay—and they were

Table 10.   Pro-natal Incentives in Bulgaria, circa 1987

	First Child	Second Child	Third Child	Additional Births
Birth payment (leva)	100	250	500	100
Monthly wage supplement (leva)	15	30	55	15
Pregnancy leave (days)	120	150	180	120

guaranteed to receive their previous position on returning to work. As McIntyre (1975:374–75) points out, it is difficult to assess the results of such policies because they correspond in time with changes in abortion availability, to which he attributes more significance. On an impressionistic level, these policies did seem to have an impact on village birth spacing, as two years was a very common age difference between two siblings. The limitations of these programs, however, were verified by a demographic consultant to the government who concluded a lengthy discussion of the details of the system by advising me not to bother remembering them, as "the system is not really working and is being changed."

Incentives were only one side of the strategy to increase fertility, for they were combined with disincentives to celibacy and childlessness in the form of special taxes. Men and women who were not married by the age of twenty-one were required to pay a "bachelor's tax." The tax rate was 5 percent of their income until age thirty, then 10 percent until they turned thirty-five, and thereafter 15 percent until they married or reached the ages of forty-five for women and fifty for men. Once married, a couple had three years to produce a child. If they did not, they were each assessed a 15 percent tax on their income until a child was born. Again, such measures did not reverse fertility declines, but they may have contributed to the continuing village pattern of early marriage and the early birth of at least one child. Finally, there were moral incentives, as women having more than two children were given medals recognizing their achievement as "Heroes of Motherhood."

When questioned, many informants said that the various incentives were simply not enough to make having more children desirable. The government, for its part, was constrained in the further expansion of incentive programs by the Turkish minority and, especially, the Roma— who, as one government official put it, "will have as many children as they receive financial compensation for." The continuing failure of pro-natal policies among the Bulgarian population and the continued growth of Moslem populations contributed to the infamous assimilation campaign of the 1980s (see Bates 1994, Creed 1990).

While pro-natal policies were being implemented to promote population growth, restrictions were being formulated to keep the existing population in place. The convergent timing suggests a sort of watershed realization by the government/party in the late 1960s of some of the unintended consequences of the socialist development strategy. Officials in the town of Berkovitza said that migration regulations were imposed in 1967, and officials in Mihailovgrad said they were imposed "around 1970." A published listing of the migration regulations, however, dates most of them to 1974 (Marinov 1985). The limitations were always referred to as "temporary limits to residence in cities," but they were never rescinded in the socialist era—in fact, these limitations were extended. As of 1981 there were only 121 small towns to which the migration limits did not apply (Marinov 1985:65–66). By 1985 the regulations and updates took up nearly forty pages of print in Marinov's collection.

The regulations served a dual purpose. On the one hand, by restricting migration to urban areas, they retained village populations and limited urban expansion; on the other hand, by making urban residence a truly limited good, officials were able to offer it as an incentive or attraction for positions and jobs that were otherwise undesirable. The restrictions limited migration to most large towns and then granted various dispensations to people who worked a certain number of years in a specified job or place. The following entry from Marinov's collection is representative: "workers and service personnel who have worked at least 6 years at the radio-relay and television station, 'Botev Peak,' upon a motion by the Ministry of Communication may be accepted as residents by all restricted cities except Sofia" (Marinov 1985:53).

Two villagers from Zamfirovo were involved in similar labor activities and were planning to relocate when their time was served. One was working as a construction worker on a nuclear power plant near the town of Kozloduy on the Danube and planned to move to Mihailovgrad. The other man was working in a lumber enterprise in Berkovitza and planned to move there permanently. This would be possible after five years of service with a promise to work five more. In the meantime he commuted from the village. There were numerous other exceptions granted, including those for spouses, government and party officials, career soldiers, and people designated as "heroes of socialist labor" in particular occupations.

A major exception was made for "young specialists," that is, young people fresh out of specialized occupational training, provided that their skills were needed in the place they intended to live and not needed at their current place of residence. This possibility provided an opening for the creative career planning described earlier. Young people were able to assess the situation and compete for specializations that were not needed in their village. They usually did not succeed, as these areas were also the most competitive and villagers were generally less prepared than urban youth, with less access to the relevant network of social connections. Still,

they tried. One village youth told me he was going to the University of
Sofia after he got out of the army. Several months later I overheard a
telephone conversation in the town hall where the director of the cooperative farm was assuring this young man's mother that he had taken care of
the necessary procedures to get the son into technical school in Mihailovgrad on the basis of the needs of the farm and his future village employment. In contrast, another village young person was successful, gaining
admittance into the Economics Institute in Sofia by arrangement of a firm
in Berkovitza, where she was supposed to work after graduation.

Another specification allowed towns to admit new residents to fill "labor shortages." Given the chronic nature of this problem in the socialist
economy, it is not surprising that the number of such positions was controlled by organs of the central government. A planning committee at the
national level allotted each town a quota of workers they could accept
each year for labor needs. The towns then allotted these positions to local
enterprises according to their needs and their importance in the local
economy. Villagers who worked on contract with these enterprises, usually
for about ten years, received town residence status. Berkovitza received an
average of twenty-seven such positions annually, plus seven positions for
"needs of a social character"; Mihailovgrad averaged one hundred workers and sixty positions for social needs.

This system clearly created a field for the mobilization of social relations. Without going into every case, we can generalize that many of the
opportunities for migration described above were not granted blindly. For
example, when I told the young man with university ambitions that I knew
a professor in his field at the university, he immediately asked me to arrange for them to meet. He then proceeded to tell me how difficult it was
to get into the university because of the role of personal connections in
the selection process and that it would be a great help to him if he could
meet a professor. Knowing the faculty member well, I did not have the
same impression of the importance of personalistic relations in the selection process, but I do not doubt they were operative to some degree.
Another village youth got an industrial job in a Sofia factory and moved
there because his father was related to the local director of a branch of
the factory located in the village. Finally, the several cases of villagers
working abroad for hard currency in the 1980s was understandable given
that an influential village expatriate was married to a woman who helped
coordinate international labor arrangements. As one villager put it, "She
arranges it for our men."

Several villagers insisted that those determined to leave the village could get out, either through official loopholes in the regulations or through unofficial connections. Still, the prospective difficulties involved may have discouraged such determination from ever developing. Furthermore, as regulations tightened, the social connections required to circumvent them inflated, often beyond the network "capital" of average villagers. Such a crackdown was evident in 1988. A village man assured me that it was getting much more difficult to migrate to cities than it had been in the past: "Factories used to have housing and everything, and it was not too difficult to migrate. Now it is very hard." In Sofia, posted advertisements for less-than-desirable jobs, such as transit driving, specified that applicants have official resident status, whereas previously these jobs were offered as a vehicle for acquiring such status. A new regulation promised to tax Sofia enterprises 2,000 leva for each nonresident employed by the firm on a temporary resident permit. A Sofia student complained that a friend of his was having problems getting a new temporary residence permit and was considering changing his official residence to a village outside of Sofia, where residence was not restricted, and then living illegally in the city.

Villagers felt the restrictiveness of the new regulations, particularly as migration had been a mechanism of socioeconomic mobility, and this sense of deprivation fueled discontent. Certainly many villagers defended rural life on various grounds, but many others complained about not being able to move. The predicament heightened their resentment of urbanites discussed previously. Given the perceived cultural superiority of urban life generated by socialist development, migration restrictions seemed to ensconce villagers at the bottom of a caste system from which they or their progeny could never escape. Regulations also further isolated villages ideologically, as they became less integral to national development than they had been in the past when they provided the urban workforce.

Luckily, at the same time, socialist policies and reforms also improved rural life. Pensions for the elderly, extensive maternity leaves for mothers, and salary supplements for children were combined with agricultural reforms—such as increasing cooperative assistance for personal production and *akord* contracts—to sustain village residents and enhance their standard of living. All these actions reveal the domestication of socialism at work. By restricting their fertility, migrating to towns, and withdrawing into household subsistence activity, villagers pushed the socialist state toward reforms and policies that ameliorated rural life, even if restricting exit from it. This result was predicated on the state's total responsibility for the entire society and the need to respond to the negative rural fallout of previous policies. One of the major actions in this regard was the attempt to industrialize the countryside itself. The next chapter takes up that project in detail.

4

INDUSTRIAL
REVOLUTIONS

In response to some of the population trends discussed in the previous chapter, and the attendant agricultural problems discussed in Chapter 2, the government began in the late 1960s to promote the idea of dispersed industrial development, whereby industrial enterprises were to be set up in rural and small town locations. Zamfirovo not only benefited from this initiative but was transformed by it. The results were immediately evident on entering the village. The cooperative farm buildings and the machine tractor station were the first structures one passed on the road leading into Zamfirovo, but immediately beyond them stood the village factory. With its factory name and requisite socialist slogan ("Restructuring: Deed and Destiny of Everyone") emblazoned across the front, the building testified loudly to the industrializing project. Together with the adjoining cooperative farmyard, it conveyed the agro-industrial foundation of the village economy. The idea for such industrial dispersion developed from state policy, but its implementation in the village engaged local factors that, when examined, further enliven our understanding of the interaction between the local and the national in processes of socialist reform and domestication.

To the extent that rural industrialization was itself an attempt to improve village life, it was a direct contribution to the domestication of socialism. Yet, it also threatened to introduce new unpleasantries, such as the notorious work discipline associated with industrial regimes. This possibility was countered, however, by the conflicting complementarity of socialism, which forced industrial accommodations to the agricultural activities of both the cooperative farm and village households. A village acquaintance summarized the interaction one day as I tried to extricate myself from an unpleasant (and all too common) discussion about finding me a girlfriend. In an effort to escape, I said I had to go talk to workers in the cookie factory—it being the first workplace to come to mind. "There is no need to go there today," he countered. "It is probably not working. They are all in the fields harvesting strawberries on *akord*." He mistook my pained expression at having my exit strategy blocked for either disapproval or confusion and went on to explain:

> You see, the cookie factory is part of the village Commerce Cooperative, which is responsible for the exported strawberries. They have to wash and sort them and pack them into the barrels for the truck. To finish the work they have to have strawberries, so the managers let the workers pick during the day. Maybe they take vacation days, but maybe they don't. Regardless, they then get to work overtime processing the strawberries. The possibility to harvest during the workday makes the [*akord*] contract more attractive, and they can take more land. So the farm produces more strawberries, the Commerce Cooperative exports more, and villagers make more money. Everybody profits.

There were, however, some losers. Certainly, cookie production suffered, at least temporarily. Additionally, a village schoolteacher complained that by the time she got to the fields in the late afternoon, farm officials had already stopped accepting strawberries for the day because everybody else had been picking during the workday. As she put it, "Children can't be turned off and left like a sewing machine."

Such relations between agriculture and industry were highly determinate in the rural (and national) economy, but they were extremely elusive to macro-level analyses focused on distinctive economic sectors. This chapter fills that vacuum with ethnography. It begins with an extended description of the nonagricultural enterprises in Zamfirovo in the late 1980s and the related role of commuting. This is followed by an examination of how nonagricultural activities interacted with farming requirements to fuel the cycle of reform and compromise symptomatic of socialism as a system of conflicting complementarity. The outcome was the adjustment of industrial discipline to the exigencies and needs of rural agricultural concerns—the opposite of what is often assumed to occur with capitalist industrialization.

While clearly redressing the rural dynamics discussed in the previous chapters, it can certainly be argued, as Konrád and Szelényi (1976) do, that dispersing economic enterprises was as much a response to urban concerns as to rural ones, notably the dilemma of urban population growth in the context of communist distaste for infrastructural investment. As Smollett (1980:53) optimistically phrased it for the Bulgarian case, "these rural factories will reverse the growth of urban congestion, and allow people to work in industry while enjoying the pleasant conditions of village life."

In fact, the urban connection is just another of the numerous related factors that made rural industrialization an extremely attractive and economical prospect. Village depopulation, the strain on the urban infrastructure, and the continuing need for ever more industrial workers in a context of soft budget constraints and extensive growth could all be addressed by locating industrial employment in villages. The existing rural infrastructure, ample if less than desirable, could be used to support industrial producers. Reciprocally, industry should provide some workers for agriculture, whether from the families of industrial workers or from local enterprises supplying agricultural brigades. Industrial work would allow villages to absorb educated and skilled young people. It also would prevent the proliferation of nonfunctional villages that had to be provided with basic infrastructural supports for diminishing nonproductive populations, a drain perhaps even more unacceptable than urban infrastructural investment.

Clearly, these arguments were broadly related to a socialist ideology that required all people and places be provisioned. In fact, dispersed development fit perfectly into the ideological structure that I have suggested was so important in both the makeup of socialist political economy and the reform process that accompanied it. To begin with, it redressed the ideologically unacceptable rural-urban inequities that had emerged in the headlong rush for industrialization at the expense of agriculture and rural society. It did so without sacrificing the industrial bias that was also virtually an ideological tenet of socialism. In addition, it promoted equal regional development by advocating a more even geographical distribution of productive activities, thereby increasing equality among individuals and between regions. In a real sense, then, the policy itself was a reform necessitated by historical developments in the context of socialist ideological and economic objectives.

Of course, implementation proved more complex than planning. In some areas the strategy never even materialized, and where it did, as in Zamfirovo, conflicts accompanied it. Arising as an answer to problems of socialist development, the process of rural industrialization generated other problems that called forth further adjustments or reforms. At the same time, the establishment of industrial activities altered conditions affecting agricultural output, injecting additional considerations into the agricultural balancing act described in Chapter 2 and thereby contributing to agricultural reforms. Thus, in contrast to the suggestion Ho (1979) makes for Taiwan, rural industrialization in Bulgaria was not really a way of "maintaining the rural social fabric" but, rather, a way of altering it drastically in order to make it more durable. In order to see this process, however, we must look at the actual nonagricultural enterprises in the village. Starting from this point, we not only get a close-up view of the implementation of state policy but a new perspective on political and economic processes that includes a greater role for local factors and social relations than it does for state fiat.

Nonagricultural Enterprises in Zamfirovo

The primary nonagricultural enterprise was the previously described village factory, which assembled stators for electrical motors. It was actually a branch of a large machine plant in Sofia, which owned the equipment, dictated production plans, and provided the necessary materials—primarily sheet metal, bar aluminum, and electrical wiring. The productive process involved molding the base of the stator from molten aluminum, cutting sheet metal into pieces that were stacked into aluminum forms, and attaching the necessary wiring. The factory produced about 15,000 such units a year. The stators were picked up by the parent plant and trucked back to Sofia, where they were assembled into electrical motors for various types of machinery, ultimately destined, I was told, for Africa.

The factory employed about 150 shift workers, consisting of ninety women and sixty men, divided between morning and afternoon shifts. Women were primarily engaged in two activities: operating the presses that cut the sheet metal into appropriate pieces and attaching the wiring to the final product. Men were involved in making the forms, assembling the pieces, and hauling the materials and products around the factory. The factory also employed about thirty salaried personnel, including the

factory managers, their administrative support staff, and skilled technicians.

Workers functioned on the norm system, which, as we saw for agricultural workers, required a minimum production per day, although there
was a guaranteed minimum wage should they fall short. In line with the
situation described by Haraszti (1978) for Hungary, norms continually escalated (see also Burawoy 1985:167–71). As the director explained it to
me, "There are increases in the norms with improvements of machines or
improved organization, and so forth." Workers described the norms as
"difficult but possible." Despite the difficulty, the average monthly salary
for workers was a respectable 250 to 300 leva a month. Although this was
considered a good wage, the work was hard, which may explain why there
was substantial turnover in the workforce. I do not have employment statistics to verify employee turnover, but based on the large number of people I spoke with in other contexts who had worked in the factory in the
past, I suspect there was significant fluidity. One middle-aged man working in another village enterprise told me he had made more money in the
factory but had changed jobs because the work was too monotonous and
strict. A current factory employee said he was in the process of looking for
another job for the same reason. Apparently, the wages attracted people
to the work, but some tired of the difficult and more rigorous regime and
eventually looked for other jobs, perhaps even less lucrative ones. The
technicians did not work on the norm and received a flat salary, "slightly
higher than that of the workers."

These salaries reflected a significant increase in 1986. Before that the
maximum wage for workers had been 200 leva, and certainly many were
below that mark. The salary increase also reflected changes in the system
of remuneration. Wages had always been tied to production by some
mechanism, but until 1988 salaries were determined by the factory's total
output. That year, the factory began working on a brigade system in which
the workers were remunerated according to the productivity of their particular brigade rather than the factory as a whole. Furthermore, brigades
acquired individual responsibility for the distribution of pay among their
members. This reflected national reform policies intended to tighten the
link between individual worker productivity and salary.

These reforms actually dated back to 1978 when the Party Conference
mandated the brigade organization of work for all productive enterprises,
including the idea of brigades being self-supporting in terms of cost accounting. According to Thirkell (1985), 70 to 80 percent of manual work-

ers in productive industries were organized into such brigades by 1983. It was not until 1986, however, that the brigade unit took on real social significance. In that year the new Labor Code was adopted, with self-management as its modus vivendi. Brigades of a "new type," created with a smaller number of members, were now charged with direct participation in decision making and execution (Stoilov 1987:26, Petkov 1987). The new system of brigade remuneration was one of the vehicles intended to unite the interests of the newly self-managing brigades and the enterprise as a whole. As we shall see later, it was not a perfect marriage, but it was indicative of the reach of centralized planning that all these various national industrial reforms affected a small local branch factory and village workers.

The factory first opened in late 1969, following the national campaign to set up rural enterprises. In an attempt to understand the mechanisms by which this national policy was implemented on the local level, I asked questions about why and how the factory ended up in Zamfirovo. The answers inevitably focused on some characteristics of the village that made it an appropriate choice: "We are a large village"; "There are lots of people here to work"; "We are not too far from Sofia"; or, "We needed it." Regardless of whom I asked, I could not get beyond such explanations. I was soon left with the impression that the plant in Sofia had, perhaps because of a national directive, decided to establish a branch assembly shop, examined all the villages within a certain geographic radius, and had chosen Zamfirovo based on particularities of location and perhaps demography.

Later in my stay I was having dinner with a family in the village on the occasion of a visit by their friends from another part of the country. On this occasion as on others, I was questioned about my impressions of the village. In lauding the diverse opportunities for work in the village, I mentioned the factory. The conversation then turned to it, and one of the guests asked the host, "Who is responsible for the factory being here?" I knew at once that I had been asking the wrong question all along—the issue was not *why* but *who*, and not just who had decided but who was responsible. When the question was asked in this way, the host answered directly, telling of a villager who, having ascended to the upper ranks of the national government, had official relations with the parent plant in Sofia and through them arranged to have the branch built in Zamfirovo. So my conception of the process went from one extreme to the other in a matter of seconds: local connections were in fact the driving force, with the national level doing little more than providing the basic policy in support of a local initiative. Later I discovered that the local initiative was actually a cooperative effort between village leaders and the villager in the national government; the former instigated the process and the latter facilitated it. Similar processes figured in the history of other local nonagricultural enterprises.

Two other important nonagricultural enterprises in the village were actually units of the local Commerce Cooperative. The cooperative's primary responsibilities included provisioning the village stores, running the village restaurant, and buying up various products produced by villagers in their personal economy. Responsibility for purchasing most agricultural items from villagers had been transferred to the cooperative farm, but the Commerce Cooperative retained responsibility for some goods, notably sheep and goat skins. It also supplied local shops and the restaurant through direct contracts with productive enterprises, primarily in the district and county but also from other areas when necessary. This responsibility put it on the firing line when there were shortages of various products in the village. Villagers, however, maintained an accurate monitoring system of the national economy. Thanks to extensive out-migration, they had contacts with people in various places and were able to determine when shortages were systemic and when localized. Thus, they could distinguish cases when the local cooperative was to blame for shortfalls from cases when national or enterprise problems were at fault. Since purchasing contracts between cooperatives and enterprises tended to be maintained over time, most shortages were, in fact, the result of production problems rather than a failure of the local cooperative. Occasionally, however, the cooperative director would be taken to task for not finding alternative sources of products when traditional suppliers failed.

The village Commerce Cooperative did not attempt to supply the variety of goods available in nearby towns, but it did provide all the basic needs of villagers, as well as a few nonessentials. There was a fairly large general store with housewares, clothes, furniture, and farming supplies. In addition, there was a central grocery store with a small meat section and several satellite kiosks that sold nonperishable items throughout the village. There was also a fish store that operated when fish was delivered and a fruit and vegetable store that never operated because there was no one to work there.

Shortages and lines for products in short supply certainly existed, but they were not endemic. At any given time there was likely to be some standard product unavailable, but such lapses were usually temporary, due to either a problem at the factory or demand patterns that peaked at particular times. For example, sugar might become short during the wine-making season, or soft drinks might be in short supply before holiday feasts. Lines did not necessarily indicate an absolute shortage of a given product. Meat was delivered to the village twice a week, so if you wanted or needed meat, you had to line up, and since there was only one distribution outlet with limited working hours, the lines were made longer. Nevertheless, many times I returned to the store later to find the product still in supply after everyone had been served. It is true that such lining-up behavior was a response to the larger system in which supply and demand were not coordinated, and shortages did occur. Still, we should be aware that the infamous lines of socialism were not simply the result of product scarcity.

A good example of the multidimensional aspects of lines is the case of bread buying in Zamfirovo. There was no shortage of bread in the village during 1987 or 1988, even though it was sometimes purchased in large quantities to feed pigs being fattened for sale to the state. Despite apparent bounty, there were often lines at the bread bakery, for several reasons. The buyers' preference for very fresh (preferably warm) bread, the somewhat limited hours for selling bread at the bakery, and the working schedule of the consumer all conspired to create lines in the absence of a shortage.

The bakery was one of the two enterprises of the village Commerce Cooperative engaged in production. It employed eight workers divided into two shifts (one all-male and the other all-female), producing over 500 loaves per day. The workers were paid according to the number of loaves they produced, and monthly salaries ranged between 200 and 250 leva. Production was automated, with mixing, kneading, and portioning all done by machine, but the machinery was antiquated, and villagers complained constantly in the late 1980s about the quality of the bread. Its texture, they pointed out, was coarse compared to that available in Sofia or even in the smaller village of Burziya, located between Sofia and Zamfirovo. Situated on the main highway, the Burziya bakery was a common stopping point for travelers in either direction. Apparently, attempts had been made to improve the Zamfirovo product, as there was a large new dough mixing machine covered up with plastic in the corner of the bakery. Unfortunately it had never worked right. When I asked why it had not been returned, one of the bakers gave the one-word explanation "bureaucracy." By 1992, however, such problems had apparently been overcome, for the bakery was producing a high-quality product.

The other productive enterprise managed by the Commerce Cooperative was the previously mentioned cookie factory. It was the second most significant nonagricultural enterprise in the village, preceded only by the machine factory. While the bakery made bread almost exclusively for village consumers (which no doubt accounts for its lack of concern with quality), the cookie factory produced cookies that were sold by the Commerce Cooperative throughout the county. The factory made twelve different kinds of cookies and produced about 560,000 boxes per year, with a leva value of approximately 1,250,000. The cookie factory employed approximately sixty people, mostly women. This number included the supervisor of the factory but not other administrative workers, as these jobs were handled by the office workers of the Commerce Cooperative. This number also reflected a ten- to fifteen-person shortage of labor in the late 1980s. Wages, tied to production, averaged around 180 to 190 leva a month—not bad but less than many other jobs in the village.

The work was not difficult, though perhaps monotonous. Most of the factory production was devoted to making waffle-type cookies, which were assembled by hand with the workers applying a glutinous sugar filling between large sheets of a thin wafflelike pastry. After several layers were assembled in this manner, the large block was mechanically sliced into small cookies and packed in boxes. Some types were covered in chocolate. The linchpin of the enterprise was the large, Austrian-made waffle machine. It was almost fully automated and required only one full-time worker to sit and take out the waffles while a long conveyor belt, fitted with several irons, moved by. She quickly removed the waffles, which were then taken to be assembled into cookies.

As with the motor assembly factory, the initiative for the cookie enterprise came from the village, although the purchase of the machine could not have occurred without the mobilization of people in higher positions. The president of the Commerce Cooperative researched the machine and pushed through its purchase using personal political and business connections. Financing came from proceeds of village agricultural production along with the backing of state loans. Integrated into a national network of commerce cooperatives, the village cooperative was well positioned to initiate such endeavors. Sixty percent of the materials needed for the cookie factory were provided by the Central Commerce Cooperative office in Sofia. The remaining 40 percent had to be secured by the village cooperative itself through contracts with primary producers. They obtained sugar from the sugar beet refinery in Lom, and most other ingredients came from firms in Sofia. Once established, these contracts were usually self-perpetuating.

All prices were set by organs of the central government and, with the exception of sugar prices, were fairly stable. Sugar prices were raised in 1979 and again in the summer of 1988. This was clearly threatening to a cookie factory, but the director told me that the state reimbursed them for the increase in sugar costs so that the selling prices of the products could remain the same. Given such subsidies to enterprises, the price increase in sugar was apparently directed at consumers who used it for home canning and, perhaps more to the point, for wine making, which was under official attack following Gorbachev's anti-alcohol measures in the Soviet Union.

The marketing of cookies was done by the local cooperative through contracts with the other fourteen village cooperatives in the district. Distribution was basically restricted to these outlets by state policy stressing regional self-sufficiency in various domestically produced products. As with similar reforms in agriculture (see Chapter 2), the underlying motivation was to cut down the extent of transport in order to conserve limited domestic energy resources (a concern reflected in the refusal, discussed in the previous chapter, to transport high school students to school on a daily basis).

The Commerce Cooperative previously included other productive enterprises, but in 1983 these activities were constituted into a separate unit called the *bitov kombinat*. *Bitov*, somewhat difficult to translate, basically means "related to everyday life"; hence, such a sector produces goods and services related to everyday needs. These activities had begun one by one in the late 1960s and 1970s, initiated by local management of the Commerce Cooperative. In 1983, with several different enterprises operating, the director decided the Commerce Cooperative was overloaded and sought authorization through higher-level connections to form a new economic unit, the *bitov kombinat*. The timing was perhaps not coincidental, as it followed the institution of the New Economic Mechanism, which promised to decentralize productive enterprises. The new enterprise remained a unit of the larger Central Commerce Cooperative system and was managed by the previous director of the local Commerce Cooperative, who was replaced at his previous post by his assistant. The *bitov kombinat* also included within its responsibility various services such as a barber, a beautician, a cobbler, a woodworker, and a tailor, but the Commerce Cooperative retained control of the important brandy distillery.

The production activities of the *bitov kombinat* were divided into three main units: one making small metal buildings, one making plastic lids, and the other making children's toys and costumes. The metal buildings were used for retail outlets throughout the county by the Central Commerce Cooperative, which also provided the necessary materials to the local workshop; the workshop employed thirty-seven men. The plastic workshop for lids employed about twelve workers, both men and women; their lids were sold to other enterprises in the area.

The largest of the three units, employing approximately fifty women, made children's toys and games. In 1987–88 its main production item was costume hats that simulated the heads of various animals and insects. The annual production was approximately 20,000 hats, sold in sets of five. All were hand cut and sewn together on simple sewing machines. A box of such caps sold for over 100 leva, mostly to the productive division of the Scientific-Production Organization in Sofia, which provisioned the elementary schools and kindergartens around the country. In 1986–87 they also exported 5,000 hats to Czechoslovakia through a contract with the Central Commerce Cooperative, but this was rare. To compensate for the limited domestic market, they changed products every two to three years. In 1988 they were planning for a line of children's professional uniforms (doctor, nurse, fire fighter, and so forth) to replace their hat line.

With the exception of the metal workshop, the *bitov kombinat* had to secure all raw materials necessary for production. This was done through contracts often negotiated or concluded at the annual contract fair in Plovdiv. The director complained of the difficulty he had guaranteeing the necessary materials and said that resulting shortages were the main constraint on his production: "It is very hard when we have to get the necessary materials ourselves. Very hard. There was a period last spring when half of the people in the firm were not working because of lack of materials." This situation represents a reversal brought about by the installation of the New Economic Mechanism around 1982. Moving toward the NEM's goal of raising the efficiency of production and the quality of products, reforms reduced the state's role in distribution (Crampton 1988:340). Enterprises previously supplied by the state had to find both suppliers and customers through direct contracts. This strategy was intended to inject competition into the system, but in practice, it simply shifted the locus of constraint. Previously, the main problem had been locating markets for the products; after the reform the limiting factor was securing raw materials. According to the manager, the latter difficulty was more constraining and detrimental.

Another objective of the NEM reforms was to increase the role of enterprise managers and workers in the planning process through a requirement for "counter plans" (Thirkell 1985:36). The state drew up its plan, but local organizations were to develop a counterscheme detailing the application of the general targets. Although "the counter-plan was not to be used as a surreptitious method for increasing work-norms or plan targets" (Crampton 1988:338), the locally generated plan had to be approved by higher levels in the village and the Central Commerce Cooperative, both of which expected increases. According to an enterprise accountant, "The plan we propose must be higher than theirs. . . . it's expected." This trend multiplied the problem of locating materials.

These developments illustrate how the reform process, responding to problems and inefficiencies in the system, created new problems and inefficiencies. Low worker productivity and the one-sided concern with quantity eventually led to calls for competition and decentralization. The transferal of acquisition responsibilities to the enterprise, however, made it difficult for them to acquire necessary materials, which seems to have reduced production and possibly undermined local motivation for initiating new productive activities. Clearly village-level production was declining somewhat in the late 1980s.

The workers of the *bitov kombinat* received an average monthly wage ranging from 160 leva to about 200 leva a month. This variation was attributed generally to variations in productivity and problems with material supplies. Thus, a reform theoretically intended to increase worker motivation by providing wage incentives actually prevented people from realizing this possibility by simultaneously restricting their access to materials.

Subsidiary Enterprises of the Cooperative Farm

All nonagricultural enterprises in the village provided workers for agricultural brigades to help the cooperative farm during peak periods of labor demand. The *bitov kombinat,* for example, annually contributed 320 workdays of grape harvesting and 45 workdays of tractor driving. Village enterprises with more employees provided more assistance, those with fewer workers provided less. The possibility of expanding this latent agricultural labor pool motivated cooperative farm leaders to initiate their own supplementary enterprises, some related to the farm's agricultural production and others completely distinct. Of the former the most significant was the processing of animal feed. This involved the drying, grinding, and/or mixing of various grains, hay, straw, and other fodder into a concentrated "flour" feed or a mixed fodder food. Some of the feed was used by the cooperative livestock farms and the rest sold to cooperative farms in the area. The percentage sold depended on local needs and the availability of alternative foods for livestock.

Most of the raw materials for feed production were grown on the Zamfirovo farm, but supplements were sometimes brought in from elsewhere in the APK. The output for the year 1987 was nearly 3,000 metric tons of feed—a significant decline from 1980, when 4,000 metric tons were produced, about 3,000 of which were sold to enterprises outside Zamfirovo. The cause of the decline was not clear, but workers complained most about the machinery, which they said was primitive, too old, and in poor condition. The annual farm report stated that the grain-drying oven was very worn and needed to be replaced. This problem was compounded by the lack of adequate storage facilities, including warehouses and silos. Consequently, grain left exposed often blew away or was ruined by rain. There was a great deal of head shaking and complaining about the fact that several tons of wheat from the bountiful harvest of 1988 rotted from dampness.

The cooperative farm operated two other agriculturally related enterprises. One was a dehydrator, built in 1989 after I first left the village, to dry the farm's walnut crop for export. This enterprise rendered the orchard much more profitable than suggested in Chapter 1. The final agricultural processing enterprise was a small cannery, which opened in 1962. Like the feed processing plant, its machinery was antiquated and worn. Jars were packed and capped by hand, then fed into a mechanical sealer. They were then loaded manually into large round metal cages, which were transferred by overhead crane to a large pressurized vat for processing. There were two such pressure cookers, but only one was operative while I was in the field, and it was used without pressure since the top was defective. Consequently the jars had to be cooked much longer, often throughout the night. The maximum production of the cannery was about 2,500 jars a day. It operated for approximately six months a year, with an average yearly production of approximately 200,000 jars.

The cannery was never intended to be a major supplier—the larger and more modern cannery of a neighboring village served this role for the local APK—so most Zamfirovo production was consumed locally. In fact, a significant portion went to the village school cafeteria and to the canteen of the cooperative farm. The rest was sold through the county branch of the state purchasing agency in Mihailovgrad, destined mainly for Commerce Cooperative outlets in the immediate region but occasionally for export. In 1988 the cannery sent 17,000 jars of pickles to Czechoslovakia. The previous year they exported a load of plums to the Soviet Union and a load of pickles to Poland. Export agreements for canned goods were handled by the state purchasing organ, but the local enterprise was made aware of the arrangements so that goods for export could be packaged differently. As the director put it, "It is better for us if they are not exported because for export we have to pack them into cardboard boxes with separators [instead of the standard metal crates], which is a lot more work." Either way, the cannery received the same payment from the purchasing organization.[1]

Supplies of jars and lids were provided by the APK, as was some of the raw produce, notably cucumbers, which were not a major crop in Zamfirovo. For the most part, however, the produce came from the village's cooperative farm itself, connecting the output of the cannery closely to that of the farm. The cannery employed eleven workers during the summer and fall, when fresh produce was available for processing. Of these, only the female manager and her male assistant were permanent employees of the cooperative farm. The rest were retired women who worked seasonally to supplement their pensions. They received 3 stotinki a jar, which divided between them came out to approximately 7 or 8 leva a day, or about 150 per month. Their products sold for 48 to 68 stotinki a jar, with the exception of strawberries, which brought 1.25 leva.

Masked by the rather limited production capacity of the cannery was its significant role in salvaging farm products that might otherwise have been wasted. It could, for example, preserve fruits and vegetables that were too ripe or otherwise unsuitable for shipping and sale as fresh produce. In fact, after telling me about this possibility, a friend of mine winked and said, "Now you know why everybody prefers to can their own goods," suggesting that the quality might therefore be questionable. I was aware of

1. Since trade within the Soviet bloc was conducted primarily on the basis of negotiated balanced exchanges, it required a centralized coordinating purchasing system.

cases where strawberries refused by the purchasing organization ended up being canned by the cannery, although just because they were not accepted as fresh does not mean they were beyond preserving. Additionally, batches of fruit with only minor deficiencies were sometimes refused by larger processing facilities because they lacked the labor for the time-consuming processes of selecting and sorting. Returned to the farm, these products could be sorted by the workers at the cannery and the acceptable portion processed there.

Indirectly, then, the cannery contributed to the farm's output, but it did not redress the shortage of field labor, especially since the cannery and the fields required labor at the same peak periods. A better fit in this regard was achieved by the farm's sponsorship of two enterprises unrelated to agricultural products, the employees of which were available for brigade work in the fields during the peak agricultural periods.

The major subsidiary involvement of the cooperative farm was referred to as the "textile enterprise" and actually included four different textile-related activities. The workshops were located in two buildings on the cooperative farmyard. Two of these activities were branches of urban textile factories, while the other two were smaller, local enterprises primarily devoted to servicing the local and district populations. The former two operated on a subcontract basis with factories in Mihailovgrad, in much the same way as the village motor factory. One of the two units spun polyester and nylon threads into thicker plies and transferred them from the spools of the manufacturer onto the spools used by the knitting and weaving machines, which were provided by the Mihailovgrad factory. This unit employed about twenty-five women, divided over two different shifts, who loaded and unloaded the spools, transferring about 340 metric tons of thread a year. There was an identical though smaller workshop in the neighboring village of Purlichevo, which was also included within the Zamfirovo cooperative farm.

Workers in the Zamfirovo workshop made over 200 leva a month, but this was not enough to resolve a serious shortage of workers, which the 1987 annual report of the cooperative farm blamed on the noisy and dusty working conditions. The report also cited problems with the machines and the sporadic delivery of inputs from the Mihailovgrad factory. The parent factory agreed to replace four machines, but there were no promises regarding the flow of materials. This reveals the subordinate position of Zamfirovo in such subcontractual arrangements; there was little the village could do about the factory's breach of contract short of

Problems of No camp

terminating the relationship altogether, which clearly would have been counterproductive.

The other subcontracting textile arrangement was with a clothing factory in Mihailovgrad, itself a branch of a large Sofia-based clothing manufacturer. The Zamfirovo workshop, inaugurated in 1979 and located on the floor above the spooling shop, received fabric pieces precut in Mihailovgrad, which thirty-two young women at individual sewing machines assembled into dresses. The work was organized on an assembly-line basis, with each operator doing only one procedure, such as putting in the zipper or sewing on the sleeves. The workshop operated only one shift and assembled about 72,000 dresses a year. All production was exported to the Soviet Union. Workers were paid according to their own production, but the enterprise as a whole received a bonus of 40 percent if it reached the given production norms at an acceptable level of quality. This dividend was divided between workers, creating peer pressure to work quickly and efficiently. The resulting average wage was 240 leva a month, which was good, but the work was tedious and difficult given the time pressure. Furthermore, the wage premium was made less achievable by Soviet perestroika, which upped the ante of quality for what it would accept in economic trade from eastern Europe.

After walking through the sewing room, one entered another workshop of the textile enterprise, which presented a drastic contrast to the hectic hubbub of people and sewing machines. Here one heard only the subdued voices of a few workers and the occasional dull sound of a loom's crossbar being engaged. This workshop produced hand-woven tufted wool rugs that were used primarily as bedspreads and furniture covers. Nine women worked on individual, handmade wooden looms, weaving designs created by the brigade leader herself and hand-drawn on papers hanging over the looms. The women annually produced about 200 full-sized spreads on a made-to-order basis. The client ordered the spread and provided the requisite 8 kilograms of wool.

The juxtaposition of these two workshops was almost a metaphor of the changes in the village economy and culture over the past few decades: modern machines on the one hand and handmade looms on the other; mass-produced, identical dresses on one side of the wall and individually designed and produced traditional Bulgarian spreads on the other; young women born after 1944 at rows of sewing machines in one room and older women, close to retirement, at the hand looms in the other. The comparison extended to wages as well, with the seamstresses getting a modern wage of 240 leva and the weavers only 150.

In reality, however, the weaving workshop was as much a product of development as the sewing shop. The weavers produced a traditional Bulgarian product in a traditional way, but such a workshop would not have existed in "traditional" times; this is because until the 1960s most households had both their own loom and someone who could use it to produce any spreads needed for the household. The fact that this workshop was opened in 1970 reveals the degree to which Bulgarian handicrafts had declined in the village and the extent to which market relations had affected household production. In other words, these very different workshops also bespoke similar and related economic processes.

At the same time, the difference in the salaries of the weavers and seamstresses reveal the devaluation of indigenous products in comparison to that of factory-produced, modern goods. A village report in 1987 suggested that the pay of the weavers be increased, although to my knowledge it was not. There was a local market for the spreads, but many urbanites I knew found them provincial and not worth the cost. Urban consumers would also have had to provide the wool, which would not have been impossible given their rural connections, but it probably contributed to their general lack of enthusiasm for what I considered very beautiful pieces.

The wool used in making the spreads was usually processed by the fourth and final workshop of the textile enterprise—a shop that carded and spun about 7 metric tons of wool per year. Most of it came from the personal economy of villagers, as the wool produced by the cooperative sheep farms was sold to the state purchasing agency. Wool working was thus a service to the village population, but since not every village or town had such facilities, it attracted customers from the surrounding area. It was common in the summer to see older women arriving on the bus loaded down with large plastic bags of wool to be processed at a cost of 2.10 leva per kilogram. At the workshop the wool, cleaned at home, was fed into large combing machines that transformed it into a smooth, nearly translucent blanket. This felted product made a perfect filler for the warm comforters basic to Bulgarian households, and many people took it home in this form. Most, however, had the wool sheet turned into a coarse thread by the spinning machines of the workshop, which separated and spun the blanket of combed wool into about twenty separate spools of thread. Finally, there was a dyeing facility where the thread could be dyed if desired. Often people preferred to do this themselves at home. The thread could be used to produce the tufted spreads mentioned above or, more commonly, knitted into the warm socks and sweaters valued by older villagers and soldiers. Like the tufted spreads, these hand-knitted products were not commonly seen in urban areas or, for that matter, among the village youth.

There were three combing machines in the workshop, but usually only one was functional. The workshop employed only a few workers, and the conditions were considered bad, primarily because of the noise and poor air quality. I was also struck by the insufficient lighting of the workshop, which was in a long, low building adjacent to the other textile building. It was so dark that even flash photographs did not come out very clearly. The annual report of the cooperative farm listed the former two conditions as problems in need of correction but did not mention the issue of lighting. The report also suggested that an increase of wages was due to the workers, as the pay scale had not been reevaluated in ten years.

In terms of working conditions and salary, clearly a better situation was available in the pharmaceutical packaging workshop, the second of the cooperative farm's nonagricultural subsidiary activities. This workshop employed approximately twenty women. When the workshop opened in 1984, these positions were to be filled by older women who could not do strenuous work, but by the late 1980s there were many younger, healthy women working there. They were attracted by the relatively easy labor, which involved packaging different kinds of medicine—or, as those jealous of these positions phrased it, "putting pills in boxes." The medicines (which included tubes of ointments and liquid medicines) were manufactured in Sofia at the state pharmaceutical enterprise. The cooperative farm sent drivers to Sofia to pick up the products and the cartons. The women then assembled the boxes, filled them, and wrapped several together into a package. The wrapped packages were trucked back to Sofia in exchange for another load of materials for village packaging.

Supplies from the Sofia factory were not always reliable, and workers were periodically out of work. Nevertheless, even when accounting for an average amount of downtime, wages averaged around 200 leva a month; given the nature of the work, this was extremely attractive. Since these were usually second, third, or fourth incomes in their respective households, the possibility of longer periods of unemployment was not enough to render the position less attractive. Whenever I was forced to accept wages for work I did on the cooperative farm, the embarrassed commentary equated my salary for a day of manual labor with that of half a day's salary in the packaging workshop. The point of such comments by my coworkers was to emphasize the devaluation of agricultural labor, but it also revealed their favorable view of the packaging workshop.

The pharmaceutical factory in Sofia maintained subcontracting arrangements with several towns and villages. Thus, the manager of the village workshop was adamant that the driver get to Sofia early on the day of his pickup and delivery in order to assure that he got products before they were given out to other villages. This meant departing the village at 4:00 A.M. to be in Sofia by 6:30. From the point of view of the Sofia plant, it was important to negotiate contracts with enough places to ensure adequate supplies of packaging for maximum production at the factory. Since the production was often below maximum, however, a competition between subcontractors emerged, and if one did not fare well, local employees had less work and less pay. Being an early bird was a necessary, although not the only, condition for succeeding in this competition. In addition, the director of Zamfirovo's workshop insisted on going in person with the driver, claiming his presence was required to secure the goods.

The latter fact reveals the personalistic nature of the contract arrangements. The local manager could acquire goods because of his personal relations at the Sofia factory; without those relations the village could not have maintained the workshop. In fact, the workshop owed its very existence to the personal relationship between the local director and a party leader at the Sofia pharmaceutical plant who migrated from Zamfirovo in the 1960s. The long-standing connection between these two men provided the inspiration for the arrangement, and the elevated position of each in his respective domain facilitated its realization. Their relationship also gave the village a privileged position in getting supplies, compared to other villages having similar workshops. Finally, social relations with these men influenced employee selection at the workshop and clearly took precedence over the reputed objective of the workshop to employ older, disabled women.

The social relations that served as the basis for initiating these enterprises could be expanded or passed on to successors. For example, the man who started the cookie factory used his connections to guarantee the supply of materials and to purchase the waffle machine. When he moved to the *bitov kombinat*, the same relations were then taken up by his assistant and successor. Certainly, the new manager lost many of these connections, but he was also able to initiate others through his own personal network.

The importance of these relations secured the position of the manager at the same time it guaranteed employment for villagers. The latter benefit—a dedication to the village and its future—was repeated to me many times as the primary reason for setting up nonagricultural activities. I do not doubt the social goals of those who pioneered nonagricultural possibilities for the village, but such activities had individual benefits for them as well. Ultimately, these developments proceed from an interaction of numerous factors, including individual motivation, social relations, government policy, restrictions on migration, the lack of fuel resources in the country, and the location of the village, which limited the role of commuting as an alternative to rural industrialization.

Commuting

The role of commuting has been a central theme in analyses of rural eastern Europe. Daily commuting provided a means of increasing the number of urban industrial laborers without attendant investments in the urban infrastructure. Thus, in many ways, it was an alternative to establishing rural industrial enterprises. There were of course costs, primarily in time and energy.[2] The extent of commuting in socialist Bulgaria was not entirely clear. One sociological study interviewing 3,819 village residents from middle-sized villages found that nearly 25 percent commuted to work in locales at least 4 kilometers away, but two-thirds of that number traveled no more than 15 kilometers. People commuting over 15 kilometers made up only 8.6 percent of the sample (see Table 11).

The extent of commuting, of course, varied from village to village, depending on the location and internal economic possibilities. Zamfirovo was not ideally located for commuting. Not being on the main road through the region, residents could not take advantage of the more numerous bus routes running to and from Mihailovgrad and had to rely only on those buses specifically destined for the village. There were three such

2. It is not surprising that Romania, well provided with domestic energy resources in the 1970s, was noted for its extensive degree of commuting (Moskoff 1978:443, Cole 1981:78–79).

Table 11. Commuting Workers by Distance and Settlement Type for a Sample of Bulgarian Villages

	District Capitals	With a Mayor but Not a District Capital	Without a Mayor
Villagers interviewed	200	3,819	144
Retired or not working (%)	44.00	43.70	48.61
Commuting up to 3 km (%)	6.00	5.08	13.19
Commuting between 4 and 15 km (%)	9.00	16.18	15.28
Commuting more than 15 km (%)	3.50	8.59	0.69

NOTE: Zamfirovo falls into the second category of villages.
SOURCE: Tsentralno statistichesko upravlenie 1998: 345–46.

buses going to Mihailovgrad daily, with a fourth returning at night, and four going to Berkovitza, with a fifth returning at night. Day laborers had to catch the morning bus, which in either case was very early—5:45 or 6:30 A.M. In addition, the buses were not reliable—I waited for many buses that never arrived, and each time workers lost a day of work. An additional bus was sent around in the morning by a Mihailovgrad construction enterprise to collect workers from the villages in the area. This was only for construction workers, however, and no other enterprise provided such a service to Zamfirovo. Many villagers owned cars, and some drove them to work in neighboring towns.

I took the 6:30 A.M. bus to Mihailovgrad once a week along with forty to fifty other passengers, some of whom were going to town for activities apart from work. I was usually waiting for that bus when the bus for construction workers arrived and picked up its dozen or so riders. I also took the 5:45 A.M. bus to Berkovitza numerous times, accompanied by some ten to twenty workers. Taken together, and allowing for commuters in cars, my estimate of the number of daily commuters from the village was between 125 and 150, almost all men. This is slightly lower than estimates I received from villagers, which varied from 150 to 200.

With regard to workers' views of commuting, most claimed not to mind, and younger men said they appreciated having less time to work in the village—the return bus to the village did not leave Mihailovgrad until 5:35 P.M. and the bus from Berkovitza not until 6:00 P.M., giving commuters free time in town after work and less work time on arriving home. Most, however, complained about the early hour, the unreliable bus system, and the inconvenience of conforming to schedules. This does not mean, however, that they all would have preferred to live in the city, as Konrád and Szelényi (1976:177) insist. While many would have preferred to move to the city (and they said so, as we saw in Chapter 3), others would have liked to have their existing workplaces in the village vicinity. Two villagers I knew had given up better jobs in Mihailovgrad for jobs in the village. This last option was of course shaped by the availability of nonagricultural work in the village. Villages with fewer work possibilities and those closer to towns were likely to have a higher rate of commuting. Many villages, for example, were so close to towns as to be analogous to suburbs, and in these cases a large percentage of villagers commuted.

Zamfirovo's location was no doubt a factor in the attention village leaders devoted to securing rural enterprises in the first place, this in turn obviating the need to commute. In short, we should not view commuting as a homogeneous option that is either desirable or undesirable. Local circumstances affect its appeal. More important, individual household and personal factors make commuting more or less attractive for different individuals at different times.

Juggling Industry and Agriculture

As a result of commuting and rural industrialization, a paradox was created whereby Zamfirovo was conceptually equated with agriculture and was still significantly agricultural (see Table 12) yet was sustained by non-agricultural enterprises. This situation is not unique to Bulgaria. It has been documented for farms in Hungary (Rupp 1983), China (Byrd and Quingsong 1990, Sigurdson 1977), and Israel (Schwartz et al. 1986)—albeit through different relations in each case. The interaction of agricul-

Table 12. Annual Output of the Zamfirovo Cooperative Farm by Sector, 1984–87 (in leva)

	Agriculture	Livestock	Subsidiary/Industry
1984	1,540,000	1,792,000	1,421,000
1985	1,226,000	1,619,000	1,345,000
1986	1,806,000	1,666,000	1,641,000
1987	1,170,000	1,748,000	1,197,000

SOURCE: Zamfirovo cooperative farm.

ture and nonagricultural activities is also not new. Indeed, in the interwar period the increasing number of craftsworkers in Zamfirovo continued to be tied to agricultural production. Socialism made this combination an issue for every village household, and even for many urban households whose members often tended gardens on the outskirts of town or in their villages of origin. Socialism also expanded the consequences of agro-industrial interaction through state integration.

Interaction, however, does not imply complete compatibility. The various activities of villagers came into conflict at numerous levels. The conflicts between commuting and agriculture were perhaps the most obvious, but rural industrialization generated its own conflicts. Friction developed between individuals, between various levels of administration, and between sectors of the village economy. Furthermore, the establishment of industrial or nonagricultural enterprises in the village brought the problems of socialist industry directly into the local arena. In Italy, Douglas Holmes (1989:31) found this interaction to be nearly unidirectional, with the factory regime subjecting the peasant to its disciplined order. In Bulgaria, however, the interaction worked both ways, so that industrial discipline was affected as well by the rural context, making concessions to rural exigencies and needs. This was not just accommodation to worker "resistance" (Holmes 1989:183) but a more interactive process. Thus, in the Bulgarian village there was less imposition of industrial discipline, and it worked the other way as well, with industry making concessions to rural life and its agricultural base. The primary mechanism of this interaction was the official administrative structure that linked agricultural and industrial activities. Whereas such structures are often cited as a problem constraining industrial development at the national level under socialism, in the local context they emerged as important to the successful balancing of agriculture and industry for the greater benefit of the village as a whole. The problems involved were important factors in the development and outcome of reform processes and sometimes even led to conflicts between various reform programs. The remainder of this chapter will look at these problems and conflicts and how they interacted with reform processes.

Such conflicts surfaced in an attempt, made while I was doing my fieldwork, to set up another village enterprise. The initiative was thoroughly local. A village leader began discussions with friends in Sofia, whom he knew through his previous management of the village Commerce Cooperative. His idea was to set up a village juice extractor that would process the strawberries and plums grown by the Zamfirovo cooperative farm, as well as apples and other fruits raised by neighboring villages. The only major requirement for such an enterprise was the extracting machine. A delegation of cooperative farm leaders made a trip to the annual international technology fair in the city of Plovdiv, where they determined that the most appropriate machine was a joint British and French product that extracted the natural juice and packaged it in nonperishable containers. They subsequently made a trip to the city of Varna to examine the operation of a similar enterprise.

The main obstacle in the way of the workshop was the price of the machine. The makers wanted 300,000 dollars plus 1 million leva credit toward the purchase of Bulgarian products. Although the dollar amount was less, it was by far the greater obstacle. Discussion with the national agricultural purchasing and exporting agency, Bulgarplod, revealed the possibility of the cooperative farm getting a loan in foreign currency from the National Bank based on the potential of the enterprise to produce for export, which meant that repayment could be made in dollars.

The need for dollars exposed a conflict. The initiator of the endeavor was under the impression that the village cooperative farm had several thousand dollars in the bank from the sale and export of strawberries to west European countries, which could be used as a down payment for the juice extractor. As he explained it,

> I was told that the strawberries brought in several thousand dollars, but now I find out we do not have any of those dollars and that the village Commerce Cooperative sold the strawberries under contract to the Berkovitza Commerce Cooperative for leva. They should have gone directly to Bulgarplod and gotten a contract for export. Then we would have gotten a percentage of the hard currency. Instead they simply made a contract with Berkovitza, and Berkovitza made the contract for foreign sale with Bulgarplod, and Berkovitza got the foreign currency. The easy and stupid way.

Why did the village Commerce Cooperative do this? Basically, because of its ambiguous political position vis-à-vis the district Commerce Cooperative. By selling directly to Bulgarplod, the village would have received more benefits, but doing so might have antagonized the district director of commerce cooperatives. Although the village unit enjoyed some autonomy, this could have damaged other relations between the village and the district director, as well as the career prospects of the local director. Individuals did not necessarily see their best interests as identical to those of the populations they served. Objectives were in conflict.

This particular conflict reflects a larger strain between the various levels of administration. Establishing the new enterprise required not only money but also connections with higher-level administrators who could finesse bank loans and help overcome bureaucratic obstacles. The individual initiating the enterprise had such connections with people in Sofia, but these connections irritated district-level administrators who were bypassed in this village-capital dyad.

The conflict between the district and local level became more explicit as the discussions around the potential enterprise became more serious. The APK in Berkovitza was supportive of the idea and offered a financial contribution with the condition that ultimate control and financial accounting reside in Berkovitza, not in Zamfirovo. Its officials were probably attracted by the potential profitability of the enterprise, but they were no doubt equally concerned that the amount of fruit to be channeled into it might subtract from the fresh supplies they expected from the village. This concern was particularly threatening given that restructuring programs in 1987–88 promised to remove grapes from the state's purchasing monopoly, freeing them up for local disposition. In fact, the instigator of the project told me in confidence that this prospect had inspired his initiative. Consequently, he would not hear of APK control and continued to work with higher connections beyond the district level.

His ability to snub the APK also reflected reforms. While the possibilities and supports for small enterprises dates back to reforms in the late 1970s (McIntyre 1988b, 1989), the new program of perestroika was interpreted as opening the way for greater local control of such enterprises. Such decentralization was in fact one of the major points stressed in the party's presentation of restructuring, and it is unlikely that the villager would have insisted on such independence outside of this new context. Furthermore, the local concern to produce something that had export value for hard currency also reflected restructuring in that local leaders interpreted the program as guaranteeing them a greater share of any hard currency earned by local enterprises. The promoter of the juice machine continually referenced restructuring programs in addition to earlier reforms as the official grounds for his proposal. The project collapsed with the communist system in 1989, but along the way the negotiations had inspired a less-expensive project—the dehydrator described previously, which provided an important resource for private enterprise in the postcommunist period (see Chapter 6).

The experience with the juice extractor verifies that reforms may have laid the basis for productive developments, but implementation required local initiative and local connections. The divergent agendas of various individuals in the village then created conflicts that shaped the ultimate outcome of the reforms. These conflicts between individuals reflected an analogous struggle among the various levels of integration, especially between the village and the district units into which it was incorporated. The APK and the district Commerce Cooperative encompassed the village cooperative farm and the village Commerce Cooperative, respectively. Both were involved in the nonagricultural enterprises of the village, facilitating production by providing products and marketing systems yet simultaneously constraining the village by attempting to siphon maximum profits to higher levels. How village leaders responded to district officials varied considerably, depending on their stance vis-à-vis financial gain, career ambition, ideological devotion, and commitment to the village.

The divergence of objectives at local, district, and even higher levels was perhaps pervasive throughout the country, but different locales were in different bargaining positions in this struggle, due to variation in the economic or demographic importance of villages and the density of their social connections with higher-level officials. However, these considerations changed over time. For example, particular social relations or connections may have facilitated the placement of industrial enterprises in a particular village. Subsequently, these relations could sour or could disappear through death. In the meantime, the various benefits extended to the village became important in their own right, giving the village some clout in resource negotiations with higher levels.

Zamfirovo offers a particularly interesting example. The ability of some local leaders to sidestep, so to speak, district levels was a consequence of the village's administrative history. Its administrative position was changed by the reforms of December 26, 1979, from that of an *obshtina* (district) capital, to a simple village within the Berkovitza *obshtina* and newly formed "settlement system" (see Smollett 1985). Until 1980, then, Zamfirovo was on an administrative par with Berkovitza, and village leaders whose tenures predated the change were subsequently loath to submit to direction from this new center. At the same time, these village administrators had connections, established when they were district leaders, with higher-level administrators, and these connections allowed them to circumvent to some extent the new formal hierarchy.

This history explains why the Zamfirovo Commerce Cooperative was never completely subsumed by Berkovitza. Over the course of the interviews I conducted and my trips to other villages, it became apparent that this institution enjoyed a degree of independence that was unusual for village commerce cooperatives. When I asked local directors about this, they alluded to informal processes, suggesting that I ask one of the directors who was in charge at the time of the administrative reorganization. These directors had the higher connections necessary to protect and advance their claims for continued independence. Equally important, they had the economic leverage in the form of the cookie factory and the *bitov kombinat* to justify or back up their claims for special treatment and continued autonomy. This also explains the generational conflict, which surfaced in the strawberry controversy, between successive directors of the Commerce Cooperative. Those who took over in the 1980s had never served as district managers and were understandably more intimidated by district-level administration. Their more empowered predecessors simply could not appreciate this concern.

Conflicts between individuals and levels of administration were often accompanied by conflicts between different sectors of the village economy. Economic diversification provoked tension between the new divisions, primarily between the farm and nonfarm sectors. Given a situation of limited resources, each found itself in competition with the other. For example, the pharmaceutical packaging enterprise was without any work for over a week because all trucks owned by the cooperative farm were busy with agricultural business and could not be spared for the full day required to deliver and pick up the products in Sofia.

Such competition for material resources was common enough, but the competition for labor resources was perhaps more evident. Establishing industrial and nonagricultural enterprises in the village contributed greatly to keeping would-be migrants in residence. These people, however, worked for the most part in nonagricultural jobs, leaving unresolved the shortage of agricultural labor that was one of the ostensible conditions prompting rural industrialization. Thus, we can see that the agricultural reforms of the 1970s described in Chapter 2—integrating personal plot production more intricately with the cooperative farm structure and establishing the *akord* system of agricultural production—were intricately tied to the development of nonagricultural activities on the local level. When industrial labor failed to spill over into agriculture as was hoped, it became clear that increasing agricultural output required ways of incorporating the free time of the increasing number of villagers not employed in agriculture. The *akord* system and greater integration of personal plots with cooperative agriculture were means to this end. These reforms did not compete with industry for labor but, rather, attempted to tap the free time of industrial workers.

This approach, however, was not completely benign as far as industry was concerned, since enterprises lost worker productivity when workers arrived already tired from the previous night's work in the fields. Beck (1976:372) mentions that the Romanian workers he studied were known to nap on their jobs to catch up on sleep lost to farmwork. I did not hear of people sleeping on the job in Zamfirovo, but managers did complain that workers were often tired as a result of their agricultural work. Zamfirovo villagers were more like the young workers in Polish "farmer-worker" households described by Nagengast (1991:166) who simply took time off altogether for major agricultural events such as the harvest of grapes or strawberries. Given the importance of such events to the cooperative farm and the entire village, an enterprise manager could scarcely complain.

In fact, for the same reason, the nonagricultural labor force in the village was often given over completely to agricultural production in the form of temporary work brigades. As previously noted, the enterprises described in this chapter provided temporary labor brigades to the village cooperative farm during the summer and fall harvest periods. Enterprise directors evaluated brigade duty as a drain on their enterprise but did not question its necessity. As one director put it, "It is difficult to meet production plans when workers have to spend time on agricultural brigades, but agriculture is the basic activity of the village."[3]

The assistance provided to agriculture by the other sectors of the village economy was essential, but there were negative consequences for agriculture as well. The very presence of nonagricultural employment rendered the agricultural occupation even less desirable or necessary, further eviscerating the permanent workforce of the farm. The only conclusion to be

3. His comment includes a play on words lost in the translation. The expression he used for agriculture was *selsko stopanstvo*, which, though commonly used for agriculture, actually means "village economy." Thus, he said literally, "The village economy is the activity of the village." This usage reflects the naturalization of the cultural equation between villages and agriculture.

drawn is that the economic sectors of the village were in a very delicate balance—a balance maintained by continual reforms, each one adjusting to the consequences of the one before. Thus, when rural enterprises failed to bring more agricultural workers in their wake, new reforms integrating industrial and agricultural activities were promoted.

One reason village labor never trickled down to agriculture is that the nonagricultural enterprises soon developed their own labor shortages. As described before, the socialist emphasis on output rather than labor efficiency created a nearly infinite demand for labor, which was difficult to curtail through reform processes because of the ideological commitment to full employment. Consequently, the nonagricultural enterprises soon fell victim to the same labor shortages as the agricultural sector. The shortage was evident in an episode at the village motor parts factory, when two fired employees had to be rehired because there was no one to replace them. The director of the cookie factory was the most straightforward about the difficulty of securing labor, claiming that the factory was understaffed by at least ten to fifteen people. "We do not have enough working people. Several workers retire and there is no one to replace them. We have enough work for more people but there is no one to hire." As mentioned earlier, the shortage of labor was also cited in annual reports of the spooling workshop. One of these reports went on to recount that a possible solution had been achieved in negotiations with the parent factory, which had promised to supply new machines requiring fewer workers. Interestingly, this reflects a reversal of the original objective of rural enterprises, which was to employ more village residents. Clearly, the delicate balance had to be continually adjusted.

There was no guarantee, however, that a balance would be achieved. In the previous chapter we examined the demographic background to the labor shortage. Among the strategies for increasing the birthrate, and by extension the future labor force, was the liberal maternity leave extended to mothers. Discussions with enterprise directors, however, revealed this to be one of the main sources of their labor shortage. While directors never cited maternity leaves as a problem, it was obvious in that nearly every enterprise had a sizable percentage of its workforce out on maternity leave. To give only two examples where I have exact statistics, the *bitov kombinat* had eighteen of its approximately one hundred workers out on two-year maternity leaves in the summer of 1988, and the sewing workshop had eight of its thirty-two seamstresses out during the same period. Theoretically, the planning system of socialism made it possible to have a simultaneous shortage of workers and a shortage of materials for them to process, hence the aptness of the economy of shortage concept. Directors scrambled to get the materials they needed in order to meet production plans only to face labor shortages in the production process. Even before restructuring, this dynamic was produced by the erratic distribution system, which kept many enterprises oscillating between labor and material shortages.

The high demand for labor in at least some village enterprises gave villagers a certain power analogous to that described by Sabel and Stark (1982) for socialist industrial workers in general. More recent analyses suggest that we treat this characteristic as less than paradigmatic of socialism: Mitchell (1992) shows that the nature of socialist industry varies in different countries; Burawoy and Lukács (1992) illustrate how it varies across industries within a single country; and Kertesi and Sziráczki (1985) have described how behavior can vary even between workers within a single enterprise. Still, the general shortage of workers and the high value placed on flexible workers combined to ensure most Zamfirovo laborers some degree of autonomy and power. This power allowed them to negotiate work requirements and to generally ameliorate their work environment. If adequate concessions were not forthcoming, they could quit, confident in their subsistence production and their ability to find some other job. Thus, a rigid workplace faced greater difficulties keeping workers, and given limited consumption options and secure subsistence production, there was only so much that higher wages would do to counter these negative qualities. This helps account for the high turnover in the village factory. The situation, however, also forced stricter workplaces to soften their conditions. This domestication of industry, then, was both a microcosm and a major component of the domestication of socialism.

Many of the adjustments that cumulatively resulted in the domestication of industry and socialism acquired added impetus from the gendered division of labor. As the reader may have noted, the majority of workers in the nonagricultural enterprises described here were women. This was partially the result of factors noted by Cernea (1978) in accounting for the feminization of agriculture in Romania: since men were most likely to commute or migrate, women outnumbered men in the village workforce. More important was the fact that several of the Zamfirovo enterprises specialized in activities that were traditionally considered women's work— such as cooking and sewing. The opposite gender bias assured that men got other jobs in the village. For example, with the increasing mechanization of agriculture men took the new jobs in the transport section of the cooperative farm and the local branch of the machine tractor station. The predominance of women in nonagricultural enterprises, then, spurred domestication of industry precisely because women were under the most pressure to meet multiple labor demands. They usually held down a full-time job, took care of most domestic chores, and worked extensively on the household subsistence plot. Despite the fact that these responsibilities were often divided between a woman and her mother-in-law, all able-bodied women were busy, especially during the peak seasons of agricultural labor. The large number of women in the workforce in a context of such triple labor burdens can only have increased pressures for relaxed discipline and domestication.[4] Women were assured of some concessions because their contribution to both household and village economies was certainly recognized, if not always acknowledged, and also because the official pro-natal policies of the state defended maternal responsibilities.

These various sources of power allowed women and men to disable or limit the effects of reform processes. Reforms that threatened to make their work more difficult, less lucrative, or less compatible with involvements such as agriculture could not be implemented by managers for fear of losing workers. Any instituted changes could be ignored by workers more or less with impunity, for workers were not easily replaced. The episode of the two factory workers who were rehired is a case in point: they were originally fired as a direct result of reforms implementing the brigade system of remuneration in the factory.

As we have seen, the brigade idea predated restructuring (see Walliman and Stojanov 1988, 1989) but was incorporated into the restructuring agenda and reemphasized as a way of making factories more self-sufficient. The brigade wage system was intended to improve labor productivity—long the Achilles' heel of Bulgarian economic development—by tying wages more closely to worker output. The factory then left it up to the brigade to divide the pay between individual workers. At one and the same time, the new arrangement increased the financial incentives and the peer pressure for higher productivity. It also avoided ideological dilemmas by granting the brigade itself the authority to decide the basis for pay distribution, and those instituting this arrangement probably assumed

---

4. Kligman (1992:374) notes that the greater flexibility of agricultural work was a factor in its feminization. If so, one can suspect that women took this concern with them to non-agricultural jobs when agriculture was somewhat re-masculinized by mechanization.

that brigade members would be more merciless. The poor job performance and high absenteeism of the two factory employees who were fired
diminished the income of their fellow brigade members, leading to the
two employees' dismissal. But they were ultimately rehired because of the
factory's needs. So, the power granted to workers by the systemic labor
shortage allowed them to circumvent reforms. Were these reforms en-
forceable, they would have ultimately undermined the power of workers
by making factories more dependent on the efficiency of labor, thus diminishing labor demand. I have no evidence that workers envisioned this
long-range consequence of the reform, but I do not question that they
did. A survey of several enterprises in a town south of Sofia, for example,
revealed that a quarter of the employees interviewed had no desire to
participate in self-management (Stavrev 1988:35).

The brigade system also came into conflict with the local social fabric,
as good relations between individuals constrained the self-discipline of
the brigade and bad relations rendered cooperation difficult. Here again
the same factory episode is illustrative. The two employees who were fired
were in conflict with other brigade members about an unrelated village
incident. Thus, in spite of Petkov's (1985:308) claim that the labor collective had a unity of labor interests, brigade members were sometimes divided on the basis of other issues. If not, the opposite obstacle of mutual
protectionism arose. Walliman and Stojanov (1989:365) claim that brigades developed a sort of "defensive type solidarity, evident in the tendency to adhere to the norm of equality, and to close ranks against the
disciplining of individuals." This added a further component to Krumov's
(1986) suggestion that the outcome of brigade organization would be affected by the particular productive situation in each enterprise.

This premise was verified in Zamfirovo. The same system of labor remuneration was installed in the metal kiosk workshop a year earlier, with
what the director said were very successful results. This prompted me to
pursue the contrast with the motor parts factory. From conversations with
the metal workers it became clear that this success was a limited one and
incentives were not operating to the maximum intended result. Granted,
the system had improved and stabilized the output of the enterprise, but
it was not driving the workers to maximize production. As one worker
explained it to me, "We [the brigade] get together and decide how much
we need to earn apiece this month, usually it is around 300 leva, then we
figure out how many pieces we have to make to earn this amount, and
then we make that many." These workers have organized to reap benefits

from the reform while limiting its impact. The irony does not stop here. In summarizing their strategy, the worker said, "We do it just like the government, with a plan. We make a plan and then fulfill it." The workers had internalized an idea or concept from socialism that was clearly limiting the impact of reforms directed toward removing or softening socialist structures. This turned out to be a preview of transition developments.

The success of the metal workshop required good relations between all those involved, allowing coordinated planning. As is evident by now, this was one of the defining characteristics of rural enterprises—their utter subjugation to village social relations. As we have pointed out, the ability of individuals to set up rural enterprises was often based on their connections at higher levels of administration. These connections were essential for the continuation of the enterprises, ensuring a place of value for the contact person regardless of job performance. Other directors were appointed by village leaders, primarily the party secretary—a relationship that could make them immune to performance criticisms.

The political nature of enterprise management often led to a limited investment on the part of managers in particular enterprises. Managers were interested neither in investing in updated technology nor in designing new products attractive to contemporary consumers. When one enterprise began to fizzle, they were content to find another. This process was behind the interest in the new village juice extractor and the history of other village enterprises, such as the textile workshops. In the 1970s the textile building was occupied by a jacquard rug enterprise that made floor runners and small area rugs on East German machines. By the end of the decade the machines were getting old and the technology itself was so antiquated that it became impossible to get spare parts. Simultaneously there was a drop in the demand for the rugs, which came to be viewed as old-fashioned and "rural" by consumers. So the directors of the farm began to cut back production and to look for other enterprises for the displaced workers. The sewing shop was the first contract they arranged in 1979. It began with only a few sewing machines, but gradually more and more workers from the jacquard shop took up sewing. In 1982 arrangements were concluded for the spooling workshop and the jacquard weaving enterprise closed. Assured of a position in the next enterprise by political connections, directors had limited investment in a given enterprise as a continuing business entity.

Connections and complicated social relations were not the sole prerogative of the managerial class. In fact, all involved in the enterprise knew one another and were connected by a multiplicity of neighborhood, family, and friendship ties. Any conflict or problem at work had repercussions throughout this network of connections. This possibility constrained interactions. Social relations played an important role in the nature of industrial activity in the urban context as well, but there the social ties were not so thick and, consequently, not nearly as constraining.

Conflicts like the ones described above were a preponderant consequence of the diversification of the village economy. At the same time, the links connecting the various sectors, both the structural ones and those based on the intricate network of social relations, made it possible to achieve a complementarity. This was no mean achievement and deserves greater appreciation. Given the conflicting demands at the local level, the links were adaptive rather than an additional constraint. Certainly the links ensured that general village needs were given priority over what might have been best for a single enterprise, individual, or sector. A clear example is the provisioning of labor brigades for agricultural work by nonagricultural enterprises. This balance operated for the benefit of the village.

Reform processes were often aimed at these very links, with severe consequences. Such was clearly the case in the early restructuring campaign, which, in an attempt to make enterprises more profitable by making them more independent, cut them loose in an economy of shortage from links that supplied them or guaranteed their supplies. The result was a decline rather than an increase in production. The cookie factory in particular felt the pinch early. In October 1988 a somewhat dejected director told me that they were not going to fulfill the plan this year even though they had overfilled a similar plan the year before. The problem, he said, was a shortage of materials. The government had reduced the importation of some important items, notably cocoa, and they were having trouble getting domestically produced materials as well. When I inquired about the cause of these developments, his immediate, one-word reply was "restructuring."

Some villagers and Bulgarian scholars alike suggested that the difficulties created for local enterprises by restructuring may actually have been intended. They believed that the problems of rural enterprises, including their fractious internal structures, had led to the abandonment of the idea of rural industrialization. Villagers saw this in the decline of their industries, such as the rug plant and subsequently the cookie factory, where problems derived not only from crises of supply but from an aging waffle machine that kept breaking down. The managers said it was increasingly difficult to repair because the antiquated spare parts were unavailable. Having concluded that it was futile to fix it, their solution was to put it up for sale—a sequence reminiscent of the jacquard enterprise and a tiny village soft-drink firm before that.

Villagers saw this as an ominous trend. Similarly, several scholars who were often barometers of official government attitudes were saying in the 1980s that the idea of rural industrial activity was inefficient—compared to urban enterprises of scale—and would not persist in a more rationalized economic system. Certainly, the attempt in 1979 to integrate villages with central towns through "settlement systems" suggested a shift in policy from the provisioning of individual villages (Smollett 1985). One villager with a conspiratorial mind insisted to me that the government, having imposed the strict migration restrictions discussed in the previous chapter, was de-emphasizing rural enterprises in order to force stranded villagers back into agriculture, which was more lucrative for the state.

As we will see in Chapter 6, this scenario came to pass not as a result of a communist government conspiracy but because of the collapse of communism. The latter proved even more ominous in that the very links keeping the various sectors of the system in balance were threatened. As the official connections between units of the village economy were severed, the conflicts and contradictions between sectors and units went unchecked, wreaking havoc on most of the enterprises described here. The attendant threat to village life and industrial identities was elemental to the emergence of socialist electoral support after 1989. Whether market forces can bring the units back into a stable relationship is yet to be seen. Even if stable relationships can be reconstructed, the diminished role of village administration may reduce the general village benefits ensured by socialist conflicting complementarity. However, some of the linkages among sectors of the village economy, as well as between the village and other administrative units, transpired through so-called informal routes, which may well continue. The next chapter takes up informality directly.

5

INFORMAL
PROLIFERATIONS

The nearly universal combination of agricultural and nonagricultural activities in the lives of villagers, and the dispersal of village social relations into towns through migration, provided a fecund context for the proliferation of arrangements integrating these various people and their productive involvements. Such arrangements multiplied to fill every interstice in the political and economic structure, creating a very different social reality from that formally defined by the structures themselves. This difference was explicitly recounted by a villager to whom I complained about a bureaucratic obstacle. Tossing his head back to demonstrate his dismissiveness, he commented, "Here [in Bulgaria] you hear only that this cannot be done and that cannot be done, but the truth is in Bulgaria everything is possible, everything can be arranged." These contrasting worlds, where nothing and everything is possible, correspond roughly to what social scientists often call the "formal" and "informal" sectors.[1]

Informal activities have a long history in Bulgarian villages, often predating by many years the establishment of socialism. For example, what was traditional craft production in the interwar period was recast as informality under socialism. Smith (1989:308, 312) has argued generally that activities become defined as "informal" only with expansion of the state's purview. In the Bulgarian case this expansion came with the installation of a rigidly defined socialist state apparatus, creating by default an expansive informal sector. Since that time, however, the activities excluded from

1. Other terms for the informal sector include the informal economy, the second economy, the shadow economy, the gray market, and so on.

the formal structure continued to interact with it in a complex way, generating new informal arrangements. In so doing, informality provided both inspiration for socialist programs and avenues for circumventing and ameliorating the same. Thus, informality is the quintessential illustration of socialist domestication through conflicting complementarity. Clearly, informal proliferation conflicted with the system of centralized bureaucratic allocation, but by filling in the gaps, informality shored up that very system. For this reason it was tolerated by the state, and that toleration made state socialism more endurable for Bulgarian citizens. This interaction was particularly evident in reform dynamics, as informal activities were alternately both models for and targets of reform therapies.

In situating informality squarely within these larger processes of change, I want to draw attention to several characteristics. The first is the flexibility of the informal sector. One strength of informal arrangements was that they escaped many of the strictures confining the formal economy and therefore could respond quickly to changing circumstances, perhaps eventually inspiring changes in the formal sector. This dynamic underlines another essential factor—the continuing interaction between formal and informal sectors. These two worlds were in fact two dimensions of a single reality. Whereas many researchers acknowledge such an interaction and reject the idea of a dual economy, they often see the influence as unidirectional or unidimensional, with problems in the formal sector provoking informal responses. These responses may then ameliorate problems for informal operators (Roberts 1976), underwrite formal processes such as surplus accumulation (Davies 1979, Moser 1978), or exacerbate in a vicious cycle the formal problems that generated them (Lomnitz 1988). These ideas are important, but they are not necessarily mutually exclusive, and they certainly are not exhaustive. They overlook other interactions between formal and informal activities, especially the ability of the latter to transform the former. To capture this possibility, we must keep the interaction between sectors as a primary focus.

It is this interaction, in fact, that Stark (1989) believes distinguishes socialist informality from the capitalist variant. This difference, in turn, explains how informality can be a force of domestication under socialism and yet often an arena of exploitation under capitalism. According to Stark, capitalist informality is congruent with the formal market principles of the economy; it is informal because it circumvents the regulatory bureaucracy of internal labor markets, avoiding trade union and state protection. In contrast, activity is informal under socialism because its market-type relations are *in*congruent with the formal bureaucratic principles of the centrally planned economy. "As an alternative institution in which skills and effort often find a higher rate of return, the second economy increases the maneuverability of labor" (Stark 1989:641).

The proliferation of informality throughout socialist society, however, depended on its articulation with state objectives, specifically its contribution to fulfilling state responsibilities. This fact was verified in Bulgaria by the beginning of perestroika, which loosened state control over the economy. Consequently, informality no longer contributed exclusively to the state sector, and as it became less complementary, official attitudes toward informal activity shifted. In other words, as the state shirked responsibility for the economy, it was less willing to sacrifice resources to informal activity, even if it helped the economy generally. This threat was somewhat reversed by the transition, which destabilized the formal sector and gave what had been informal relations free rein. Still, since socialist informal activity depended on the formal system, the transition also threatened informal arrangements, even as it made them more important. This certainly accounts for some of the village ambivalence that developed around the transition.

While it moved out of the shadows during the transition, informality continued to operate predominantly through prior social relations. This underlines a final aspect of informality—the importance of incorporating various social factors into the analysis. Thus, for our purposes we cannot limit ourselves to the concept of an informal economy defined on the basis of "income-generation" (Castells and Portes 1989:12). To do so would be somewhat distorting for the countries of eastern Europe, where an elaborate official structure connected the economy to political considerations at every level. In such situations political leverage is an economic resource, and economic resources may facilitate political posturing. Moreover, both political and economic objectives intersect with diverse social obligations, such as those to kin or friends (see, e.g., Sampson 1987:132). Indeed, the role of such social relations in informal transactions helped sustain the importance of kinship in Bulgarian society. Thus, contrary to modernization theories, economic development and a welfare state did not erode kin obligations. Rather, because socialist development depended on an informality that operated heavily along kin lines, socialist development actually enhanced certain kin connections. At the same time, then, culturally shaped commitments to these kin provided another force driving informal activity.

Keeping these various considerations in the foreground requires a flexible approach to informality. As a base of operations we can define the informal sector as a collection of processes, incompletely regulated by the political and economic apparatus of the state and used by individuals to pursue social, political, and economic ends. At least as important as what these processes are, however, is their role in the larger political, economic, and social systems in which they operate. From this perspective the informal sector emerges as a means of integration that brings together many different dimensions and units of society that are otherwise compartmentalized. Thus conceptualized, such a sector is likely to be especially instrumental in socialist societies, where the state attempts to regulate all manner of political and economic activity through highly compartmentalized bureaucratic structures integrated vertically (Hirszowicz 1980). Likewise, given Kideckel's (1993) insights about the autonomy of socialist households, informal relations may be especially significant as one of the few means of integrating households. Integration, in turn, facilitated the development of complementarities.

The following pages give ethnographic examples from Zamfirovo for each of these characteristics of informality. I begin with a discussion of various types of informal activities, followed by a description of weddings and house building as major "happenings," engaging multiple forms of informality. I then examine the social relations involved in informal processes and the benefits of informal activities for the formal system. Finally, I look at the ways in which informal activities may have figured into reform processes leading to the transition.

Informal Activities

There are numerous activities in Zamfirovo that one might examine to get at the nature of informal processes. Perhaps the area most commonly discussed for other east European cases is subsistence activity. I chose to examine such production in the context of village agriculture in Chapter 2, reflecting what I saw as its official articulation with the state agricultural system. Nonetheless, personal plots also supplied possibilities for unregulated activities that can be seen as part of the informal sector. One of the most pervasive was the informal exchange and sale of subsistence products and services that exceeded consumption requirements. Obviously, participation in such activity varied according to productive output. Many agricultural products circulated in this way, among them peppers, tomatoes, grapes, and, to a greater extent, animal products such as meat and eggs. Yet the amounts were not substantial. Because climate was the major factor in crop yield, most villagers experienced roughly equivalent fortunes in their personal production. When it was a bad year for peppers, most of the village and region were short on peppers, and people did not have any extra to sell. When there was a bumper crop for tomatoes, most people had more than they needed and there was little market for the excess.

This dynamic was less determinant for the three major crops—wheat, corn, and grapes—for which there was nearly perpetual demand: grains were fed to livestock throughout the winter, and grapes were made into wine, which sustained villagers throughout the year. Greater demand for these products fueled more activity in the informal arena. Corn cultivation was more labor intensive than wheat. Plots were usually plowed and planted by machine, although some people still did so by hand, aided by only a horse- or donkey-drawn plow. Regardless, the subsequent hoeing and harvesting had to be done by hand. This significant labor requirement and high product demand led to at least a few cases of sharecropping, which was officially prohibited. A village family would let someone else grow corn on their personal plot and receive half of the crop in return. Since most villagers wanted more corn than they could produce on their land, such arrangements were not widespread. If anything, the significance of sharecropping lay in its contribution to the social security of older villagers, who found themselves with progressively diminished possibilities in the rural economy. Unable to do the strenuous work of hoeing, harvesting, and cutting corn stalks, they could lease their plot on shares and still get a little corn.

Since wheat was cultivated mechanically, it did not generate such arrangements. It did, however, occasion informal activity in the process of getting machines and drivers to do the work. Since timing was important and demand was concentrated at peak periods, getting a tractor or combine driver to work one's plot often required good social relations and possibly gifts as an enticement. Meadowland, which included alfalfa plots as well as grassland, fell between wheat and corn in this respect: it required some labor in harvesting but relatively little other input. Like wheat and corn fields, meadows were valued for the animal food they yielded, in this case, hay. I was aware of people purchasing the right to harvest other villagers' alfalfa and grass in exchange for money or meat.

Vineyards were perhaps the most valued and the most labor intensive of the crops grown on personal plots, and also the least integrated with the formal cooperative sector. There was a high demand for grapes by town residents who wanted to make their own wine but did not want to do the work of viticulture or could not get access to a personal plot. Residents from nearby towns would appear in the village toward the end of the harvest period searching for anyone with grapes to sell, pursuing leads, as it were, through the grapevine. More often, sales were arranged by villagers on behalf of urban relatives or friends. A villager with no surplus grapes who had an urban friend or relative wanting to buy might use his or her village connections to arrange a purchase.

The extent of these exchanges fluctuated with annual output. My first grape harvest in the village was a bad one, and the only grapes available for sale belonged to a few individuals who could not drink alcohol for health reasons. The second harvest I witnessed was a bumper crop, and there were several commercial transactions as a result. Such transactions took place toward the end of the harvest, after villagers were certain of fulfilling their own consumption needs. Officially, the yield from personal vineyards was intended for household consumption, but no local administrators attempted to track down grape sales. The informal market in grapes was somewhat limited by factors similar to those limiting the vegetable market. First, even though the attempts of some villagers to augment their own vineyards were successful, plots were small and therefore the amount of possible product was limited. This combined with high demand on the part of the producers themselves to ensure that few grapes were offered for sale.

Urban demand was also mitigated somewhat by the fact that many townspeople had access to vineyards in the village. The common pattern was for the children of a household to migrate to town during their young adulthood and then, after their parents' deaths, continue tending the family vineyard, perhaps even using the house as a weekend villa. If they lived in a town near the village, they might desert the ancestral house altogether, returning only on occasional day trips during the agricultural season to work the vineyard and possibly the garden but allowing the house to fall into ruins. The resulting incongruous sight of a dilapidated and deserted house surrounded by a manicured vineyard or garden testi-

fied to the value of these personal plots. Since many Bulgarian townspeople were of village origin, this type of activity was an important source of
grapes for urban households. In addition, the People's Councils in most
towns granted residents small plots of land on the outskirts of town in
what was referred to as the "villa zone." These plots, however, were rarely
sufficient in number for all those desiring them.

The value of personal plot production led to all manner of strategies
for extending access to land beyond the legally prescribed half hectare. If
a family moving from the village were to abandon its personal plot, relatives remaining in the village would take it over for their own use. A more
common extension was the use of the personal plots of relatives who had
died, or of older relatives who were no longer able to perform agricultural
work. The former case would be restricted primarily to the garden plots
around the house and possibly the vineyard. In the latter case, when a
parent or grandparent was still alive, the descendants in the village might
jointly work all the plots and divide the produce, or they might simply
divide the plots among themselves.

Clearly, these possibilities were based on kinship, but political connections and perhaps even petty bribery helped officials overlook the continued utilization of land by individuals who no longer had official rights
of access. Rights to the grapes of a vineyard planted and tended by a
close relative were informally recognized. Also, the personal vineyard was
often on land not easily utilized for mechanized agriculture, so it did
not behoove the farm to reclaim it when the "owner" died. Nor was the
demand for vineyards completely unlimited. They required a lot of work
to ensure optimum output, so much so that villagers said they had to be
"cared for like children." Given the other labor requirements of villagers, they simply could not work unlimited amounts of vineyard. This
limitation was verified by the fact that three-generation households no
longer divided just to acquire more personal acreage (each household
being entitled to the maximum). Informal machinations were usually
sufficient to expand land access to the point of full household labor utilization.

It might be argued that the attempt to extend access to personal plots
and the consequent overproduction of crops reflected an entrepreneurial
strategy for producing a marketable surplus. My experience suggests that
this was not the case for most Zamfirovo residents. The two growing seasons I witnessed were quite different, resulting in shortages the first year
and a small surplus the next. Thus, as suggested long ago for Melanesian

societies (Vayda, Leeds, and Smith 1962), overproduction was more likely
a hedge against bad years. The surplus of good years could then be invested in various informal connections.

There were only a few cases of private entrepreneurial agricultural production in the village. One family had planted their rather large yard with
fruit trees and sold most of the fruit. Another household had done the
same in the past, but the elderly couple were no longer able to tend the
orchard adequately. What little the trees produced was taken by their son,
who lived in Sofia, to underwrite his participation in the ubiquitous urban
economy of favors—itself a major aspect of the informal sector that I will
discuss later. The other case of private entrepreneurial agriculture was
that of a former village family who had migrated to a nearby town and
used their rather large yard in the village to grow tulips, which they sold
in town on holidays.

Not only did villagers generally eschew surplus production, they were
often to be found on the other side of the equation—buying privately
grown products in the markets of Berkovitza or Mihailovgrad. In 1988 the
village itself did not have a market, but entrepreneurs from other areas
sometimes trucked their produce in, setting up a stand near the central
square. Such vendors, although not uncommon, usually came one at a
time and only on weekends during the summer and fall.

I constantly asked villagers why they did not grow food for the market
and was uniformly told it was because the village was poor. Further elab-
oration revealed the meaning of this expression to be "agriculturally
poor," for the hilly terrain of the foothills, the rocky content of the soil,
and unreliable water resources in the region were cited as proof of the
village's poverty. According to sociological estimates (Kyuranov 1987:413),
however, Zamfirovo was not unusual in its limited degree of market gardening: of the nearly 40 percent of Bulgarian families who farmed personal plots, only 4.8 percent sold any fruits or vegetables on the market.
Even assuming significant underreporting, this number is quite small.

This statistic may mask significant regional variation resulting from the
agricultural conditions cited by Zamfirovo residents. This possibility is
supported by the fact that many families (16 percent) sent animal products to market (Kyuranov 1987:413), animal raising being more viable in
marginal areas. Regional variation in market gardening was also suggested
by personal experience. I visited villages in the south-central plain, for
example, where nearly every yard was given over to plastic-covered green-
houses producing tomatoes and cucumbers for the market. Indeed, cars

bearing license plates from these areas were common at the markets in Mihailovgrad and Berkovitza.

There were also vendors from areas less agriculturally endowed, some in fact from regions with ostensibly worse agrarian conditions than Zamfirovo. When I pressed Zamfirovo residents with these examples and again asked why they did not try such activities, their common retort was either that there was "no tradition" of it, or that villagers were "too lazy." In actual fact, it was neither village deficiencies nor indolence that underlaid their entrepreneurial ambivalence. Quite the contrary, the village was advantaged in the number of lucrative nonagricultural possibilities (discussed in the preceding chapter), and far from being lazy, villagers spent extra time earning cash on the *akord* system, growing strawberries for the cooperative farm (as discussed in Chapter 2).

What we might call nonagricultural entrepreneurship was more common in the village, and most villagers supplemented their official income with some type of informal activity. As my next-door neighbor explained it to me, "You must have a skill in order to live well. Without the extra [income] you cannot do anything." She was trying to convince her daughter to apprentice herself informally to a friend of the family who was a part-time seamstress. Her husband, having been trained as a veterinary assistant, got extra income from castrating pigs throughout the village.

While most villagers plied such trades on the side, there were a few cases of more extensive involvement in entrepreneurial endeavors. One was a retired couple with two home knitting machines and a sewing machine; the wife knitted and the husband sewed. The living room of their house was given over to a small-scale workshop from which they produced knit shirts and sweaters on a made-to-order basis. Despite the fact that knitting provided a lucrative income, it was not a common activity, probably because machines were expensive and required some degree of skill and training to operate. The knitter described here benefited from this fact in that she had acted as master to several village women wishing to learn the trade. These informal apprentices provided help and labor while learning. Only one of the apprentices, however, persisted to the point of mastering the craft. She subsequently purchased her own machine and began producing sweaters and shirts to supplement her official job at the local school. She and the woman who taught her were the village's only machine knitters, and there was ample demand for both of them. They received 30 leva for a shirt, and the clients supplied the material. Their products were highly valued for several reasons: they were of good quality; the close machine knit resembled commercially produced material rather than the sweaters hand knitted by everybody's grandmother; and people could request particular styles to suit their own tastes.

Except for the older generation, more and more villagers were placing a high value on appearing fashionable. In addition to favoring the business of the knitters, this contributed to a high demand for seamstresses as well, especially around ritual occasions such as weddings and graduation balls. The latter was particularly important, as every female graduate had to have a new dress in which she paraded through the streets of town from the school to the restaurant where the ball was held. In the spring the three village seamstresses were kept busy making these dresses. Other periods were slower, although there was still enough demand to occupy their spare time.

Some older women wove the tufted wool spreads described in the previous chapter and either sold them or gave them as gifts. The large wooden loom was still a dominant presence in some kitchens and was likely to have a spread on it in some state of completion, with the pattern drawn on paper and hanging overhead. The spreads were produced strictly on a made-to-order basis, and the price depended on their size and the complexity of the pattern, although none were cheap. A plain white spread the size of a single bed cost upward of 100 leva. Obviously, larger and more elaborate versions could be very expensive, and, as with the other trades, the price did not include the raw materials, which the client supplied. The profits might seem significant, but the work was time-consuming and monotonous, making it less attractive as an entrepreneurial activity. Furthermore, most women had other responsibilities and could not devote themselves to it exclusively, even if they were so inclined. Primarily an activity of older women, such weaving may in fact be dying out; certainly there was little evidence of younger women learning the craft. Many women's crafts, however, were only taken up in old age, making it hard to predict their continuity.

Perhaps the male counterpart to women's quasi-entrepreneurial textile activities was woodworking. In 1987 there were two woodworking shops in the village. One ran all day, for the operator was officially retired from his principal occupation; the other functioned as an auxiliary job for a middle-aged man employed in the state sector. The retiree inherited his trade and much of his equipment, which included an electrical band saw and a circular saw, from his father, who had learned the craft from his father before him. He supplied villagers with wooden implements, but most of his work involved cart construction and wheelwrighting. The part-time woodworker specialized in construction materials—processing tree trunks into building lumber and a limited amount of the decorative lumber that was popular in new house construction. A few of the newer houses in the neighborhood of the workshop had this carved wood paneling covering part of the standard plaster facade, usually the upper floor or attic. He was also occasionally commissioned to produce simple wooden furniture such as tables.

As with textiles, woodworking was a producer's market made unbalanced by raw material shortages and limited spare time. One had to negotiate with the artisan to get a commitment to do the work, and even this often depended on a personal connection and the ability to provide the necessary materials. One could pilfer enough wood for small projects from secluded forests. An example of this occurred during a camping trip to the mountains; I was struck by the precision with which two of my companions set about cutting a tree into makeshift stools. They were extremely particular about the size of the tree, and after selecting it were just as meticulous about the size of the pieces to be cut. It seemed like an excessive concern over something to sit on for two days in the woods. When we were packing up to leave, the basis of their concern became clear: the pieces of logs were destined for the village, where they were made into small stools. Obviously it was much more difficult to manage similar feats with larger quantities of wood, which likely would have attracted official attention.

A final example of informal entrepreneurship comes not from the village but from a nearby town. I include it here because the man involved was a migrant from Zamfirovo who maintained extensive socioeconomic connections in the village, and village residents made up a significant percentage of his clientele. Given the aging of the rural population discussed in Chapter 3, the village was a particularly promising market for his product—marble tombstones. At his home in town he had an electric sander for polishing marble and an electric chisel for cutting, engraving, and carving out a place for the picture of the deceased. He was in his mid-thirties and worked on tombstones after hours and on weekends. Bulgarian tombstones are approximately 3 feet high and vary in width from about 2 to 6 feet. However, they are very thin, usually 2 to 3 inches, so they did not present a major problem for handling and transporting.

The tombstone maker also supplied the materials, which he acquired from a nearby marble quarry, the region being a major source of marble

for both the domestic and international markets. Because of this abun-
dance, the town itself, although relatively small and not wealthy, had a
large public square completely covered in pink and white marble. The
tombstone maker also used scrap pieces to make a mosaic marble stair-
case in his house. He was emotionally transported when I told him that
such a feature would be extremely expensive in the United States and
certainly a sign of wealth. He assured me that such was not the case in
Bulgaria, where granite was the more valuable stone, but he was nonetheless very pleased to discover that something he owned would be highly
valued in the United States. He was at that time adding onto his house a
new room, which included a fireplace inlaid with green marble imported
from Cuba. He had acquired it from the marble quarry but was uncertain
for what purpose it had been imported.

The above descriptions of entrepreneurial activity may seem trivial
compared to the "socialist entrepreneurs" of Hungary (Szelényi 1988),
but the full significance of the Bulgarian case only comes out through a
long-term life-cycle perspective. Since the Bulgarian state has neither advocated nor facilitated private enterprise to the degree found in Hungary and elsewhere, villagers continued to work for the state, with their
involvement in entrepreneurial production limited to after hours. However, over the life cycle this changed. Many people who devoted their
free time to entrepreneurial endeavors turned to it full-time once they
retired in order to supplement their state pensions. Since the official retirement age was only fifty-five for women and sixty for men, they were
able to devote at least a few years to nearly full-time private production,
tapering off again as they became infirm. This process is exemplified by
the knitting and woodworking cases described above: retired villagers
worked full-time at their crafts, while younger individuals did the same
jobs on the side. The tombstone maker also commented that his skill
would give him something to do when he retired. Many insisted that
such work was essential, for pensions were inadequate. Because such activity varied over the life cycle, its overall importance is easily under-
estimated—only a small portion of village residents were fully engaged
at any one time. This is an important consideration not only for Bulgaria
but in all attempts to analyze informal sector activities. Since most studies
of informality delineate the sector and analyze it structurally, this factor is
often missed.[2]

2. Roberts's (1989) study of informality among the urban poor of Guadalajara is some-

The importance of entrepreneurship may also be further masked by ethnocentrism. Because many products and services never make it to a market, they may escape detection. In fact, many of the products and services discussed above were exchanged between people already connected—in many cases along the same paths as excess agricultural production. This was true for full-time as well as part-time producers. The full-time knitter had many more clients than the one who knitted only part-time, and the social distance between the former and some of her clients was greater. Still, almost every client had some connection to her. This also ensured against state surveillance and regulation for tax purposes.

The personal nature of such exchanges facilitated agreements between the parties involved, but it could also allow for a degree of manipulation that approached bribery. For example, the knitter often made sweaters for her doctor at no charge, expecting better treatment instead. We have already alluded to the parallel necessity of bribing tractor drivers to get them to service personal plots. A similar gratuity was expected by the attendant at the village distillery in order to get an appointment for making brandy. The brandy itself then joined lamb as a primary commodity in the traffic in influence, a somewhat reduced version of the role of vodka in Poland (Hann 1985:88–89). The term bribery, however, suggests a thoroughly negative valence on an activity that was much more ethically ambiguous for Bulgarian villagers. They did not consider such arrangements either ideal or "good," but they did not judge themselves or others too harshly for engaging in them. While they might complain about the fact that such gifts were necessary, they also acknowledged that it was foolhardy not to participate. As Verdery (1983:62) points out, bribery may actually be a rational form of investment in an economy with few profitable uses of surplus earnings.

We should point out here that it was the ubiquitous rural-urban separation in Bulgaria that gave the local currencies of bribery much of their value. Products like brandy and lamb worked in informal transactions because they were less available in cities, while the number of urbanites with village relatives provided informal avenues for the flow of such goods. Since agriculture provided some of the most significant currencies in the informal economy, one of the main consequences of informal prolifera-

---

what of an exception, although in that case the major variable over the life cycle was the labor contribution of children.

tion was the further expansion of agrarian influence throughout Bulgarian society.

On the other side of the coin, there were many urban items that made their way to the village, softening the distinction between givers and takers. The city, for example, had a decided advantage in access to black market goods and activities, which could be a valuable currency of influence in all areas of the informal sector. This advantage was especially characteristic of large cities like Sofia, where a pervasive black market was provisioned by numerous foreigners. Notable among these were thousands of Vietnamese workers, sent to Bulgaria on temporary work contracts in exchange for Bulgarian products. Driven by low wages, these workers became famous for their traffic in black market goods, especially counterfeit Western clothing, some of which trickled down to the village through migrant connections in Sofia. Clothes were the most common black market item seen in Zamfirovo, but there were also Western videotapes, including pornographic ones. In general, however, the black market activity in the village was limited. Videotapes, for example, were only useful to those few villagers with videocassette players—primarily villagers who had worked abroad and earned hard currency.

Western cigarettes were often seen in the village, but as they were available in hard currency stores in towns and sometimes even official state stores, they were not necessarily evidence of black market activity. Villagers, though, sometimes transformed them into such by smuggling them in on excursions to Romania and then selling them for exorbitant prices. As the village was located in northern Bulgaria, such excursions were not difficult to arrange, and while ostensibly organized as recreational tours for workers, they bore a closer resemblance to business trips. People would load up on cigarettes—preferably Kents, but Bulgarian brands would do. If they got them across the border without being caught by customs agents, they sold them for Romanian money, which they used to buy whatever they could find. The payoff of such smuggling had apparently declined with the deteriorating Romanian economy; while I was in the field, veterans of previous trips returned from excursions complaining that there was nothing to buy in Romania and that they were not going back again. Such reports also assuaged local discontent with the Bulgarian economy.

Having crossed the line of legality in our discussion of informal activity, I will proceed to what is ironically one of the most talked about activities of the informal sector—theft. People repeatedly cited theft as a problem for the village, especially the cooperative farm. Of course they did not cite their own exploits in this regard, but they did finger others. The cases of theft I observed directly involved cooperative property. Theft of private property was less common, although certainly not unknown. Villagers complained about cooperative theft so commonly that it was hardly news, whereas private theft was a major event. For example, word spread throughout the village when thieves picked two peach trees in a villager's personal garden clean, but the denuded plum trees along the edge of the cooperative plum orchard failed to provoke comparable excitement. If violated fruit trees attested to the presence of thieves in the village, in other regions of the country where busy roads traversed large orchards, signs along the highway forbidding drivers to stop made the same point.

Zamfirovo officials posted guards on fruit and vegetable plots around the clock as the crops approached maturity, but they were not entirely effective. During the grape harvest of 1988 the police stopped a car leaving Zamfirovo by night and found it loaded with grapes stolen from the cooperative farm. The thieves were from a neighboring town. In conformity with Bulgarian law, the car used in the theft was taken by the state. Most guards also had relatives and friends, and it is questionable how vigilant they were against theft by one of their own. There was also the potential for theft by the guards themselves, cases of which were reported. Finally, there was the possibility of village political leaders arranging for people to purchase cooperative products, a transaction that was officially circumscribed. One morning before dawn, while waiting for the bus to town, I saw a station wagon come from the direction of the strawberry fields loaded down with strawberries. The cache was covered with blankets except for an exposed corner that passed right by my eyes. Such a large haul had not been acquired without some official collusion.

Since the products used for animal feed were highly valued as crops in personal plot production, it was inevitable that they would be among the products stolen from the cooperative farm. This was evidenced by the speech of the cooperative farm director at the annual meeting of cooperative farmworkers in 1988. He cited the theft of these resources as one of the major drains on productivity and insisted that it was unnecessary, for the farm would provide workers with animal feed. Apparently, he had forgotten the Bulgarian proverb that "theft is clear profit." Whereas the farm might supply animal feed, it also charged for it or required the return sale of animals to the farm. The relative advantage of theft in this regard eventually forced preventive measures: before I left the village in

1988, the director prohibited anyone from driving his or her horse cart or donkey cart into the cooperative farmyard where grain and straw were stored. A prior personal experience helped me understand his action. One day I was offered a ride home from the cooperative farmyard by a neighbor with a horse cart. We passed by the cattle shed just as a worker was feeding the calves. The timing was too auspicious to pass up, and since the driver knew the woman, he asked her to throw a few bucketfuls of feed into his cart "for the lambs." The amounts taken in such acts were small, but if repeated on a regular basis or reenacted by many parties, they could account for a significant loss.

Keeping carts out of the farmyard might have cut down on the theft of the most valuable fodder, but it did not stop people from stealing hay and straw directly from the fields. While observing the gathering of straw one day, I wandered off and came across several bales of it hidden behind a stand of bushes. Clearly, someone in the group of workers had stowed the bales, intending to pick them up later. A more comic example transpired while I was on a nearly full bus returning to the village from a nearby town. We passed a cooperative meadow that had recently been mowed— the grass left to dry prior to being gathered and baled. The bus driver, after making sure the coast was clear, pulled over to the side of the road, pulled out two large plastic sacks, jumped out of the bus and ran into the field where he hurriedly stuffed hay into the bags. When the bags were full he hauled them back to the bus, loaded them inside and continued on his route. My fellow passengers, who waited patiently on the bus watching the whole episode, had various reactions to it, ranging from ambivalence to amusement, but no one was horrified or indignant. As he told an inquiring passenger, the hay was for his two lambs.

In sum, theft was clearly a problem, although I am not convinced that the magnitude of the problem was as great as discussion and comment suggested. The focus on theft in colloquial conversations and official pronouncements had other bases related to psychology, identity, and the nature of socialism. On the one hand, the pervasive role of communal ownership (Comisso 1991) made villagers sensitive to theft of what amounted to *their* resources. On the other hand, constant accusations of theft allowed people to rationalize their own informal machinations in this regard: if common property is not being respected by all, then all must take their share. The resulting theft also provided an example of how one could, if not beat, then at least manipulate and make use of the system. A similar tension and dynamic can be found in the *Hitur Petur* (Sly Peter) stories of Bulgarian folklore, in which the distinction between cleverness and criminality in Peter's interactions with the Ottoman Turks is not always clear. The same uncertainty was evident in the colloquial use of the word "sly," which was attributed to people both for cheating ability and for cleverness. Such slyness was often presented as a particularly Bulgarian trait. At the official level, the focus on theft provided an easy excuse for poor performance of the system—an excuse that obviated the necessity of looking for more serious, systemic, or solvable problems.

Theft was often connected to other informal activities, as goods that were stolen sometimes ended up in other exchanges. In fact many of the activities described above interacted with each other extensively in particular contexts. In the next section I take up two such contexts—house building and weddings.

Informal Happenings

A particular endeavor that set the whole system of informal activities spinning was house building or remodeling. It is not surprising, then, that this has been a focus of previous studies of the informal sector in eastern Europe, of which Kenedi's (1982) is the most popular (see also Sik 1988). The Bulgarian cases I witnessed did not approach Kenedi's experience of house building in Hungary, in either its tragic or comic aspects, but his work is unique as a detailed insider's description of Hungary's hidden economy and thus merits comparative comment. It provides a vivid descriptive overview of the breadth of informal activities that no analytical discussion of the topic has achieved. This said, Kenedi's experience with house building must be contextualized. He is an urban intellectual, and this clearly affected his experience in the informal economy. While he entitled his description "Do It Yourself," he repeatedly reveals that he actually did little of the work on his own: "As we progressed from the roof to the groundwork, I began to realize that using grey matter might be more fruitful than learning manual skills or even higher crafts" (1982:45).[3] Leaving aside the fact that learning a "higher craft" also requires using one's mind, we get the gist of his meaning from his account of roofing the house: "I was standing on the rooftop hammering away—no small feat considering that in my childhood I'd suffered from vertigo, when the

---

3. The book's title had other meanings, but the contradiction remains.

carpenter's mate suddenly said he would be willing to do the entire job for 3,000 forints. I almost fell off the roof and had to grab his hand, thereby closing the deal. . . . He was a country boy, not used to the high prices prevailing in our area."

Kenedi did do some of the work himself, but nothing to compare with the amount that a Bulgarian villager or even a transplanted Bulgarian villager in the city would do. This reflects the fact that villagers acquired at least rudimentary skills in a number of trades in the course of village life and were capable of doing many jobs themselves. Even when they lacked the skill, they attempted to minimize the hiring of skilled labor. One informant, a villager who migrated to the city in the 1950s but maintained his village house and garden, was engaged in building a house in the city during the time of my stay. We became good friends during his periodic trips to the village to help his parents and in-laws maintain his village house and garden. I also visited his family on trips to the city, marking the progress of the new house. He and the rest of his family worked every evening and all day Saturdays and Sundays on the house, to the point that it became a bone of contention, taking precedence over visits to the village and the fulfillment of village social obligations and work requirements. This conflict was sharpened by the fact that my friend depended heavily, and quite literally, on the fruits of village agriculture to support construction. Each year he imported fifty gallons or more of wine in addition to other foods from his village relatives. These village resources were important to his strategy of minimizing hired labor, for some urban friends and acquaintances were willing to help in exchange for this rural bounty.

When it was absolutely necessary to hire a skilled worker for any specialized task, my friend would work closely with the craftsman, watching everything he did and learning as much as possible. After a day or two of working with the specialist he would inform the worker that he had run out of money and could not afford to complete the job. The skilled worker might be slightly irritated, but for most craftsmen there was more than enough work, so he departed telling the owner to give him a call when he could afford to continue construction. The owner then used what he had learned to finish the job himself. This strategy was problematic only when large or specialized machinery was required. In such cases it was necessary to pay the worker for the whole job. When the machinery was less specialized and less expensive, it could often be acquired on temporary loan without an operator from either individuals or state enterprises. The mobilization of state property for private use was another common element of the informal sector. Here again, gifts of village produce to employers or friends facilitated such favors.

In contrast to my friend, Kenedi's urban background forced him to go to much greater extremes to find skilled laborers and materials. A Bulgarian villager would also acquire these necessities through informal channels, but he or she would have less difficulty locating what was needed. I do not want to give the impression that the process was easy in the village: it was very difficult and could take a long time. One had to negotiate social relations with anyone in a position to provide necessary materials, either formally or informally. When goods were very scarce, this could be an uphill struggle, as those with access were less willing to provide them. I followed one case where a man was able to get cement through his work connections but told a neighbor who asked for some that he could not get any more. Some items might not be available in the country at all, so acquiring them depended on connections with someone who traveled abroad. In addition, skilled workers were busy, and one had to conform to their schedules. I knew one family who bought a new hot water heater and waited a year for the only village plumber to get around to some rather complex piping and installation.

These difficulties were manifested in a large number of unfinished houses: some were complete enough to be occupied even though no further work was under way; others never having reached that point stood empty. These contrasted with numerous houses on which construction was proceeding, if slowly, and a large number of remodeled or completed dwellings that were quite elaborate. The ambiguity evinced by these differences was reflected in two commentaries on house building frequently offered by villagers. One was a joke about a widower who comes to a village hunting for a widow to marry. He asks a man on the village square who the widows are in the village. The man points in various directions and says, "See those new houses? There are the widows"—implying that the demands of house building killed their husbands. A contrary suggestion is found in the common village claim that the state with all its resources takes much longer to build a structure than a private individual utilizing informal relations. Together, these comments point to the hardship required to build a house and the success possible when informal arrangements are used.

Another village event that could shift informal mechanisms into overdrive was a major ritual celebration, such as a christening or a wedding.

The amount of resources required for such events, especially weddings, caused families to engage in all sorts of informal action. The extent of the requirements will be most evident in an abridged description of one wedding.[4] The groom's family and friends gathered at his home with a band early in the morning on the day of the wedding. This group of over thirty people made its way boisterously to the bride's house, where her family and close friends had gathered for a morning feast. Despite the early hour, this was not brunch; it was a full meal replete with the requisite brandy and wine. Eating, drinking, dancing, and some ritual enactments—such as a simulated bride capture—consumed most of the morning. Then the procession reassembled, now including the bride and her relatives and friends, and made its way to the town hall, where an elaborate civil ritual was performed.

From this event the procession returned less ceremoniously to the groom's home, where the couple was presented with a seemingly endless array of gifts. The couple positioned themselves in front of the door on the second floor, their arms joined around each other's neck to form a sort of bar. The entire wedding party gathered around to watch as the groom's mother started the presentation. She began laying gifts across the couple's linked arms. As the gifts piled up, they would be taken into the house by someone standing in the doorway behind the couple. First, the groom's mother loaded on heavy gifts, such as rugs, blankets, and comforters. Then came tablecloths, towels, and every conceivable household textile. Finally, she bestowed clothes for both the bride and groom. There were so many gifts that it took twenty minutes of rapid piling to get them all presented. After she finished, other female relatives of the groom followed suit with fewer but still numerous gifts. One person gave over twenty-five pieces of bed linen, and this was only a fraction of that given by the groom's mother.

After the groom's relatives had finished, there was a break. At this point I thought the exhibition was finished, but they were only gearing up for the presentation of gifts from the bride's mother. The number of gifts was phenomenal. Although I was well acquainted with discussions of dowry in southern and eastern Europe (Fél and Hofer 1969, Friedl 1963, Grossiaux 1987, Schneider 1980), I found myself drawn instead to comparisons with

---

4. For more details, see Ivanova (1984) and Silverman (n.d.). For a comparative case, see Kligman's (1988) eloquent analysis of Transylvanian weddings. While there are many differences in details, a similar structure is clearly detectable.

Kwakiutl potlatching. There were several room-sized rugs, numerous heavy blankets and bedspreads, and more than a lifetime's supply of bed linens and clothes. Not surprisingly, given the amount of goods amassed, almost all items had been commercially purchased, and they still had their price tags to prove it. Older villagers verified that such largesse, which was typical for village weddings, was not characteristic of dowries twenty or thirty years earlier, when most items were made by hand.

After the couple had received all their gifts, the mother and father of the groom took their place and accepted about three armloads of linens and clothes from the bride's mother. The bride then joined her mother and other relatives to present similar gifts in a similar manner, first to the sister of the groom and her husband and then to the groom's grandmother. The wedding party then went to the village restaurant for the wedding banquet—the crowning event of the wedding ceremony. Complete with an orchestra (see Buchanan 1996), the banquet was attended by over 200 guests, who were plied with as much food and drink as they could consume. Guests reciprocated with a cash gift, given as the couple passed through the restaurant toasting each guest in turn.

Clearly, large amounts of money had to be accumulated by both sets of parents to stage such a wedding. One woman told me that her daughter's marriage cost 4,000 leva. This expense obviously required advance saving, but it also meant escalating involvement in supplementary income-generating activities. The importance of informal processes in providing for such events was made clear to me by a villager's statement in a conversation about the man who castrates pigs before and after work: "Why do you think he gets up before dawn every morning to operate on pigs? He's got two daughters over there who will marry soon." Such events could also require increasing production of agricultural and animal products needed for the feasts, which might necessitate theft of animal feed from cooperative sources or informal purchases of products from other villagers. Getting adequate supplies of soft drinks, which were mixed with wine, and of food, a portion of which was purchased through the restaurant, often required connections with someone in the Commerce Cooperative, and maybe even gifts to repay them for their help. These are just some of the possible informal involvements. This example also shows clearly that cultural requirements could drive informal involvement as much as economic or political motives. Informal activity, in fact, reflects the interaction of these various concerns.

Social Relations and Informality

What is apparent from the preceding descriptions is the near total reliance of informal activity on interpersonal connections and its reciprocal role in socially reproducing the same. Through the expansive network of social relations created or maintained by such activities, various individuals, groups of people, sectors of the economy, and even regions of the country interacted. This was an essential contribution to a socialist system in which official political integration was predominantly vertical and where village households were increasingly self-absorbed (Kideckel 1993). Informal activity in Zamfirovo clearly reflected household interests, from building a house to marrying off children. They also reflected household resources. At the same time, the importance of informal relations connected households within the village and beyond, providing lateral integrations and forcing some qualification of the household autonomy thesis for the case of Zamfirovo. To appreciate the integrative role, we must start with the social relations through which it was achieved.

As previous examples revealed, most products and services moving through the informal sector, whether agricultural surplus or bribes, traveled along lines of personal connections. This fact increased the value of the products and services. Producing goods and providing services were not simply moneymaking activities; they were intricately connected to, and given value by, the system of mutual exchange and personal connections that integrated society. A product or service of limited availability not only brought a price, it also generated obligations and long-term connections between the parties involved in its exchange. For example, the high demand for knitted shirts meant that the maker acquired other valuable goods and services to which her clients had access.

The knitter could select her clients or decide on production priorities on the basis of the potential differential return from different people. On one occasion, the knitter's husband was taken ill and could not hoe part of his garden plot. The wife agreed to knit a sweater in exchange for a neighbor's help in hoeing their garden. The neighbor agreed but then vacillated, eventually telling the knitter that she simply did not have time to do the hoeing and instead would pay whatever was necessary for the sweater. The woman told her she did not need the money: what she needed was someone to hoe. Subsequently, the knitter recounted the story, telling me that she was not going to knit the sweater.

This example illustrates the limits of labor commodification and the greater value of goods and services over and above cash in informal exchanges. I do not, however, interpret this either as the decommoditization of the economy or as a complete undermining of the cash nexus, as suggested by Sampson (1983:52). It was certainly true that commodities become personalized in informal transactions, but that does not necessarily mean they were always removed from their cash basis. Many informal exchanges or barters between individuals were expressed in explicit cash values, each side estimating the cost of the items or services exchanged. Furthermore, in many informal transactions cash payment and noncash exchanges coexisted peacefully, the latter neither vanquished by the cash nexus nor substituting for it. Only in a few cases was cash completely irrelevant.

The view that rational market exchanges are completely commodified and necessarily devoid of informal obligations, or, conversely, that informal relations are thoroughly decommoditized, is somewhat ethnocentric, reflecting the persistent acceptance of an innate opposition between informal and formal sectors. In an economy of shortage, by contrast, even the *sale* of a product or service for cash may be seen as a favor. In other words, when something is in short supply, someone is doing you a favor by selling it to you—even at a high price—rather than to someone else. Thus, a skill or product in demand could generate nonmonetary as well as fiscal resources. To sell products on the market was to squander this alternate source of value—a situation that may have accounted for the limited market participation of Bulgarian villagers cited above. In any case, value derived from personal connections was not necessarily antithetical to cash interactions; in many cases Bulgarian villagers were able to have both. Certainly, skills provided both monetary income and nonmonetary obligations from clients. Socialism maintained commoditized and uncommoditized relations, even in a single transaction.

The connections between informal activities and social relations worked in numerous other ways as well. Bulgarian villagers sometimes mobilized existing social relations to facilitate informal activities. At other times they engaged in informal exchanges expressly to establish relationships with individuals perceived as potentially useful in other endeavors. At any one time the existing profile of good relations shaped what was possible informally and may have even stimulated informal activities. Bad relations could restrict what was possible and could block formal avenues, necessitating the use of informal ones. At the same time, certain activities could transform good relations into bad. At the societal level the informal sector as a whole was shaped as much by this vast network of social relationships as it was by the structural delineation and regulation of formality. In this sense, Sampson (1983) is correct to emphasize that the second economy is above all a social economy (even if the term "economy" is limiting).

While some social relationships seemed to be based primarily on informal interactions, most informal relations were grounded as well in other attachments, such as friendship, neighborhood, or collegiality. The most common bedrock for informal relations was kinship—a connection Smollett (1989) has characterized as an "economy of jars," in reference to the large number of home-canning jars that moved informally between kindred. Kin relations were important to all the informal activities and exchanges previously described. They provided preexisting connections that were always there and that did not have to be sought after or maintained with the perpetual exchanges required for non-kin-based relations.

In many ways the domain of kinship shrank in Bulgaria during the socialist era for the same reasons it contracted in cases of capitalist development. As a result there was a restriction in the group of kin that one could freely call on for assistance. This did not, however, result in a general decline in the importance of kinship in the informal political economy. For example, while one might have lost touch with the second cousin who was promoted to an important ministerial post, one could still rely on one's grandmother to relay the need for a favor to her sister, who would in turn make the matter known to her son, who would pass it on to his son in the ministry. In this way kinship remained more important in the informal political economy than it often appeared in the society at large. Conversely, the role of kinship in the informal sector and the general importance of informal activities combined to sustain or reinforce kinship relations in the face of other forces undermining them. Such conflicting pressures on kinship relations may have contributed to the intermittent tensions between rural and urban family members recounted in Chapter 3.

Fictive kin relations of godparenthood and marriage sponsorship provided another base for informal relations. The godparents played important roles in the wedding described previously and gave lavish gifts to the couple. Such relations, however, were themselves affected by the informal processes in which they participated. The most evident effect was a decline in the perpetuity of fictive kin relations. Hammel (1968) describes such relations in Serbia as being passed from generation to generation, and Bulgarians told me the same had been true traditionally in Bulgaria. But in the 1980s there was much more flexibility. People chose new god-parents for their children, and those children often selected their own marriage sponsors. Freed of predetermined linkages, fictive kin provided a wonderful resource in establishing social relationships of value in the informal sector. As the latter became more essential, the manipulation of fictive kinship increased.

In one case, a family chose a Sofia couple—rather than anyone from the family of their own godparents—to be their child's godparent be-cause they felt it was more useful to have godparents in Sofia. As the father said, "If she goes to university when she grows up, she will have a place to stay." Another example shows how various social relationships interacted. A young man chose as his wedding sponsor a middle-aged man who had migrated to town, pointing out that this man was the son of a past village leader. He was clearly considering the close kin connection between son and father in asking the son to be his sponsor. He was not disappointed. One of the largest gifts presented at his wedding was from the sponsor—a large electric stove that had been acquired gratis from the sponsor's father, who in turn had received it as a retirement gift from an important business connection.

These examples reveal the fallacy of modernization arguments com-mon in explanations of socialist reform programs. Such arguments see the extensive informal sector as one of the drains on economic develop-ment necessitating reform therapies. More often than not, they lay the blame for the expansive informal sector at the feet of such "cultural tradi-tions" as kinship obligations. The data presented here show that such arguments are wrong on two counts. First, rather than being simply the cause of informal activities, kinship, both fictive and real, was maintained and perpetuated by its important role in informal activities. Second, these so-called traditions were actually transformed by changing political and economic forces and were different than they had been in the past. The informal sector in the Bulgarian village was thus an excellent example of how culture and economy interacted through continuous reciprocal rela-tions, as opposed to one determining the other. This same point is veri-fied by the wedding recounted previously. It was culturally defined ritual requirements that drove much informal activity, but these cultural re-quirements had escalated in response to new economic possibilities for buying dowry products and the decline in the number of children for which such outlays had to be made.

Looking at social relations also helps make sense of villagers' ambivalence about theft. As mentioned before, people complained extensively about the problem of theft while simultaneously participating in it. I previously suggested that the former provided a rationalization for the latter, and while this was certainly true, it is not the whole story, for the criticism of theft came in different intensities. People sometimes criticized others severely for stealing, although at other times the condemnation was almost jocular, accompanied by an elbow in the side and a wink. This variation reflected the social relations involved. Without exception those who were condemned for theft were individuals unconnected to the speaker. The closer the connection the more benign the evaluation of theft—thievery perpetrated by a closely related individual was described as sly, in the *hitur Petur* mode, while that of unconnected villagers was just considered bad. When relations changed, so did the evaluations of theft. This process was most obvious when good relations soured between individuals, for accusations of theft often followed. Thus, in a political and economic situation where theft was something of a necessary evil, its necessary and evil attributes were assigned differentially on the basis of social relations.

Social relations operated within what might be seen as strictly formal parameters as well. As we saw in the previous chapter, social relations were important in ensuring the supply of scarce materials between enterprises. Here we see a clear parallel with the role of social relations in capitalist economies—whether called the "personalist ethic" in South Korea (Yun-Shik 1991), "patronage" in Mexico (Lomnitz 1988), or simply the "old boys' network" in the United States. Such connections, however, are more likely to be cast as informal in the socialist context, where the state should be taking care of such arrangements according to principles of rational planning.

Formal Benefits of Informality

While informal relations can be seen as contributing to the incapacitation of official structures, they also facilitated the operation of the formal sector. For example, the previously mentioned role of informality in redressing socialism's overly vertical orientation clearly helped shore up the formal system, as in the case of village enterprises where directors used informal social relations to secure supplies. There were numerous other ways that informality actually benefited formal operations. These contributions emerge exactly where the formal and informal sectors interacted. For example, the cases of informal village entrepreneurship described above provided goods and services to the village that were hard to find through state outlets. Yet, in each case the endeavor was wedded to the formal sector. The man who made tombstones in his free time worked by day at the marble quarry, which accounted for his access to the necessary raw materials. Similarly, the man running the lumber mill had a day job in the forestry service. The older village knitter and her tailor husband acquired their skills in their formal jobs before retirement. While the young knitter acquired her skill through informal relations with the older knitter, the demand for the product motivating her apprenticeship reflected aspects of the formal structure: at the macro level it followed from a limited variety of desirable clothing in the shops; at the micro level it connected to the presence in the village of the spooling workshop and its parent thread factory in the nearby town. A number of important social relations between villagers and townsfolk facilitated the informal movement of both customers and thread from the town factory to the village knitters. More directly, some of the thread delivered to the village workshop for transfer never left the village, at least not on spools. Thus, it was no surprise to me or anyone else when the young knitter left her relatively easy job in the village school to take up work in the thread workshop.

Such possibilities clearly benefited the workers, but they also benefited the enterprise and the wider economy. Perquisites of this sort helped secure a workforce by attracting workers to otherwise undesirable occupations and keeping them there in a system that was perpetually labor hungry. This role fits well with Gabor's (1979) classic suggestion that the informal economy arose from a shortage of labor rather than a shortage of goods. I pointed out in the last chapter that the thread workshop was considered an undesirable place to work and had some difficulty keeping workers. Now we can see how its connection to informal activities made it more attractive for some and mitigated this difficulty to a degree.

Another case makes the same point more decisively. One of the cooperative farmworkers I knew had used his connections with the farm administration to get a particularly desirable piece of land as his personal plot. The plot was near a large block of irrigated cooperative land, and whenever the weather was dry, the farmworker tapped into the nearest irrigation outlet and piped the water over to his personal plot. As he told it, the director of the farm confronted him and insisted he stop irrigating his plot. Having read *The Milagro Beanfield War* (Nichols 1974), I was primed for a combative response, but socialist reality proved to be much more banal and efficient than capitalist fiction. He simply told the director that if he could not water his plot, he would quit his job on the cooperative farm. He continued to do both until the transition. Similarly, participants in fruit-picking brigades often took home a bucket or two of the harvest for their own consumption, usually but not always paying for it. Either way it was an incentive for them to devote a day to brigade activities.

Interactions were multidirectional as formal occupations and political considerations also led to informal activity. For example, the villager who bought up eggs and animal skins for the Commerce Cooperative sometimes helped people butcher sheep and kids with the agreement that they sell him the skin so that he could fulfill the norm for his job and thus increase his formal income. This informal maneuver brought in products for the formal sector. Similarly, the relatives of the village meat purchaser raised extra pigs for the state to help him meet plan targets. Of course, as sellers they may have benefited from his position as well.

Several of the above examples include the possibility of theft and thus challenge the idea that theft is completely antithetical to the formal sector or simply a unidirectional drain on state resources. As the above cases suggest, the possibility of theft may have attracted and kept workers in enterprises vulnerable to labor shortages. But the formal benefits of theft were not limited to the labor dimension. If we look at what was stolen and what happened to it in the wider economy, we can see further symbiosis. The most common resources stolen from the cooperative farm were animal foods. In many cases people who stole such supplies did so in order to feed a greater-than-average number of animals, some of which were likely to be sold to the state, as described in Chapter 2. This was the case with the man who gave me a ride home in his cart—he was raising several sheep for eventual sale to the state. The same held for the man who irrigated his corn illegally. Obviously, theft increased the cost of animal production for the state, but in a context where the demand for meat was much greater than the supply, the higher cost may have been a small price to pay for the added production it facilitated.

In some cases theft appears to have provided benefits at no cost to the formal sector. As previously mentioned, a major problem for the cooperative farm was adequate storage facilities for grain. When there was a bumper crop of wheat, as in the summer of 1988, there was no place to store the excess, and it was often left exposed in large piles. In the summer of 1988 the whole village square was given over to a pile of wheat for several weeks, until it could be taken away by the state. This pile was the first to be picked up; others, however, were left for longer periods of time, and consequently several tons of grain actually rotted. Such improvised storage depots were obviously the most vulnerable to theft, and no doubt grain theft increased in proportion to their presence. Since some of the stolen wheat was certainly fed to animals destined for sale to the state, and since the wheat that was taken was especially vulnerable to rot, theft may have actually salvaged resources for the state.

The same was true of cooperative fruit and vegetable crops. Because there were often not enough workers in the cooperative farm, at harvest time a percentage of produce might be left unharvested until too late. There were, in fact, reports on Bulgarian radio from other villages where large amounts of crops were lost due to shortages of workers to pick them. Under such circumstances theft cannot be viewed solely as a loss to the cooperative. Once we are disabused of the idea that theft was a one-way affair, then the extent of the activity is more understandable, as is the ambivalence that villagers exhibited when discussing theft and the state's apparent hesitation to stop it.

Informal activity also benefited the formal system by integrating regions of the country directly, expediting economic functions by circumventing the centralized bureaucracy. I mentioned in the previous section that the nature and degree of informal activity, such as market gardening, varied from village to village. Such variation reflected the variety of constraints and possibilities in different regions, leading to distinct economic activities. The different products of these endeavors were exchanged informally through social networks crisscrossing the country, thereby providing a means of lateral integration in a system formally structured around vertical linkages.

Regional variation, however, suggests a more general role for the informal sector as an arbiter between local and national political and economic administration. The socialist system was often criticized for its centrally determined plans that did not adequately consider or allow for local variation. Informal activities may represent local adjustments to national policy that were both more rapid and less constrained than official mechanisms such as counterplans. In this view, informal activities were a response not simply to the systemic problems of the formal sector but to its homogeneity as well. Such local adjustments were essential to the functioning and reproduction of the formal system. The contribution of these potentially negative factors to the system's operation makes informal arrangements the ultimate expression of socialism as a system of conflicting complementarity and a major mechanism for ameliorating socialist life.

The Dynamics of Informality

Integral to the idea of conflicting complementarity is that conflicted arrangements were unstable, prompting perpetual readjustment. As informal activities were elemental to the process, they too varied. This change had two dimensions: change resulting from a redefinition of the formal sector, and change resulting from fluctuations within the formal sector as defined. The latter might include a fluctuation in the supply of particular materials from the formal sector, provoking informal production or black market activity. Such changes were fairly frequent, contributing to the amorphous nature of the informal sector. The bane of an analyst, such flexibility was one of the strengths of this sector in general, and all the more so in an economic system not noted for its quick-response capabilities.

Long-term and extensive activities of the above type might provoke economic planners to make formal adjustments, with indirect consequences for the informal sector. This possibility is of utmost importance, for it represents an avenue of feedback in state economic planning that is denied in top-down or bureaucratic models of socialism. Just because the informal sector was unofficial does not mean it escaped official detection or recognition. Economic planners were aware of aspects of the informal sector, and they implemented policies in response. In this regard it was uncanny how closely the official prices of some products conformed to black market exchange rates in the late 1980s (see *Sofia News* 6/28/90). American cigarettes were occasionally available for 4 or 5 leva per pack, and Bulgarian wine intended for export was sometimes sold domestically for 9 to 12 leva. Both were about four times their dollar value in the United States at the time, conforming to the then current black market exchange rate of 4 leva to the dollar.

In many cases the governmental response to informal processes took the form of policies curtailing such activities. Alternate responses, however, included changing the conditions of the formal sector thought to be generating informal activity or even attempting to incorporate informal resources into the official system. If we combine these possibilities with the previous suggestion that informal activities represented local adjustments to state planning, then we have an indirect means by which local populations influenced national policy.

A primary player in this interaction was the reform process. Reforms were the quintessential alteration of the formal political and economic system and thus were likely to provoke some realignment in informality. Despite this obvious connection, the interaction between informal and reform processes has not been a major theme in the literature on either subject, probably due to the limited ethnographic attention to reform programs.

Contributing to this oversight is the fact that informal and reform processes are often presented in the literature as resulting from the same formal stimuli. The standard economic explanations for reform programs are replicated almost identically in accounting for the expansive role of the informal sector in socialist societies. Like reform, informality is explained as a response to the endemic problems of the socialist economic system. Recurrent shortages, universal price controls, inefficient production, poor distribution, corrupt authorities—all of these are cited by Grossman (1989:152–53) in accounting for the informal sector of the Soviet Union. Any one of these phenomena is just as likely to be touted as an explanation for the institution of reform programs, or their failure. Such parallel conceptual maps make an analytical intersection unlikely.

Maria Łoś (1990:213–19) achieves a temporary intersection in her attempt to characterize the informal activities of Marxist states during four different stages of economic development, one of which is the reform stage. Drawing on Grossman (1982:262) and Cassel and Cichy (1987:142), she actually suggests that the informal sector is "a surrogate for reform" during what she refers to as the "monopolization" period of socialism, when problems of the formal economy were still considered temporary (Łoś 1990:207). Although the idea of stages limits the appreciation of ongoing systemic integration, Łoś does point out one of the important connections in the interaction between reform and informality: the fact that via reforms, informal activities were co-opted and integrated into the formal sector. A paramount example in Bulgaria was the change in the rules governing personal plot activity. The state moved to gain output from the personal plot—actually to stimulate personal plot production so it could acquire the surplus—by formalizing existing informal arrangements. Through a series of reforms it authorized cooperative farms to provide mechanical assistance to personal plot production and to return concentrated feed in exchange for animals sold to the state. Existing informal activities, such as the theft of animal feed, were probably additional motivations for such policies. The reforms increased sales of livestock to the state but did not eliminate theft, since it was "clear profit." In short, the informal sector motivated reforms that led to greater state-private interaction, even if the full objectives of the reforms could not be realized.

The interaction between informal and reform processes is even more obvious in the development of the famous *akord* system. In a sense, this reform program aimed to get more informal household production into the formal state sector. As we saw in Chapter 2, it was very successful in Zamfirovo for strawberries but floundered when attempted with other crops, where it did not fit as well with preexisting formal and informal activities. In this case, informal processes were an inspiration for reform programs that then had differential results as they interacted with both formal and other informal involvements. The difficulty in expanding *akord* arrangements beyond strawberry cultivation no doubt contributed to the subsequent attempt to link these contracts with access to personal plot acreage.

Similar interactions were evident in the industrial sector as well. The attempt to make local enterprises more autonomous and self-sustaining actually led to an increase in informal activity. Enterprise managers, forced to secure their own materials of production, resorted to networks of social relations and informal arrangements to do so. Reforms did not necessarily create these networks; as Sampson (1987:128) points out, they were a response to the requirements of plan fulfillment generally. Indeed, in the Soviet Union informal networks of managers who helped each other were so much a part of the system that they were known by a special term—"family circles" (Sampson 1987:128). Similar networks were no doubt in place in Bulgaria, but their importance and role was extended by decentralizing reforms that transferred more responsibility from the state to enterprise managers.

Similarly, at the village factory the concept of worker self-management, implemented in an attempt to improve worker productivity, sometimes had the opposite effect. Workers used their increased control to enhance informal rather than formal production. Bićanić (1990:89–91) suggests the same for self-management in Yugoslavia, citing petty theft as a consequence. In Bulgaria theft preceded self-management and from my observations was not exacerbated by it. Instead, Bulgarian workers used their increased role in decision making to facilitate more work time for their informal activities at the expense of their formal ones. For example, the self-management of factory brigades allowed brigade members to cover for each other when they took time off for informal activities. Similarly, we saw in the preceding chapter that metal workers used the brigade system to set their own production targets, and while their plans did not exceed previous production levels, they accomplished the same amount in less time, the difference being deployed in informal activities. Such results were acceptable to managers because of the importance of informal processes to the village and country as a whole.

This factor takes us back to the previous chapter and provides another reason why what Holmes (1989) sees as the rigors of industrialization did not have the same effect on Bulgarian villagers that he suggests for Italian peasant-workers. The intricate connection between formal and informal sectors in Bulgaria meant that factory workers were excused for agricultural work and social requirements. They were not held to the discipline of the capitalist factory because, as I have tried to demonstrate, their alternate informal activities were also important for the formal sector. Given the intense integration of informal and formal processes, official reforms had to strike a balance with informality. Brigade reforms among the metal workers show such a balance. The workshop maintained its production, while the workers and the larger village economy benefited from their increased informal activity.

Such adjustments were permanently thrown off balance by perestroika, which granted more weight to formal rationalization than to informal concerns. Much of the restructuring program was directed toward separating the economy from state control, making it more self-sustaining and self-regulating. In the socialist case, where the state and economy were indistinguishable, the costs of an expansive informal sector were not so detrimental, for informal activities still contributed to the economic provisioning of society, which was ultimately the state's responsibility and the basis of its legitimacy. Even if labor or material resources were lost by the state to the informal sector, they were likely to be directed eventually to this provisioning. In Zamfirovo this connection was recognized in the general cooperation between sectors: people were let off work to harvest their strawberries and additional absenteeism was tolerated, as was petty theft. These concessions exemplify again the conflicting complementarity central to the system. If the state and economy are separated, however, resources lost by the state sector do not necessarily resurface in an area or sector where the state is responsible. In such a context, informal activity becomes less integrated with the state sector and thus more suspect in the view of administrators.

Under capitalism as well, the state is often in collusion with informal activity, but what I am suggesting here is a conflict that is particular to a period of socialist reform—the period of dissociation between government and economy that began with perestroika but continued into the transition. In this period, many economic inputs are still coming from the state sector, but since the state has begun to transfer custody of the economy to an emerging private sector, the outputs are no longer contributing solely to an area of state responsibility. Not surprisingly then, with the attempt to rationalize the economy by removing state controls and state monopolies, there is a simultaneous attack on the informal sector. Thus, in a magazine interview conducted in 1985, Soviet Ambassador Grekov, criticizing the Bulgarian economy, zeroed in on Bulgarian workers for concentrating their energies on their second jobs (cited in Pitassio 1989:204). Subsequently that year, an article in the Bulgarian Communist Party newspaper claimed that the equivalent of 30,000 jobs were being wasted by absenteeism while the black market and illegal operations of a semiprivate nature involved as many as 10,000 people in Sofia alone (cited in Crampton 1988:348). The same theme was evident in the village as well. At a meeting of the Zamfirovo cooperative farmworkers in 1988, the director complained that the average workday of farm employees had dwindled to four hours, the rest being spent on personal and informal work. Such comments were perceived as an ill-wind regarding the government's attitude toward the relationship between formal and informal sectors. Given the importance of informal processes for Bulgarian villagers, their anxiety about restructuring was understandable.

Ironically, the greater threat in this regard was not the attack on informal processes but the collapse of formal structures. The shock to formal structures in 1990 provoked informal processes into hyperactivity. The increased strain on informal connections may have led to some retrenchment of informal connections, but those that remained became more important. At the same time, we must acknowledge that the prior expansion of informal processes contributed to the vulnerability of the formal system. So, while the integrations and adjustments achieved by informal routes were adaptive locally and empowered villagers, they were also detrimental to the system as a whole. As state institutions and labor were rendered less significant vis-à-vis expanding informal activity, the practical and ideological foundations of state socialism were further weakened.

Barring an economic miracle, however, the informal processes we have described here will not simply wither away. As long as there are severe inadequacies or difficulties of any type in the formal economy (whether called socialist or capitalist), people will pursue alternate avenues to satisfy their wants and needs. Certainly the transitional Bulgarian economy could be said to have such problems. Letters from the country in 1990 described grocery stores with nothing in them whatsoever. In 1991, when prices were decontrolled, letters told of ample goods that few could afford. Subsequent inflation made matters continually worse, reaching crisis proportions in 1996. By early 1997 an average monthly pension hardly covered a month's supply of bread. Through it all, villagers continued to rely on their agricultural production, the animals they raised, and their informal networks. As one informant wrote in a letter to me in the fall of 1990, "There is nothing to buy in the stores, but like other villagers we will kill a pig at New Year's and we will have meat this winter." I am sure his daughter in Sofia, who did not raise pigs, also had meat for her family. At the same time, their dependence on these resources reinforced their commitment to the agricultural system that made such production possible. As we will see in the next chapter, this put many villagers at odds with ideas of transition.

6

RURAL RESTITUTIONS

The pervasive importance of agriculture described in the preceding chapters perpetuated a political interpretation of agriculture in the extreme. Since at least the interwar period agriculture has been less an area of policy concern and more a facet of political identification. Once particular agrarian arrangements become elemental to political definitions, however, real negotiation or innovation is constrained. The reforms being experimented with in 1988, for example, were the first to really challenge the association of cooperative production and socialism in Bulgaria, but the socialist system collapsed before they could develop, preventing any meaningful dissociation. At the same time, the constant tinkering with agriculture through reforms kept it central to perceptions of socialism. As a result, when the antisocialist coalition, the Union of Democratic Forces (UDF), gained power in 1991, one of their first targets was agriculture. UDF leaders set their sights on the cooperative farm system, which symbolized socialism in the countryside and which they believed sustained socialist sentiment among villagers. This conclusion reflected the election results from 1990. The UDF performed poorly in the countryside, and leaders assumed that villagers, dependent on resources allocated through cooperative farms, were intimidated and manipulated by communist farm administrators. The solution, then—symbolically, politically, and economically—was to get rid of the cooperative farm system. Just as collectivization answered numerous problems faced by the Communist Party after World War II, decollectivization resolved multiple difficulties faced by the UDF in 1991.

Their policy reflected an accurate recognition of the important role of agriculture in the society but an incomplete appreciation of the intricate connections involved. During the previous four decades of conflicting complementarity, agricultural considerations infiltrated all dimensions of the society in multiple ways. While some of these connections probably made it an attractive target for those wanting radical and rapid transformation, other connections doomed such a strategy. Generally, the integrative nature of socialism made surgical corrections impossible: there was no place to make a start without wreaking havoc everywhere. This was especially true for agriculture, since it was so thoroughly connected to the rest of Bulgarian society in so many ways. Having followed the preceding analysis from a village perspective, the reader probably appreciates this fact better than did the leadership of the UDF.

I returned to the village in 1992 at the beginning of the UDF's decollectivization program, which consisted of the explicit dismantling of the cooperative farm structure underlying most of what I have described in the previous chapters. Villagers were very agitated; indeed, it seemed that agriculture had vanquished all other political considerations. One elderly woman who was permanently stooped from years of hoeing and harvesting was torn between anger and despondency. Despite her physical condition, she worked daily on the personal plot of her household, which included her son, her daughter-in-law, and one granddaughter. The daughter-in-law took care of all the household chores after returning home from her job in the post office, but she had heart problems and could not do heavy labor. The recently unemployed son was usually occupied hauling wood, maintaining the house or barn, or tending to the needs of livestock. The granddaughter was away at school. This left the grandmother to hoe and weed, the very activities that had nearly crippled her physically. She was understandably unhappy about the prospect of being given more land: "What are we going to do with this land? Who is going to farm it, tell me? How many decares do you think I can dig with my little hoe? In the past, when it was still possible to work the land by hand, and I was healthy, they took it away from me. Now when you need machines, chemicals, and everything else, and I am worn out, they want to give it back. Forget it. Stupidity. First the communists made us give up our land, and now the UDF is making us take it back. It is like getting slapped on both sides of your face." She dramatized the assault by turning her face first to one side then the other in a pantomime of successive blows.

Other villagers insisted that such an assault was necessary. Parroting the arguments of the UDF leadership, they claimed that the only way to change was to get rid of cooperative farm leaders who controlled local resources and resisted changes that would undercut their power. This logic followed that of a joke popular during the period of perestroika. Two Bulgarians are complaining about the stagnation of their country compared to developments in the Soviet Union. One says that Bulgaria needs a Gorbachev. The other counters that they would need a thousand Gorbachevs. "Why a thousand?" asks the first speaker. "One for every village." Ironically this reflects the limited ability of centralized authorities in Bulgaria to carry out their will, and while it suggests local authorities had more influence, we have already seen that by the 1980s, many villagers were not intimidated by village administrators either. Surely they were even less fearful in the wake of 1989. Village supporters of the UDF, however, denied this possibility and presented themselves as the exceptions.

Since many UDF supporters continued to define resistance on the basis of dissidence and anticommunism, those who supported socialism in opposition or in resistance to new threats were seen as conservative and under the thumb of communists. In other words, for anticommunists, continuing cold war oppositions rendered a socialist resistance unthinkable. However, for the villagers who had reshaped socialism and who, like the woman quoted above, were tired of being pushed around, domesticated socialism provided a handy means to resist the latest round of assaults, even if they had previously not been supporters of the Communist Party. They used the association between socialism and cooperativism to defend their agricultural arrangements and achieved some success. While the Zamfirovo cooperative farm seemed doomed in the summer of 1992, by the summer of 1993 it had a new lease on life, with over 500 voluntary members. Its long-term prospects, however, were threatened anew by inflation and fuel shortages in 1996–97, which made it nearly impossible for the farm to operate.

The rest of this chapter follows the vicissitudes of cooperative cultivation in the village beginning in 1989. I start with a rundown of national policies affecting the process, followed by a description of the general difficulties involved in implementing them. I then turn to the local consequences of decollectivization in Zamfirovo and attempt to account for village responses by relating the process to the limitations of private farming. A final section looks at other changes in the village since 1989.

The Law of the Land

One of the most important projects on the political agenda after 1989 was the restitution of property rights to landowners or their heirs. As noted in Chapter 1, those who contributed land during the process of collectivization had long ago ceased to exercise any control over their property through existing cooperative structures. All political constituencies agreed on the need to restore these rights, but they differed radically over whether or not such restitution required the dissolution of existing cooperative farms. In other words, could property rights be reinjected into existing cooperative structures, or did the structures themselves have to be eradicated? The Socialist Party maintained the former position: with member consent, old cooperatives could reconstitute themselves as real cooperatives. Individuals wishing to withdraw could do so, and those remaining would be protected by state cooperative regulations guaranteeing their rights as cooperative members. The UDF was not convinced. They saw the socialist argument as a ruse to simply reproduce old structures. According to this view, members would be too intimidated or simply too unaccustomed to ownership to exercise their property rights. The cooperative leadership would resist any loss of power and restrain member control. So the UDF advocated the complete abolition of the cooperative farm system. From 1989 to 1995, as parliamentary control shifted between the two parties, the nature of state land policy oscillated between these poles.

The original Law on Ownership and Use of Agricultural Land—or, more colloquially, the "land law"—was finally passed in March 1991. It was followed in April by more specific regulations for the law's implementation, and both documents were amended slightly in September. As these acts were passed under the parliamentary control of the Socialist Party, they reflected a bias toward cooperative cultivation. They maintained restrictions on the size of private landholdings dating from the postwar land reforms, limiting most holdings to 20 hectares, with a maximum of 30 in the northeast grain-growing area of Dobrudzha. Owners were also restricted in the disposition of land. Regulations required waiting periods before restituted land could be sold and specified particular preferences in terms of purchasers (e.g., relatives or neighbors). Owners were also required to use agricultural land for agricultural purposes or face potential fines, and according to some interpretations, they were even required to continue existing usage (e.g., pasture had to be maintained as pasture).

For those wishing to stay in cooperatives, property rights would be restored in ideal shares of cooperative land, on the basis of which rent and dividend payments would be figured. Others would receive a share of land equivalent in quality and quantity to that which they (or their parents) had contributed, although not necessarily the same land, plus compensation for nonlanded contributions such as livestock, tools, and labor. Land commissions were to be established in each municipality to receive the claims of cooperative members and decide on allocations. Where claims exceeded land available for restitution (due to the construction of roads, buildings, dams, and so forth), the amount of all claims for that village or farm were to be reduced by the percentage necessary to make total claims equal available land—a factor called the correction coefficient. The expectation of continued cooperative cultivation was given further legal grounds by the Law on Cooperatives, passed soon after the land law. It allowed the boards of existing cooperatives to re-register under new regulations specifying voluntary membership and requiring rent and dividend payments to members. The Law on Cooperatives necessarily overlapped with the land law in specifying procedures for those exiting cooperatives.

The overall program had obvious limitations. The new cooperative regulations allowed for such a smooth transfer that some carryover of old abuses seemed certain. Indeed, existing cooperatives were bound to remain the most powerful actors in agriculture, at least in the short term. As such they were also likely to be advantaged in the distribution of resources to exiting members, so that better land and resources would remain in the cooperative while the less attractive resources were offered to private farmers. This possibility itself might discourage private initiatives. Conversely, some cooperative administrators took advantage of their position in the uncertain period between 1989 and the passage of the land law to sell off desirable cooperative property to family members, informal connections, and even strangers with whom they later hoped to establish business connections. These actions, which hurt both supporters of the cooperative and those who wished to leave it, were not sufficiently regulated by either the land law or the new cooperative regulations.

Actually, there was very little time for the new policies to have any measurable effect, as parliamentary crises provoked new elections for October

1991. When the UDF emerged victorious, they immediately set about remedying the problems of the land law. A vast array of amendments were passed in early 1992. Indeed, only a minority of articles and paragraphs remained untouched. Restrictions on who could buy and sell land were reduced, and owners were given clearer latitude in the use of restituted agricultural land. All past transactions of movable or immovable property, with the exception of farm produce, were declared null and void. Limits on landholdings were apparently lifted.[1] The new amendments also promoted the restitution of land rights in so-called real boundaries. "Real" here had two meanings—historical and geographical. Historically, it emphasized boundaries that really existed in the past. Restitution was to conform to these historical boundaries "wherever existent or possible to establish" (Article 10a, Paragraph 1). When past boundaries could not be reestablished, an equivalent area of real farmland in the geographical sense (as opposed to just an ideal share) had to be allotted in the same area or in an area adjacent to the original land contribution (Article 10a, Paragraph 2). Amendments to the regulations for application (Article 18i) attempted to speed the effect of these laws by allowing owners to apply to land commissions for temporary usufruct of farmland based on their land claims. This allowed them to take possession while the lengthy process of restitution proceeded. It also allowed for substitution, so those whose land could not be restituted could use other land until a resolution was reached.

The most far-reaching provisions of the 1992 amendments provided for the complete liquidation of cooperative farms. Cooperatives registered under the earlier cooperative act were legally terminated, and landholders could only join new cooperatives with legal documentation of landownership (a deed) in hand. This possibility was further complicated by the requirement that land rights be attached to real pieces of land rather than a portion of collectively owned land. Given the situation in 1992, this rendered cooperative initiatives impossible or invalid. In a reflection of this inevitability, added to the regulations for applying the land

---

1. There is some disagreement around this issue, since it involved prior regulations (cf. Dobreva 1994:347 with Kopeva, Mishev, and Howe 1994:208). But because Paragraph 15 of the Transitional and Concluding Provisions of the land law specifies after restitution a two-year period when ownership may not exceed 300 hectares, it seems clear that the intent of the law was to eventually remove such limits. As one might expect from discussions of interwar landholdings in Chapter 1, a 30-hectare limit hardly seemed like a limit at all to most villagers.

law were several articles (and a new chapter heading) specifying more elaborate procedures for the distribution of nonlanded cooperative farm property. Cooperative members or heirs were to receive shares of cooperative assets on the basis of three contributions: the amount of land they contributed to the cooperative (adjusted for its quality and for the number of years it was used by the cooperative); the number of labor days they had worked on the farm; and any equipment or unreimbursed money paid to the farm for the purchase of equipment. The total shares for the village were then correlated with the total value of farm assets, as determined by an external panel of appraisers, to establish the relative value of shares. Former members could then use these shares to purchase cooperative property other than land. Any assets not of interest to shareholders could be sold at auction. To carry out this liquidation and ensure that all cooperatives were deactivated, the amendments terminated the activities of all managing bodies of cooperative farms and instructed county governors to replace them with liquidation committees consisting of a chairperson and three to five members. These committees were then assigned the schizophrenic task of managing farm production while liquidating farm assets.

If liquidation was intended to transcend the abuses of prior cooperative structures, it generated its own excesses. Committee members were accused of looting farms for personal profit, and even their legal activities offended villagers who saw the whole process as simply destructive. These discontents contributed to the collapse of the government in the fall of 1992. The subsequent government maintained the policy of decollectivization but slowed down the timetable, restricted some of the most offensive elements, and softened its anticooperative tone. The activities of liquidation committees were to be monitored by the Ministry of Agriculture, and some of the more suspect actions—like selling livestock—were restricted. The possibility of personal profiteering through the sale of cooperative livestock had been a lightning rod for rural anxiety since the beginnings of the transition. Liquidating committees, after they took control of the farms, became the focus of such accusations, but communist managers of cooperative farms had been accused of similar offenses prior to 1992. The new policy attempted to defuse this volatile concern. It also reflected the changed attitude toward cooperative arrangements. As cooperatives seemed increasingly inevitable, there was greater concern to protect potential cooperative property from dissipation. The new cooperatives that had been disallowed were tacitly allowed to operate, although they still lacked the necessary legal documentation of landownership. Some groups even started submitting applications to the land commissions for land to be restituted collectively rather than individually, even though there was no legal basis for such a request.

When new elections brought the Socialist Party back to power, these tendencies were expanded and given more legal backing. In May 1995 the parliament enacted another collection of amendments to the land law; not surprisingly, they reversed many UDF amendments and reinstated some elements of the original land law. The activities of liquidation committees were immediately suspended, and cooperative members were empowered to elect their own representatives to complete the work of property distribution. New cooperatives were allowed to accept land from owners collectively, obviating the need to wait for individual deeds from land commissions and circumventing, to a degree, the need to divide large blocks of land into parcels. Restrictions on the sale and use of agricultural land were also revived.

While these changes responded to previous excesses, they clearly perpetuated the manipulation of agriculture for political purposes. Indeed, President Zhelev and the parliamentary opposition appealed the majority of the changes to the Constitutional Court, which canceled nineteen amendments in June 1995. Fearful that socialist power might still advantage the cooperatives, Zhelev went on national television in February 1996 and urged villagers to form committees to take back their land. A presidential call for quasi-vigilante action against parliamentary preferences captures both the political divisiveness in the country and its agricultural basis.

Such actions could sometimes be effective because of the legal uncertainty produced by the perpetual manipulation of agricultural policy. In such a situation, whoever asserted their claims could often have it their way. This possibility was indeed part of the UDF's concern about village cooperative leaders. Apparently Zhelev decided to try the same tactics. As a colleague in Sofia, exasperated by my incessant inquiries about the law, put it in 1995, "There have been so many changes in the land law that nobody really knows what laws apply." One of the workers for the old village cooperative summarized the whole process in a more telling critique: "It's a wheel turning in the same place. Every time they change power they reverse the changes of the previous government and we end up going around in circles, making no progress. Maybe they do it for their own entertainment; maybe we're like circus performers to them. I don't know."

Problems in Restitution

The politicization of property restitution was dialectically related to the difficulty of the process. Frustrated policymakers appealed to ready-made political formulas (not unlike socialist central planners before them), and these programs only exacerbated the problems. The difficulties started with the first step in the process—the submission of land claims. The national deadline for claims had to be extended at least twice to accommodate the volume of requests and to allow claimants time to locate documentation. Given the history of migration, owners sometimes had to travel to other parts of the country to collect documents and stake their claims. In many cases land commissions had to help locate applicable documents and publish the data for villagers to use in their claim forms. In other cases, county archives sent copies of relevant documents to villagers. These documents included tax registers, lists of itemized contributions to the cooperative farm from the time of collectivization, old property documents, and bills of sale. In the absence of these reports, claimants could use witnesses, ideally owners of neighboring lands, to verify prior ownership. The land commission in Berkovitza, which was responsible for Zamfirovo, also reported using village elders who remembered which land belonged to whom. As the president of the land commission said, "You would be surprised how much some older villagers remember." Unfortunately, different villagers sometimes remembered things differently, so this resource generated problems as well as solutions.

The same history that made community knowledge so useful also affected the accuracy of official documents. Prior to collectivization, villagers often relied on common community knowledge of boundaries and ownership rights. Major disputes over land usually concerned inheritance, which involved the creation of new boundaries and divisions rather than disagreement over existing ones. Thus, many villagers treated the official registers used to calculate their tax or requisition burdens as manipulable. People could understate their holdings or contributions for the purpose of reducing these burdens without endangering their land claims, which were communally recognized. Villagers also underreported their contribution to the cooperative farm for the same reason. As recounted in Chapter 1, by the time of massive collectivization, the real cooperative elements of the farms were already disappearing. In such a context, and given that everyone was being forced into the cooperative, precision seemed unnecessary, so some people purposefully underreported their contribution for fear they might somehow be taxed on what they had contributed. As the most complete documents, however, tax registers and cooperative farm inventories became central to restitution calculations, and villagers who had underreported their holdings often lost claims.

Even with documents and good memories, there were still problems. As Verdery (1994) demonstrated in detail for Transylvania, the very features of the physical environment seemed to have changed, making it hard to locate the exact amounts of land in the same places they were before collectivization. Stones, paths, and balk lines that previously marked boundaries had all been removed. Stands of trees had been cut back by villagers pilfering fuel or building materials. Even waterways may have shifted course. In the last two cases the historical markers remained but no longer bounded the same area as before. Such shifts occurred gradually, without documentation or notice, making the results quite mysterious or, as Verdery aptly puts it, making the land seemingly elastic.

A significant percentage of agricultural land was simply no longer available. Most of the buildings constructed by cooperative farms and machine tractor stations after collectivization were built on somebody's farmland. In many cases so were factories and city suburbs. The apparent concessions to the rights of builders in early transition legislation led many to start constructions on land they had previously been using agriculturally in order to prevent it from being restituted to the former owner. Most of the irrigation reservoirs flooded somebody's former plots. New roads and paths cut through previously arable land. According to the land law, these proprietors were to receive either equivalent land elsewhere or some other compensation. Landless villagers were also legally designated to receive land by the land law, but amounts were not specified. As a result of these various requirements, the land claims in many villages significantly surpassed the amount of land available. The land law provided a solution that perpetuated processes under way since the interwar period—the privatization of common lands. Municipalities were to be restituted as owners of common lands, but they were authorized to use the land to compensate various categories of claimants. This would likely cause subsequent problems for villagers who still needed common lands for pasturage. Furthermore, given the encroachments on common lands up to the time of collectivization, the amount of this resource was limited in many villages. In cases where there was simply not enough land, the correction coefficient would reduce every villager's claim, but those being asked to give up land that was clearly theirs in the past were likely to be dissatisfied.

Even land that could be returned may have been altered in quality or category. Large tracts of land had been planted with orchards or permanent crops, supposedly enhancing its value, while other land had eroded or been overexploited by the cooperative farm, making it less valuable. Since land was supposed to be restituted in a quantity *and* quality equivalent to that collectivized, these developments caused problems. A similar problem affected land used for personal plots. If this land belonged to someone else prior to collectivization and the user had planted a vineyard or some other permanent crop, then the two individuals were likely to come into conflict over compensation or sale. The state provided regulations for former owners to compensate the cooperative farm or personal proprietor for such improvements, but former owners were not always willing to do so.

The potential problems were infinite, and often the land commission was not even aware of the barriers. The president of the Berkovitza commission said the biggest problem she faced was the lack of records regarding construction over the last forty years. "We have no idea if the land being claimed by somebody has been built on by the farm or state, and this affects whether or not the land can be returned in its original borders." This also made it difficult to evaluate cases of rapid building done solely to establish stronger land claims; without records it was hard to prove such machinations. The constant changing of the land laws was an additional impediment. Villagers were often unaware of the latest changes—a situation that made it difficult for the land commission to work with them. As one member of the commission put it, "We have to keep explaining the laws over and over, and by the time we get it through to them and they come back with some required document or form, the law may be different. We get something done and then there is a change in the law and we have to redo it. It's a never-ending process. Plus there are the endless complaints that have to be redressed. We've been at it for three years now, and we are still in the thick of it."

The commission managed to proceed by relegating some of the problems to the judicial system. The Berkovitza commission attempted to resolve conflicts over land, but if they were unable to reach an acceptable solution, they simply referred the case to the courts. They made no attempt to deal with the issue of inheritance at all. According to the land law, property rights were restituted to the former owner, living or dead. In the latter case the legal heirs had to devise their own settlement and have it approved in order to receive land rights. If they could not agree, the case went to court. People who contested a commission decision—such as those who lost land due to past underreporting—also had to take their complaints to court. The president of the land commission said it could take two years for people to get answers on such matters. Of course, new conflicts emerged at each step in the process.

The land commission temporarily sidestepped other problems by proceeding differently with land that could be restituted in its real borders and land that could not. Generally, land to be restored in real boundaries presented fewer difficulties, since, barring some of the forces mentioned above, it had retained prior boundaries and, in many cases, had been under continual use. The map of real boundary plots as determined by the land commission was posted in the village of Zamfirovo in the summer of 1994, and villagers had two weeks to submit complaints. These were either redressed or dismissed, and a year later the actual surveying of plots began. Surveying was the last step prior to issuing actual deeds. A schedule was posted at the town hall and the village bakery delineating the area of the village to be surveyed each day. Villagers with property in that region were instructed to meet the surveyors there with the documents they had received from the land commission verifying their claims.

During the summer of 1995, I accompanied the surveyors—a family of four, consisting of a husband, wife, and two young sons—on their rounds. They owned quite sophisticated computerized survey equipment and had been subcontracted by the land commission through a competitive bidding process. The wife consulted with the assembled villagers to determine the corner and midpoints of each boundary, which her husband then recorded electronically. In one case a man's land had been divided by a new path and half of it incorporated into a cooperative block. They surveyed the remaining half and told him the other amount would be dealt with differently, according to reallocation plans. Observation of several surveys revealed little disagreement. There was some debate about actual border points, but all concerns were resolved to the mutual satisfaction of those involved. This happened quickly once nearby proprietors got involved and a clear consensus emerged. At the time I accompanied them, the surveyors were about halfway through the process in Zamfirovo and said they had not yet come across any major conflict between villagers. The potential for conflict was lessened somewhat by absenteeism: as elsewhere, lots of owners did not even show up. The surveyors stopped every morning at the village square to arrange visits for those who missed their scheduled appointments, to answer questions, and to verify the official documents of villagers who had neglected to bring them to the fields on the day of surveying.

A final document specifying the actual boundaries, complete with a map of the actual plot and its neighboring parcels, was subsequently produced by the surveyors on a home computer. With this document the owner could get a legal deed. One day a representative of the land commission joined the surveyors and showed me a trunk full of unclaimed survey documents from neighboring villages. In many cases, documents were produced even for unclaimed plots because the plots surrounding them were surveyed and this, by default, confirmed the boundaries of the unclaimed pieces. The representative said that many people had moved away and did not really care about the small plots. Others had died and their heirs were not interested. Still others, he said, were afraid they would be taxed if they actually claimed the land. There was a moratorium on taxes for several years, but people were already worried about what would happen when it expired. He said they erroneously thought that by not claiming the land officially, they could continue to use it without ever paying taxes. However, they were also likely to be relieved of the property, since land not claimed after ten years reverted to municipal ownership. This was one hopeful development in regard to the crisis of village common lands discussed previously. In the meantime, however, the knowledge that certain individuals had not claimed their land or submitted land claims led to suspicions by other villagers over what was happening to this land and, more important, who was getting it or profiting from it in the interim. There were more than enough cases of villagers cultivating the unused property of others to justify such suspicions.

Rights to land not in real boundaries were restituted in principle only. In other words, owners received a document saying the land was theirs, but they were not allowed to take it over for cultivation or sale. The Berkovitza land commission had proposed some reallocation of abandoned cooperative blocks in the plan of real boundary land submitted to Zamfirovo in 1994. But the rest had to await a reallocation plan that would consolidate all fragments located in the same general area while trying to maintain equivalence of quality and quantity. Clearly, reallocation posed the greatest difficulty; as of February 1997, it still had not been attempted in Zamfirovo. Land commissions were contracting out the technical work of coming up with distribution plans, including the new roads necessary for accessing each plot. Such plans had to be announced and approved before parcels could be laid off, deeds issued, and the plots entered into the cadastral records. Decisions were certain to be contested, meaning a long process. Furthermore, the country did not have enough qualified technicians to complete the task quickly. Every delay made it more likely that the process would be halted when political power changed hands.

Most land in the country required reallocation. According to 1992 data from the Ministry of Agriculture, land still intact in former borders amounted to less than 12 percent of all land nationwide. In Zamfirovo the amount appears to be much greater. Based on a sample of 200 owners, the amount of land that could be restored in real boundaries accounted for nearly 27 percent of total landholdings. Zamfirovo's advantage in this regard may be due to the location of the village in the foothills of the Balkan mountains, where significant stretches of forests and steep terrain were not incorporated into cooperative farm blocks. Still, the vast majority of land, even in Zamfirovo, could not be restituted in real boundaries. Villagers could not use their land if it was still under cooperative cultivation, although many had been allowed to use other land, including abandoned blocks, until their own land was officially restituted. As reallocation of blocks seemed less and less likely, villagers who wanted to farm privately grew impatient, and by 1994 a telltale sign of resistance appeared across the landscape—small plots of corn or sunflowers interrupting large blocks of wheat. My suspicion about this was confirmed by inquiries; in all the cases I investigated, the surrounding land was cooperative and the violating plot that of a private owner who had taken over his or her former land for private use. Since these were clearly exceptions—a few decares in the case of Zamfirovo—the cooperatives simply worked around them and did not cause trouble. Nevertheless, the cooperative management insisted they had the right to use the land until restitution decisions were finalized, while private farmers insisted they had the right to their own land. Other forms of resistance included chopping down trees or setting fire to buildings or crops that stood in the way of restitution.

Such actions protested the lack of progress toward reallocation, but they also provided a warning in regard to the idea of reallocating cooperative blocks. Regardless of how fair the proposed plan might be, it was destined to meet with resistance from owners insisting on their former plots. There are various reasons for this. Villagers interested in private agricultural production wanted the best land available; if the decisions of land commissions compromised this in any way, they were likely to resist. Although such exchanges would consider the quality, quantity, and location of land, absolute equivalences were impossible to formulate; hence, contestation was inevitable. Also, some villagers wanted fragmented plots for the same reasons parcels were divided before, to ensure land for different uses—gardens, forests, pasture—and to minimize damage from natural disasters. For many villagers, particular plots also carried symbolic meaning and sentimental value: the land provided a physical link to past generations.

Insistence on particular plots could also represent another form of resistance to decollectivization: by contesting commission decisions, villagers created additional barriers to land entitlement. Furthermore, if they were successful in increasing the amount of land restored in pre-socialist parcels, they might enhance the attraction of cooperative cultivation, since owners of fragmented and dispersed plots were unlikely to find private agriculture attractive. This interpretation is supported by the fact that many of those who opposed plot consolidation in 1994 were advocating and supporting it in 1995, when it seemed clear that the cooperative might survive and consolidation was needed to maintain cooperative lands intact. Of course, the changes in the land law in 1995 made it less essential to reestablish plots, for villagers could enter cooperatives collectively. In this case the commission could recognize cumulative land contributions in block form, and reallocation became an issue only for those refusing to join. The incentive this gave to maintaining cooperative structures provoked President Zhelev's call for villagers to take back their land.

Overall, Zamfirovo is advantaged in the potential resolution of land conflicts, for it is one of the villages where available land actually surpassed the amount requested in claims. Indeed, the village may end up with significant increases in municipal and common lands. Villagers cited the common tendency to underreport landholdings prior to collectivization as one major factor, as well as the massive out-migration and depopulation discussed in Chapter 3. The heirs of those who left the village were less interested in the land because the village is isolated and the land less valuable than that bordering towns and cities. The agricultural value of the land is also limited by the terrain and soil quality. Having extra land gives officials more latitude in appeasing would-be private producers without completely undermining cooperative blocks.

From Liquidation to Exasperation

Clearly, for most land, the issue of restitution was inextricably bound up with the question of cooperatives. Restitution could not be finalized until it was certain whether property rights could be transferred collectively for owners wishing to stay in cooperatives. However, from the collapse of the UDF government in 1992 until the socialist amendments of 1995, the legal status of cooperatives was completely unclear. In villages where the liquidating committees were less aggressive or less politically committed to the UDF, cooperatives that registered in 1991 continued to function throughout 1992, despite being legally disallowed. When the authority of the UDF was weakened by the collapse of its government, additional cooperatives organized and began to operate more assertively, taking over the cultivation of land from liquidation committees, much as individuals had been allowed to do. Cooperative members also pooled their shares to purchase the bulk of machines and buildings from the former TKZS in the legal auctions specified by UDF amendments. This strengthened the position of cooperatives and made it difficult for individuals to compete. Rural UDF supporters and others opposed to cooperative production were forced to join together in their own cooperatives in order to compete with the successors to the TKZSs (see Kaneff 1995, n.d.). Although primarily a defensive posture, the movement of antisocialists into alternative cooperatives actually encouraged further accommodation to the cooperative idea in the restitution process. Such accommodation was formalized in the 1995 socialist amendments to the land law, but in the light of appeals to the constitutional court, and the subsequent collapse of the socialist government, the final outcome is far from certain. What is clear is that the violations and excesses of the liquidation program backfired. Instead of wiping out cooperative cultivation and socialist support, liquidation inspired cooperative sentiment.

The Liquidation Committee took over the Zamfirovo cooperative farm in June 1992. The committee consisted of two men from the village, one from the district town of Berkovitza, and the chairman from Mihailovgrad. The chairman was born in the village but migrated to town when he was young. As elsewhere in the country, the composition of the committee was the first bone of contention for villagers already unhappy about the liquidating process in general. Villagers accused committee members of being unqualified—that is, they were not agronomists or experienced farmers. This complaint was generally valid: the vast majority of Bulgarians trained in agronomy or related occupations were part of the old cooperative management structure, which the UDF was trying to purge. In addition, two members of the Zamfirovo committee did not live in the village, and this further diminished their suitability in the opinion of many. Given that the same critics assessed the two local committee members—chosen for their support of the UDF—as even less capable, it is hard to imagine that anyone could have satisfied village critics. Still, it is true that officials made no apparent attempt to diffuse potential resentment in their appointment of the Zamfirovo committee.

The major criticism of the chairman concerned his political history as a Communist Party member, which led villagers to interpret his rabid anticommunism as hypocritical, opportunistic, or both. He claimed he left the party when he realized what it was really like; others said he had been asked to leave when caught stealing. Still, villagers seemed to respect his higher education, even if it was not in agronomy, and he had relatives living in the village, which seemed to mitigate his status as an outsider (in fact, he subsequently moved back to the village). Thus, when I arrived in June 1992, villagers were taking a wait-and-see attitude toward him. As one of the most severe critics of liquidation put it, "We can work with him."

The chairman also benefited by his association with the policy mentioned earlier of allowing villagers to take over designated areas of cooperative farmland for their own use. This policy amounted to lifting the limits on personal plot acreage. Some villagers took over plots they expected to have returned to them; others were granted temporary rights to other cooperative land. Nearly every village household with adequate labor took on additional land through these arrangements in the summer of 1992. Typically, this land included small plots near water resources that were used for intensive vegetable cultivation and much larger plots of meadowland. Additional meadowland was particularly attractive, for it allowed villagers to expand their household livestock operations and increase highly valued meat and milk production without a proportional increase in labor. Still, even meadows required some work harvesting, and it seemed that everybody in the village was making hay in the summer of 1992. This also helped the Liquidation Committee, which did not have to worry about managing land it could allocate to villages. Of course, this strategy was less useful in smaller villages with predominantly older residents who could not expand their farming activities.

In Zamfirovo, at least, these possibilities kept early attitudes toward the Liquidation Committee somewhat benign. By the time I left the village later that summer, however, the situation had reversed, and villagers were increasingly critical and vocal. At one slightly drunken dinner party toward the end of my stay, the host even suggested that someone should do the committee members physical harm: "These four now control every-thing. They do whatever they want; they don't have to answer to anyone. Someone will kill them for what they're doing. At least the communists had to answer to the party. Now there is no control and no rules. They can do whatever they want. We should have done what they did in Zalapitsa."[2] Another guest asked the speaker why he did not do something himself. The speaker shrugged this off, but his wife said, "Give him a few more drinks and he will." Each successive summer visit found ever more pervasive criticism of "the liquidators," as the committee came to be known.

The turning point followed immediately from one of the first actions of the chairman. He sold the bulk of the cooperative's young sheep, which had been designated as reproductive stock, diminishing the ability of the cooperative to reproduce its flocks. Villagers who hoped to establish a new cooperative saw the holdings of the existing cooperative as their fu-ture resource base and interpreted his action as a preemptive strike. Even those villagers who were less committed to the cooperative idea be-lieved that the sheep should be returned to villagers rather than sold. Of course, the chairman was just doing his job—liquidating the farm. By the summer of 1993 there were no sheep left in the cooperative; most had been sold, but about 200 to 300 were restituted to villagers. The same process was under way with cattle, although some of the farm's dairy en-terprises were still operating because, as the chairman complained, sales had been restricted before he could finish the job. As previously noted, these restrictions came with the collapse of the UDF government in re-sponse to popular complaints about the looting of cooperatives.

Resources from the sale of farm goods were used to pay the operating expenses of the farm. Many factors conspired to increase these needs and thus fuel the pace of liquidation. Agricultural subsidies that underwrote the cooperative farm system were reduced or withdrawn, making it neces-sary for the farm to come up with more of its own resources. At the same time, the farm was handing over meadowlands—a low-cost source of ani-mal feed—to private villagers, making it harder to support cooperative livestock. The lame-duck situation of the cooperative farm made it nearly impossible to secure loans from banks for the costs of planting, so in

2. The villagers of Zalapitsa in south-central Bulgaria occupied their cooperative farm office and refused to allow the Liquidation Committee to take control. Authorities called in the military to install the committee. As I later describe, Zamfirovo residents eventually did follow the Zalapitsa example.

many cases cash had to be generated up front. Prior debts of the farm also had to be paid, and expenses such as salaries continued as usual. Thus, the seemingly schizophrenic objectives of the Liquidation Committee actually fused into a singular devouring persona: because the committee financed the continuation of agricultural production through the liquidation of farm resources, continuing cultivation itself provided the motivation for ever more liquidation.

Villagers grew more and more concerned as they watched village resources trickle away. For most villagers the very idea of liquidation made no sense. They did not understand why existing resources and structures could not be used in the new capitalist system.

> Why do we have to destroy everything and start from scratch? No other country has done that—only Bulgaria. Why not take what is there and build upon it, correct it, improve it? No, we have to tear it all down and start to build capitalism with nothing. From nothing you will get nothing. We won't be able to straighten things out and develop normally for twenty years at least. Bulgarian work. I have nothing against a market economy and private production. If you want to be private, here's your land, work it, good luck. But why is it necessary to destroy the whole system just for the sake of those few who want to be private farmers? It's stupid. You know it is very easy to tear a building down, one good push with a tractor might do it. But try building it back and it's not so quick or easy.

Defense of liquidation by the chairman of the Zamfirovo committee echoed ideas I heard from UDF supporters in Sofia. The chairman insisted that just letting people leave the cooperative farm or reclaim their land was insufficient. As he put it,

> The main thing is for people to develop a sense of private property. To get a piece of paper and know that the land is theirs and they have to decide what to do with it. This is a very difficult idea to instill. Someone came by the office the other day and asked me for something from the farm for his sheep. He has no conception that those sheep are solely his responsibility. This we have to change. . . . [Furthermore,] the old cooperative leadership was basically a family affair, one group of kin and their connections controlled everything. They had to be removed from power before any

real cooperative could be possible. Besides, they had no understanding of how to run a farm for profit. They were only concerned
about pleasing their superiors. They had to be removed so that
capable people can take leadership positions and individual farmers
feel free to make their own decisions.

In other words, decollectivization was necessary to instill ideas of private
property and eliminate politicized management, which should eventually
result in a more productive agriculture.

Of course, in the meantime one could only expect agricultural production to decline, as the system of production was liquidated. Thus, in a
perverse repercussion of decollectivization, declining production became
a reflection of the success of farm administration. If one of the goals was
to liquidate the cooperative farm, what better evidence of success could
there be than diminishing output? As previously discussed, the decline in
output meant that farms had progressively less income, which necessitated
further liquidation to meet expenses or pay debts. So, declining production not only verified the progress of liquidation, it drove the process ever
further along. Not surprisingly, Zamfirovo production declined significantly under "the liquidators." They took over in the summer of 1992
after much of the planting had been done, so output that year was relatively stable, but the following year large blocks of land went unplanted,
and perennials such as grapes and strawberries were neglected. The strawberry crop was negligible by 1993. A contributing factor was the complete
lack of irrigation—the equipment had not been maintained, and work-
able parts had been looted. The chairman explained that the committee
had not attended to such concerns because they had originally been told
the liquidation process would be completed in a year, so they never expected that they would still be managing the farm in the summer of 1993.
Besides, although he did not admit it, looting and theft actually aided
liquidation.

As the process dragged on, it generated more and more evidence of
waste and loss. With sales restricted, cows from the cooperative dairy farm
were distributed to families that had contributed cows to the cooperative
during collectivization. Several villagers immediately sold theirs, saying
they could neither feed nor take care of it and did not need the milk.
Certainly, they did not expect to use it for draft power. This upset other
villagers who saw it as another cooperative loss, even if it went through
the hands of individual members. More devastating was the destruction of

the stables and buildings where animals had been kept. With the issue of landownership unresolved, no one knew who would get the land on which these buildings stood, making it nearly impossible to sell them. The solution was to take them apart and sell the materials separately, which also simplified the restitution of the land itself. Whenever villagers passed the remaining foundations, however, they were graphically reminded of the seemingly wasteful destruction. Many of these buildings had been built manually by villagers during the early years of building socialism, when villagers were required to provide labor days for village development. They were thus intensely symbolic of the village and its labor. For those who remembered this labor, the attack on the cooperative farm seemed like an attack on the village itself (Creed 1995b:860). They gleaned similar impressions from the rusting machinery in the cooperative farmyard, most of which had been broken or rendered useless by the theft of parts. Dying orchards and vineyards along the main road to the village relayed the same message; villagers harvested what little they could while shaking their heads about the loss.

Disgust at the destruction of liquidation strengthened cooperative sentiment among villagers—the very opposite of its intended effect. A new cooperative, entitled "Dawn," formed with 546 members in October 1992, right after the government fell. Actually, much of the membership had signed up under the first cooperative law in 1991, but the cooperative had never officially registered and ceased further activity following the 1992 prohibition. The governmental collapse reenergized it. Dawn began with only about 10,000 decares of land, or approximately one-third of the amount worked by the old cooperative farm in the 1980s. Most Dawn members contributed only part of their land to the new cooperative, either because they wanted to keep the rest for private use or because it was still being used by the old cooperative.[3] It also seems clear that the largest landholders did not sign up at the start. According to a member of the Liquidation Committee, the outstanding 200 or so households had as much land between them as the 546 new cooperative members. However, as a result of liquidation abuses, limited alternatives, and tacit political support, cooperative membership expanded quickly.

With the establishment of a new cooperative, village critics of liquidation quickly changed their tune. Whereas they had opposed liquidation in

3. This makes the amount of land worked by Dawn at any one time an unreliable indication of the land the cooperative might subsequently access with the same membership.

the summer of 1992, they were hurrying the process along by the summer of 1993. The longer the liquidation process continued, the more resources it consumed, leaving less for its successor. As a result, the relations between the new cooperative and the Liquidation Committee of the old one became quite strained. The chairman of the committee saw the new cooperative as a complete subvention of his power, preventing him from doing what he was sent to do. He declared their operation illegal, and when I asked him how they got by with it, he said that nobody would stop them: "They just took what land they wanted, the best land in the TKZS, and said, 'We are many, we are big,' and nobody stops them." He implied that his own lack of action came from the top: "With the Berov government there is nothing one can do, since he is just a puppet of the socialists." Still the liquidators did what they could to divert resources from the new cooperative and make its work difficult. In 1993 Dawn was forced to rent machinery from a neighboring village where the Liquidation Committee was more sympathetic to cooperative organizing: the Zamfirovo committee either refused to provide machine services or charged exorbitant rates.

Some cooperative members suggested that other villagers were colluding with the liquidators to sabotage the new cooperative. There were extensive fires just before the wheat harvest of 1993, suspiciously affecting only the fields of the new cooperative. It was a very dry summer, so the fires could have been accidental, but villagers suspected arson. Some suggested that the land could have been desired by former owners who hoped that the fire would remove the land from "cooperative block" status and make it available for restitution. Most, however, believed it was just jealousy provoked by the cooperative's rebirth and success.

The survival of the cooperative forced many of those who advocated private production to reassess their ideas and unite in an alternative anticommunist cooperative of their own. This second cooperative was formed in late 1993. Following the politically symbolic pattern documented by Kaneff (n.d.), they named themselves "Gushantsi," the pre-socialist name of the village. The main organizer was a doctor who had returned to the village to start a business buying wild products such as mushrooms and herbs from village gatherers; he dried these products in the nut-drying facility he rented from the cooperative farm. His parents had left the village before he was born. Dissatisfied with his income as a doctor, he decided to capitalize on his restituted resources in the village. In 1993 he bought a tractor and hay baler, rented some land to augment his own, and started tending approximately 60 decares of sunflowers and meadows to supplement his drying enterprise. By late 1993 he had transformed his operation into a cooperative, and in the summer of 1994 it had about eighty members and 300 decares of land. Among the members was the chairman of the Liquidation Committee, which immediately brought Gushantsi into conflict with Dawn. As a clerical worker for the Liquidation Committee put it,

> The two cooperatives hate each other and work against each other, so they both suffer. I have 50 decares of land, which I have not signed over to either cooperative. I cannot work all the land myself, but what can I do? My boss is a member of the anticommunist cooperative and he will fire me if I sign up with the communists. And I am not going to sign up with his cooperative, because I do not trust them. Besides, my husband was a party member before the tenth [i.e., the transition] and he would not like it. So I just keep the land, and we work what we can.

When she subsequently lost her job anyway, as she knew she would, she signed over much of her land to the "socialist" cooperative (Dawn).

By 1994 Dawn was in control of nearly 13,000 decares of land, based on the contribution of over 800 members. It employed twenty full-time workers and ten to twelve temporary seasonal employees. They cultivated about half of the contributed land, primarily in wheat (approximately 5,000 decares), with significant amounts of corn (2,000 decares) and sunflowers (1,000 decares). They also used about 2,000 decares of meadows for making hay and about 1,000 for vineyards and orchards. The remainder was pasture land, apparently used by villagers for their household livestock. Wheat was sold to purchasers who called on the cooperative, and much of the rest of the production was used to feed the cooperative's 120 head of cattle (as of 1995). The milk was sold to a private firm in the neighboring town, and everyone complained about the low prices paid for it in 1995. Wheat prices were also cited as extremely low that year. Most of the limited profits were redistributed to the members: 30 percent for land rent and 30 percent for dividend payments on the basis of contributed capital and livestock. Another 30 percent was reinvested in the cooperative, and the final 10 percent designated for social needs of cooperative members. The profit of the cooperative for the 1994 year was approximately 700,000 leva, from which members received 100 leva per decare for rent—half paid in cash and half in kind (usually wheat)—and an average of "a few hundred" leva in dividends. These numbers suggest that it was not the money that attracted villagers to the cooperative—a few hundred leva was not much when bread was nearly 6 leva a loaf at the time.

The expanding membership made it possible for Dawn to acquire significant amounts of machinery when the remaining assets of the old cooperative farm (TKZS) were auctioned in the spring of 1994. The TKZS had purchased all the equipment of the local machine tractor station as well as the building itself from the APK when it disintegrated in 1990. These machines then accounted for a significant portion of TKZS assets to be liquidated. Villagers received verification of their shares in October 1993, with the sale starting in March 1994. Villagers could use their shares to purchase farm property according to set percentages in various categories. For example, if 25 percent of the farm's assets were in livestock, then members could only use 25 percent of their total shares on livestock purchases. This was intended to ensure the complete liquidation of assets. Otherwise, villagers would use all their shares to bid for the most desirable products, such as tractors, driving up the price for these goods and leaving everything else unclaimed. In Zamfirovo the percentages were as follows: livestock, 23 percent; machines, 34 percent; automobiles, 6 percent; buildings, 13 percent; permanent cultures, 16 percent; appliances, 5 percent; and "other," 3 percent. After the number of individual shares was determined, any prior restitutions, such as animals already given over, were deducted. Villagers could sell the remaining shares to others (with the percentage designation intact) or use them to purchase cooperative assets at appraised value. If only one person wanted an asset, it was sold at the appraised value; if two or more wanted the item, it was auctioned to the highest bidder. Anything not purchased in this way could then be offered for cash sale to villagers and outsiders.

If the goal of this disbursement was to get farm equipment and other resources into the hands of private farmers, it was only partially successful. Since contributions of land and equipment were small during collectivization (see Chapter 1) and since most villagers accumulated only a limited number of cooperative labor days in the wake of mechanization, migration, and industrialization, few villagers had enough shares to purchase anything as significant as a tractor. Some were able to buy shares from others or get shares from family members; others got together to combine shares in small groups; and still others solicited shares in exchange for the promise of plowing and sowing services once they got a tractor. In this way approximately twelve tractors, four trucks, and two hay cutters were purchased privately. Most of the buyers, however, did not intend to become private farmers; rather, they bought the tractors in order to service the plots of other villagers for cash. This follows from the rather advantaged position of machine drivers described in Chapter 2. Most of the buyers were skilled drivers who correctly expected the demand for their services to continue. They hoped to continue the previous system as private operators. The remaining bulk of machinery was acquired by the cooperative Dawn. This included two wheat combines, a silage combine, ten tractors, two hay cutters, and about seven trucks and vans.[4] The cooperative Gushantsi got three tractors and one truck. The remaining machines were considered too worn out to merit purchase, but prices were reduced, and several of them sold in the year following the original sale. Dawn acquired two more wheat combines and a jeep.

Dawn also bought several of the useful buildings, including the machine tractor station, one dairy firm, the textile building, and the grain storage facility. Gushantsi bought the building where its drying enterprise operated. Private individuals or groups bought six buildings including the cannery, which was purchased by a family who acquired the shares of several villagers on the promise of payment from an outside investor who had still not materialized in the summer of 1995. The workers in the wool processing plant got together and bought it for themselves, and the chairman of the Liquidation Committee bought one of the buildings in the farmyard. Nobody in the village could afford the feed plant, which was acknowledged to be potentially profitable, and outside inquiries had been discouraged in the hopes of some village interest developing.

The sale of cooperative resources generated more suspicion of the Liquidation Committee. Accusations about what had happened with unclaimed shares were continually broached in 1994. The committee chairman assured me that these shares were still there, waiting to be claimed and used to purchase any remaining cooperative property, but villagers believed they had been used by those connected to the committee or sold for personal profit. Villagers also raised suspicions about the underhanded dealings of those who had purchased equipment privately. The standard complaint was that they had access to the machines prior to

4. The numbers given to me by Dawn and the Liquidation Committee regarding machine purchases did not match, although they did not vary by much. Those given here are averages.

purchase and had stolen essential parts, rendering the machines useless and of limited value in the eyes of the appraisers. They then bought the machines at low prices because no one else could use them. Afterward, they simply replaced the stolen part and started plowing. In short, "Those who bought the tractors are those who stole the parts." This claim was recited so often that I had to remind myself that it was only gossip; no one had any evidence to back up their accusations, although most people found my need for proof humorous. Villagers were also disgusted that some of these felonious acquisitions were sold again for cash to outsiders. As an otherwise strong advocate of private farming described it,

> The idea was that these machines were bought with the labor of villagers and should stay in the village, so outsiders were not allowed to bid. I was in agreement, but then listen to what happened. Villagers bought the equipment with their shares and turned around and sold them to outsiders for cash, making a big profit. Some had purchased shares from other villagers in order to buy the machines, but they got so much money from outsiders that they still made a big profit—sometimes more than twice what they paid. If the TKZS had sold it to the highest bidder that extra money could have gone to the village for its needs. Instead it went into the pockets of those with connections to the liquidators, and the village doesn't have anything to show for it. And if you talk too much about what they did you may end up dead.

The final threat seemed melodramatic to me, although I detected an unusual silence from the other men present.

While all this was going on, the Liquidation Committee (now down to two members) was still carrying on minor farm activity, farming a couple of thousand decares in 1994. The contradictions continued to mount along with the discontent. As the chairman put it, there was no way to win: "I get it from both sides. 'Why aren't you liquidating the farm instead of spending time working the land?' and 'Why are you spending all your time liquidating the farm instead of seeing to the nation's food supply?' The worst part is that both are right."[5] By the fall of 1994 the mounting contradictions and discontent combined with the growing power of the

---

5. The complaints I heard against him in the village all reflected anger over his attention to liquidation at the expense of production, but in towns and other villages I heard the opposite complaint as well (see Kopeva, Mishev, and Howe 1994:215).

cooperative Dawn and the increasing certainty of a socialist victory in the upcoming national elections to produce action. Old village leaders organized a demonstration to oust the liquidators. Villagers occupied the square and prevented the Liquidation Committee and its support staff from entering the town hall. They then convened a village meeting and selected three people to take over the work of the committee. As one of those elected described the event to me, "I've never seen such an occurrence. . . . I was stunned and did not know what to do. I never imagined that something like that could happen here." It was under the tenure of the new committee that Dawn acquired the additional machines previously mentioned.

After the socialists won the December election, national policy followed that taken unofficially in Zamfirovo. Liquidating committees were demobilized, and cooperatives were instructed to hold meetings and select a group to take over the final disposition of the cooperative. When this law came through in 1995, Zamfirovo residents met again and voted to turn over all remaining cooperative farm assets to none other than Dawn. The official transfer occurred in the summer of 1995. Dawn also acquired responsibility for settling claims against the TKZS and for selling off remaining assets, such as the feed plant, to anyone still having shares or to outside investors. Most villagers, including some Dawn members, doubted that anything would leave the new cooperative once it was handed over. As one villager summarized the situation in July 1995, "All this activity and work over the last three years and look, by the end of the month we will be back where we started, only with a lot less resources than before. Who could have imagined such an outcome. Bulgarian work!"

This criticism is perhaps too extreme. In 1995 there were two cooperatives rather than one, providing some choice for villagers and even village competition. While the larger of the two used over 40 percent of the previous cooperative's land, it only employed about 10 percent of the former workforce. So some degree of economic rationalization was evident. Significantly, Dawn was paying small rents and dividends to its members. Still, despite these changes, even cooperative members complained that the new cooperative was operating too much like its state predecessor, especially in areas like preferential machine servicing for relatives and autocratic decision making.

By the beginning of 1997, the parallel with the past was both more and less accurate. Citing poor returns, Gushantsi had ceased its agricultural operations, giving Dawn a cooperative monopoly characteristic of socialism. At the same time, other changes, especially spiraling inflation, made

Dawn less economically viable. The farm could no longer afford the exorbitant costs of fuel, seeds, fertilizer, pesticides, and mechanical replacement parts. Farm members and administrators offered pessimistic prognoses for both the cooperative and agriculture generally. Thus, while the UDF's attempt to eliminate cooperatives actually strengthened them, the BSP's economic inertia, intended in part to sustain socialist economic institutions, eventually undermined the viability of cooperatives. Both strategies backfired.

Cooperative Versus Private Cultivation

The problems of cooperative production did not inspire private alternatives. There are several reasons for this.[6] First, most villagers had small amounts of land and did not see how they could possibly make a living as private farmers. According to village land restitution lists, the average village holding was 27.8 decares, and there were only four families entitled to more than 100 decares—one with 150 decares and the remaining three with around 112. Legal restrictions may have limited the land market, but most families needed a significant portion of their land for subsistence anyway, and they were too insecure about the future to sell the extra. Had they been willing to sell, who could afford to buy it? They were definitely willing to lease it or provide it to sharecroppers, but there were not many takers. The size and dispersion of plots also had negative effects on mechanization. As one villager told me "Why should I get a tractor? I would spend a fortune in gas driving it from one plot to another."

Most villagers lacked the investment resources needed to expand private production. Land might be leased for a share of the product, but money for inputs had to be found up front, and machinery had to be acquired in advance. It was difficult to secure farm loans from new banks because agriculture was such a bad risk. There was a new cooperative branch bank set up in the village in 1993, but, as one villager sarcastically described its tight money policy, "It's only for putting money in, not for taking it out." Even if loans were available, interest rates were exorbitant, and villagers lacked acceptable collateral. After one villager lost his house through a loan default, most decided against putting their house up as

6. See also Dobreva (1994). Many of these factors would apply to other east European countries as well (see Agócs and Agócs 1994, Hann 1993, Kideckel 1995, Singelmann 1995).

collateral. With limited capital, private farmers would still be dependent on the machine services of others. Even if they managed to purchase a tractor, they would still need combine services. Since no individual in Zamfirovo owned a combine, private farmers had to request such services from the cooperative, and unless they knew the combine operator, they were likely to be relegated to the end of the line, with each day's delay posing a new threat to the harvest. In 1995 a village friend threatened to give up his attempt to farm 40 decares privately because he couldn't get the cooperative to harvest his wheat: "I'm private, understand, and they put me off. I have just come from the fields, trying to get them to harvest my wheat without success. These combines were purchased from the labor of all the villagers, not just those that joined the new cooperative. It's not right for them to discriminate, but they have the power. I'm going to sell the tractor and hunt for work in town. Anything would be better than this. It's not worth it, not for 3 leva a kilogram for wheat."

Most village households also lacked the labor needed to expand cultivation, especially given the above mechanical limitations. They could not afford to hire labor for the same reason they could not afford machines, and they soon learned the limits of self-exploitation as well. One man's attempt to cultivate a greenhouse in order to tap the higher vegetable prices of early spring is indicative: "This year I built a small greenhouse and it was profitable. But so much work. Keeping the [wood]stove going all winter in the cold, and then it snowed and the plastic covering fell in under the weight. It was too much work. I originally thought I would start small and expand if it was profitable, but I couldn't do any more. I don't even think I will do that much again, maybe just enough for us to have a little salad on the table early in the season."

The limits of labor became apparent generally, as most villagers took advantage of 1992 amendments allowing temporary usufruct of land prior to restitution. Some added as much as 10 to 15 decares to their existing personal plot that year. As I said, this helped ameliorate early attitudes to decollectivization, but like other aspects of the program it may have backfired when villagers realized that they could not handle the extra work required. Villagers in the summer of 1992 and 1993 were working more than I ever recall, and still they could not get everything done. I was in the town hall in 1992 when a villager came to the Liquidation Committee and said that he could not possibly work all the corn he had paid to have them plow and sow and asked the chairman to let him exchange a few decares for wheat (which did not need so much work). The chairman agreed and told him to just pass the corn acreage on to somebody who could tend it because the Liquidation Committee did not want to worry about it. The limits of labor and technology were compounded by limited experience with large-scale private farming. While villagers could have picked up the requisite knowledge and skills quickly, the limitations described above made it difficult to get a start.

Villagers were especially discouraged from private production by the "price scissors"—the difference between the prices farmers received for their produce and the cost of inputs such as fuel, herbicides, pesticides, and fertilizer. Villagers insisted that there was no profit in growing products for the market and challenged each other about the profitability of their agricultural activities. By 1995 they had also had experience with a couple of years of price fluctuation, so that even profitable activities were seen as insecure and not a basis for expanding production, certainly not if it meant going into debt. In 1994 milk prices were viewed by villagers as quite profitable, reaching nearly 20 leva a liter, but they started falling precipitously in 1995 and seemed to be headed back to 1993 levels of only 4 leva. By the summer of 1995 villagers were complaining that the 7 or 8 leva they got for a liter of milk was hardly more than it cost them to buy a liter of soda, the same complaint I heard in 1993. The idea that what they earned for all the work involved in producing a liter of milk would only buy a liter of soda was unimaginable and unacceptable. Some of the price flux was seasonal, reflecting the much greater supply of milk from the spring through the fall. Prices were likely to increase again during the winter, but then there was less milk to sell, and the prices of products villagers had to buy increased steadily rather than oscillating. Inflation slowed by 1995 but revived with a vengeance in 1996 when fuel and electricity prices skyrocketed. Prices for farm products also increased—milk reached 300 leva a liter in February 1997—but villagers insisted their expenses rose disproportionately. With the price of fertilizer over 200 leva a kilogram, and tractor services costing nearly 3,000 leva a decare, it was easy to believe them.[7]

Villagers also complained about the limited markets for their products. Between socialist purchasing monopolies and the high informal demand generated by a shortage economy, villagers had little experience at seeking out marketing venues before 1989. As a result, they had limited information about potential buyers or markets and no knowledge of how to

7. Prices rose so quickly in early 1997 that it was difficult to make any cost-benefit analysis.

contact them. They remained at the whim of old state purchasers, their monopolistic privatized progeny, or the private purchasers who might come by the village. Some villagers managed to locate alternative customers, but others, especially those without transportation or prior connections through their jobs, had difficulty. One woman's experience with strawberries in 1992 (before they completely dried up) is exemplary.

> We went to harvest and there was no cart to haul them, no crates, and no one to weigh them. A couple of times some people came from Sofia and bought only as much as they could carry in their car at 5.50 leva a kilo. But they were not reliable, you didn't know if they would come or not, and when they saw people had no options they tried to lower the price even more, even though they already get over a 100 percent markup just for driving here to there. Those of us with cars were able to take ours to Vurshets [a neighboring town] to an Austrian firm we heard about. For others it was awful, and strawberries spoil quickly.

By 1995 there was only one company purchasing milk in the village. There had been two the year before, both from the county capital, but one went bankrupt with the decline in the price of milk products, so villagers with cows were left with one place to sell their milk: "For those who have more milk than they can use there is nothing else they can do with it. There is one man with five cows; what's he going to do with all that milk? He has to sell it no matter what the price. And now that the price is lower, they are even slower in paying people for the milk. We haven't been paid now in three weeks."

Several villagers spun their complaints over milk prices into dire predictions about the future of village dairying. As already mentioned, villagers voiced concerns as early as 1993 over the number of cows slaughtered or sold by newly restituted owners. As it turned out, many proprietors actually kept a female calf. They said it would be a better cow and give more milk than one that had spent its life in the cooperative stable. Thus, there were still approximately a hundred cows held privately in the village in 1994, although the number dropped to seventy-five in response to declining milk prices the following year. If this number is added to cooperative holdings, the total number of village cattle amounted to less than one-third of the former TKZS's holdings. Furthermore, some owners were discussing selling their cows because of the work required and the lack of profit.

Many villagers blamed the state for their inability to farm privately. They expected the state to help with the marketing of products, to protect agricultural markets from outside competition, and to directly subsidize production. In the words of a frustrated farmer: "Agriculture is always a losing enterprise. Under socialism, under capitalism, it doesn't matter. There is no profit in farming. That is why the state has to help. Doesn't the United States provide subsidies to farmers? Of course, and it's the same in Europe. Without help from the state you can't have agricultural production." The Bulgarian state, however, was hardly in a position to provide extensive supports.

Given the resulting difficulties villagers faced in private farming, Zhelev's appeal for villagers to form committees to take back the land seems uninformed and simplistic. The problem was not simply property rights and ownership but the structures of the agrarian economy. Under conditions in the 1990s, why should villagers have wanted their land back? In Zamfirovo, many did not—at least not if "back" meant back under private cultivation. They wanted as much land as they could cultivate, and they wanted their rights over the rest officially recognized, but they did not want to have to farm it all. From the very start of decollectivization, over 500 Zamfirovo residents were ready to maintain the cooperative cultivation of their extra land, and by 1994 the vast majority had (re)joined a cooperative.

Of course, some villagers did see private farming as an option. The story of one family reveals some of the factors influencing such a decision. The household consisted of the husband, his wife, his mother, his son, his son's wife, and two grandsons. The son was approximately thirty-five years old. The husband and his wife were both retired at fifty-five. He was able to retire early because he had worked ten years as a miner, and early retirement was part of the incentive package the state used to get people into the mines. The package also included a relatively high pension, over 2,000 leva a month in 1994. The son had lost his job in the village factory, but the daughter-in-law was still employed in the kindergarten and earning about 1,000 leva a month. Everybody was able to work extensively, including the grandmother, who was in excellent health for her seventy-five years. The grandchildren were big enough not to require constant supervision yet still small enough not to be a major expense.

The household had 70 decares of land; 20 decares of it was still in cooperative blocks awaiting reallocation, but they had received usufruct rights to other land in the meantime. In 1994 they were actually using more than 70 decares, having plowed into neighboring lands not being used by absentee owners. In all they had 26 decares of wheat, 16 decares of corn, 8 decares of oats, 2 decares of grapes, 12 decares of alfalfa, 16 decares of meadow, 4 decares of melons, and 3 decares of sunflowers, plus a small vegetable garden. They had one cow and a calf they intended to raise as another dairy cow, two pigs, two horses, five sheep, and a goat. They had purchased a tractor with their farm shares, but it was broken and needed more work than they had expected. In the meantime the husband cultivated the corn with his horse and plow and paid the Liquidation Committee for cultivation of his wheat fields. The daughter-in-law's family also helped out, but the landowners still had to hire Roma to hoe the corn in 1994. They expected to sell the wheat and corn production, and the wife suggested they might grind the wheat into flour and sell it in the Roma quarter of Berkovitza.

The husband was adamantly anticommunist. In his assessment communists only knew how to lie and steal, so they could not think about working like him. This was why more villagers were not interested in private farming—they were lazy and did not want to do the work, so they put their land in cooperatives instead. His own entrepreneurial enthusiasm was partially a product of these political sentiments, but it also reflected the particulars of his household situation. With significant amounts of land, many able-bodied household members, and four sources of cash (three pensions and a salary) the household could afford the required investments of labor and capital. However, by 1995 even he was less evangelical about the private project.

> There was no profit. The opportunities all disappeared when the communists came back to power and even before, when those blues [UDF], or rather reds painted blue, began to show their true colors. I had to pay over 5,000 leva to the cooperative for harvesting my wheat. How can we make a profit with such expenses when they buy our milk at 7.50 leva a kilo? . . . If I was thirty-five I could really work and make a profit, but I can't work like I did. Do you know what money you can make with sunflowers? I've planted 6 hectares, but you lose a lot if you don't have a combine and have to pay for that service.

He also complained that pensions had not kept pace with inflation, so his cash resources seemed to be declining. By 1997 he was in much the same predicament as the cooperative—unable to afford basic inputs. If someone so committed to private farming had lost enthusiasm, the attitude of others is even more understandable.

Several villagers continued to experiment with private commercial farming, but most simply increased subsistence activities, perhaps with an eye toward selling the surplus. With products expensive in stores and villagers short of cash, they opted to produce as many of their own needs as possible. One village woman who still had her job in village administration and lived with an unemployed husband, two teenage children, and her retired in-laws described her family economy in this way:

> Now we don't sell anything. We raise everything to eat and don't buy anything besides what the kids have to have. We used to sell lambs to Rodope, but now we slaughter them all and put everything in jars to feed ourselves. We couldn't afford to eat meat otherwise. The same goes for milk. We have a pig, a goat, five sheep, chicken, ducks, geese, everything. We use it all ourselves. We have to work more now because we no longer get feed for animals like we did when we sold to Rodope, so by consuming all of our produce we have to ensure more feed for the livestock over the winter. We are surviving fine with necessities, but the cash needs worry me. Our son is getting ready to start technical school and we need cash, not just food.

As she makes clear, subsistence production was the predominant factor in the village economy, expanding to replace wages and state supports for the personal sector. This is why there were still cows in the village even when milk production became unprofitable: they were owned primarily by larger families—especially those with children or grandchildren—who needed a lot of milk. Families that could make do with a goat and sheep got rid of their cows when milk prices dropped. Still, there had been almost no cows in the personal sector of the village in 1988 because milk could be purchased cheaply. The same shift explains increasing cultivation of sunflowers. In 1988 when sunflower oil cost 2 leva a liter, no one in the village grew sunflowers; by 1995, with the price closer to 50 leva, plots of sunflowers decorated the countryside. Villagers took the seeds to one of the mills in two neighboring towns and had their own oil pressed; the remains provided good animal feed. In the early 1990s villagers began taking a portion of their wheat to the newly renovated mill to be ground for household consumption, whereas in the 1980s they bought flour and used their wheat primarily for animal feed. As bread prices continued to escalate in 1996, many villagers elected to hand over a portion of their wheat harvest to the village bakery in exchange for coupons entitling them to bread at substantially reduced prices. In essence, this amounted to consuming their own production.

Generally, villagers took over as much land for these subsistence needs as they could manage, perhaps with the idea of selling the extra production. This accounted for larger amounts of wheat acreage than required for most household needs. But given the price scissors and market uncertainties, such endeavors remained wedded to subsistence and informal activities. There was less interest in doing something strictly for the market, and most villagers hesitated to expand production either beyond what they could manage with household labor or into areas that required significant investment. Those who did expand often depended on prior informal connections and resources. For example, villagers with connections to combine drivers were more likely to have larger holdings of wheat. Interestingly, many Zamfirovo residents continued to refer to their subsistence activity and any commercial accompaniment as their "personal economy."

Increased subsistence activity helped maintain the importance of the three-generation household. As a young village postal worker put it, "We have land, but you have to have an appropriate family situation to make use of that land—you need a grandfather and grandmother and young people able to work. My in-laws are both dead, God forgive them. Me and my husband and five-year-old daughter can't do anything. We are lucky to both have jobs right now. But this is also a limitation. We can't buy anything with our salaries because they are low and prices so high, and we spend so much time on the job that we can't grow everything we need to eat—there's not enough time." As previous examples suggested, the market profitability of any private agricultural activity was shaped by similar considerations.

Some villagers expected to be forced into more commercial production by their cash needs, but given limited profits, it is not clear that farming would provide a solution. In such a context, joining the cooperative made sense. Even if rents and dividends were small, they were better than nothing and certainly better than the possibility of *losing* money farming. In addition, the cooperative continued to provide some of the perquisites for its members that were so important under socialism, such as (preferential) machine servicing of private land and in-kind materials from the cooperative. In 1995 Dawn had promised to supply sunflower oil to members at cost, and they were looking into ways to make yogurt from cooperative milk production, which they could sell to members, circumventing the low milk prices paid by dairy firms.

Subsistence and new cooperative cultivation helped maintain agricultural production in Zamfirovo, so despite the dire predictions I heard in 1992, only about 20 percent of the village's arable land was unused in 1994 and 1995. However, it is dangerous to interpret the amount of cultivated land as an indication of support for private production, or for the agrarian transition generally, as several UDF supporters did. For some of the people farming that land, their work was a source of discontent. Two different elderly men on two different days in 1995 gave nearly identical tirades to this effect when I met them coming from the fields. Both had been hoeing corn, and this is how one responded to my casual inquiry into how he was doing:

> I'm tired. You know, one should work less and rest more when you get old, but here in Bulgaria we're mixed up—it's the opposite. I was born in this village, but I worked as a teacher in Berkovitza my whole adult life. I only came here on weekends to raise some fresh vegetables and of course grapes, but I never had to hoe corn! Write this down—under old man Todor [Zhivkov], I never had to hoe corn. Now here I am seventy-three years old, and I've come to the village to hoe corn so we can have something to eat. And not just for an hour or two but all day, for three days. And it may have to be hoed again before the corn is harvested. We're going backwards.

Of course many people *did* hoe corn under Zhivkov. Indeed, nearly all village women and many village men did so regularly. It was his urban residence, his occupation, and his gender that delivered him from the same fate, not Zhivkov or socialism. Still, his diatribe has a broader resonance in that for most able villagers, the amount of farmwork increased dramatically in the 1990s.

There were other steps backward as well. Several households disconnected their hot water heater, and some replaced an electric stove with its wood-burning predecessor. They could no longer afford the rising cost of electricity, and some even considered having it disconnected completely. Actually, such regression reflected the same interactions operative under socialism: subsistence production expanded, but it still articulated with the cooperative farm, and its expansion was driven not only by decollectivization but by developments in other village enterprises as well.

Beyond Agriculture

Agricultural developments in Zamfirovo in the 1990s were clearly connected to other factors of transition, especially inflation and unemployment. With food prices skyrocketing, villagers *had* to produce more of their own consumption needs. Salaries and pensions failed to keep pace, but even those getting minor increases were lucky, since most villagers lost their jobs completely. As previously mentioned, most farmworkers and administrators were laid off as a result of liquidation, and the new cooperative picked up only a few. Since many of the village's nonagricultural enterprises were attached to the farm, they too were threatened by liquidation. The cannery, the forage enterprise, and the pharmaceutical packaging workshop were all closed by the summer of 1992. The spooling workshop was still operating in 1995, although five people had been laid off in the summer of 1993, and the sewing enterprise shut down completely in 1992.

Farm liquidation was not the sole culprit, for unaffiliated enterprises suffered similar fates. The cookie factory was hardly operating in 1992 and continued to decline thereafter. The *bitov kombinat* had managed to survive, albeit with periods of no work. In 1997 it still employed twenty seamstresses and two cutters, plus several men in the metal workshop and one man making plastic lids. The women made clothing for a private merchant in a neighboring town who supplied all the materials and sold the products in her own retail outlet. Managers said it was a constant struggle to find work.

The village factory worked even more erratically. Anyone who could find other work had left. As one former worker characterized it, "They would work for three days and then not work. You never knew when there was going to be work or for how long. It's very hard to live like that." Like workers in other enterprises in the mid-1990s, they often did not even get paid for the work they did. They continued to go to work in the hope that some money would eventually come through and to hold onto their jobs in case the enterprise managed to improve. The same situation characterized many of the urban factories to which villagers commuted. Under such circumstances, several workers simply had to give up their urban jobs when transport costs jumped in 1996–97.

In 1994 a clerk in the village administration told me that few households had more than one salary coming in, and in many a single pension supported five or six people. She estimated that 70 percent of the working-age population was unemployed. "We are all going to be left without work. I'm all for private companies and enterprises, but why can't the state keep its enterprises too, to make sure people have work. No one wants to work the land; how are we going to live?" The Bureau of Labor in Berkovitza reported the number of unemployed villagers at 300 in 1995, but this did not include those who were technically still employed but only working erratically and often not being paid. Clearly, high unemployment contributed to the subsistence expansion described above: at one and the same time it freed up household labor and increased the need to limit cash expenditures. The connection was made clear to me while I was talking with a village friend and another villager passed us on his way to pasture his cow. My friend commented, "I didn't know they had a cow; he must have lost his job." In this context, then, what was Zamfirovo's good fortune under socialism—a diversified economy and sizable working-age population—increased the impact of unemployment and amplified the apparent damage of transition. Young displaced workers were able to move into subsistence production, but as suggested above, this often increased their discontent.

Despite high unemployment, the social relations characteristic of socialist job securities continued to protect some workers. In the village context, market and labor transactions continued to resist complete rationalization. Despite not having enough work to keep his employees working full-time, the manager of the *bitov kombinat* refused to fire a recalcitrant and lazy employee, saying, "it is not comfortable. This is a village and we have to live together." Indeed, it seemed that the manager was more concerned with keeping the workers employed than making a profit. A similar response came from an employee in the village Commerce Cooperative who was explaining to me why their stores could not compete with the new private ones, especially in terms of service: "We have one clerk who, if you go into the store, you would change your mind about buying anything and would never come back. All she does is sit on a chair outside. She may not even come in to wait on you, and if she does, you will wish she hadn't." So why not replace her? His only response was that it was "very hard and complex." The same relations can be expected to influence new firms as well, although perhaps to a lesser degree.

There were new firms and businesses in the village, but they hardly made a dent in the extensive unemployment. In 1992 the nut-drying enterprise of the old cooperative was rented to the doctor who would later become the organizer of the alternative cooperative, Gushantsi. He told me he came into contact with people in Sofia who were involved in the mushroom exporting business and told him how profitable it was. So he decided to try it out in Zamfirovo because he had land there and the area was good for wild mushrooms. He began with 5,000 leva capital (about one month's rent for the dryer), and a few months later his firm was supposedly worth 5 million leva. If this is true, it was extremely profitable. He sold the dry mushrooms in bulk to Italy, where a firm packaged them and sold them to France and the United States. He also sold fresh mushrooms to other countries. Village collectors received about 40 leva per kilo of mushrooms. He also employed nine village women to clean and slice the mushrooms and six men to haul them and to travel around the district buying them. Workers earned between 1,300 to 1,500 leva a month. The owner said it is hard for them to adapt to working for private enterprises where "they only get paid if they work. But they are getting used to it." The women said they were satisfied with their job, one adding that she was "satisfied just to have a job."

As several villagers predicted, the mushroom craze was short-lived. It was so lucrative that villagers overharvested, and few mushrooms survived to the point of reproducing and dispersing spores. So while everybody was collecting mushrooms in 1992, there were hardly any mushrooms to be found in 1993. The firm shifted to the much less lucrative but still profitable drying of wild herbs. In 1994 they found another valuable market in snails, which were exported to Greece. Snails were still around in 1997. Mushrooms returned to the area in 1996, but the firm did not switch back.

The choice of wild products was to circumvent the more restrictive policy of the European Union (EU) on agricultural imports; wild products were easier to sell to member states. Still, the owner complained about the firms he supplied and about competition with old communists. Under socialism all agricultural exports went through the state agency Bulgarplod, which had representatives in importing countries. These connections continued, and it was hard for new operators to get customers. "We are breaking in, little by little, but it's very hard. And the prices we get are so little compared to the final purchase price." He also added that he did not like doing business with Italians, which may explain his decision not to revive mushroom purchasing in 1996. As previously recounted, he expanded his activities into limited agricultural production in late 1993, which eventually formed the core of the short-lived alternative cooperative Gushantsi.

Another villager, having been a purchasing agent for Rodope prior to 1989, started a similar business purchasing animals. He reported making an average living in 1992 and 1993, but less so in 1994. By 1995 he had given up and was looking instead at opening a small store with fast-food service. He blamed the problems on the communist return to power: "The communists are back in charge, and they prevent business. Prices for animals were high and people were selling a lot, but now they are so low that no one will sell. I can't do any business with these prices." He offered no explanation of how the communists were lowering prices, but he was convinced the reductions were a result of communism.

Another businessman from the town of Gabrovo set up a small plant for making cheese in the basement of the *bitov kombinat* in 1993. He wanted to expand a successful business in his hometown by setting up branch plants in order to minimize high transport costs. The shop opened in January 1993 but only operated for four months: they could not find enough local customers and amassed a staggering debt. The electricity and water were particularly costly inputs. Villagers also said the quality was inferior. Whatever the reason, the shop remained unused and the equipment was sold off in 1996. This conclusion convinced a few villagers that the whole enterprise had been a money-laundering scheme all along.

While larger enterprises dwindled, the number of small retail and service establishments grew significantly. Several villagers started neighborhood bottling shops where they made soda from concentrates they purchased. Three new bars, a video rental shop, a mixed goods store, a small clothing store, and an appliance repair shop rounded out the new businesses. One villager's attempt to open a photocopying shop with a small machine she purchased from savings, ended when the machine was stolen. Given high village unemployment and limited cash supplies, business for most of these retailers was not great. The same problem constrained the new village market, which opened in 1991. It took place every Thursday morning at the village square, but the number of vendors was small, averaging no more than ten, and the selection of goods limited. Villagers reported that when the market first started, there had been numerous merchants and a better variety of goods, but it declined quickly, as merchants did little business. "Villagers don't have any money to spend. Even the local kiosks in the village have been shut down because there are no customers." The numerous bars in the village did better; they were sustained by young people who congregated there and had privileged access to the limited cash supplies of their families. The village mill was also doing well, due to the increase in subsistence activity. A Sofia-based company had renovated the mill in the early 1990s as a joint venture with the village. However, it was then restituted to a group of heirs, none of whom lived in Zamfirovo, and one of whom was the reigning Minister of Agriculture. Villagers commented sarcastically on the rapidity with which the minister's property was restituted compared to theirs.

Other job prospects were very limited. One villager went to pick peaches in Greece, but he said the necessary visas were difficult to get, and he failed to repeat the sojourn. Two villagers I knew went to work each summer as roofers in the Danubian town of Lom. Similar jobs were reportedly available in Sofia, but there was extensive bankruptcy and scam artistry in the construction business. Firms took cash deposits from buyers, started construction as a pretense to get more, and then disappeared with all the money, never paying the workers. This made several villagers hesitant about taking just any construction job. As one construction worker put it, "Bulgaria is a mess; nothing is certain."

Unemployment also affected urbanites, and this increased the dependencies between rural and urban family members. Jobless urbanites relied even more heavily on village relatives for basic consumption needs than they did in the past, further increasing the subsistence activities of villagers. Thus, some common aspects of capitalism—unemployment and inflation—ironically enhanced the importance of informal kinship exchanges driven previously by socialist shortages. This increase, however, generated more conflict and rural-urban tension, as some villagers felt increasingly exploited.

If economic difficulty increased the informal flow of goods, it also dovetailed with the general collapse of state authority and the advent of liquidation to expand another area of informal activity—theft. Villagers saw theft in every transaction, especially those involving cooperative property. It was not always present, of course; some villagers accused of stealing actually paid the Liquidation Committee for the goods they took, or had the value deducted from their shares. But this possibility only increased the amount of real theft by providing a cover: village thieves could tell their neighbors or other curious individuals that they had bought stolen goods legitimately. As a worker for the committee discreetly described the situation, "Those who ask for the things we are liquidating pay for them; those that don't ask, don't have to pay." Even when goods were purchased, villagers assumed buyers paid more than receipts stated, with the difference going into the pockets of the person who sold it.

The evidence of theft was all around. The destruction of buildings and machinery previously described seemed too violent and destructive to have been a legal or controlled procedure, so the ruins bespoke theft as well as destruction. A man who had been his neighborhood shepherd for a day in the summer of 1992 said it was scandalous the way people came to the fields to steal the farm's hay and straw: "The fields were full of people just stealing all they could pick up in midday without any concern. I have never seen such theft." Another villager, however, offered a different interpretation: "We don't have theft in Bulgaria; it's called privatization." Accusations of theft often followed political alliances: socialists accused the Liquidation Committee and its supporters of stealing, while the latter defined theft as a strictly communist specialization. One man joked that the acronym of the Bulgarian Communist Party, BKP, actually stood for *Bez Krazhba Propadnesh* (without theft you collapse): "They learned to lie and steal under the old system and now they cannot *not* do it."

The only new informal activity that developed in the village during the transition was also the most lucrative—black market commerce with Serbia. The village is not far from the Serbian border, so the United Nations embargo was an economic boom for villagers willing to violate it. Although no one admitted to it, villagers unanimously agreed that "others" were involved. The traffic included basic goods, such as wine and food, but the greatest profit came from fuel. The commerce transpired along isolated border regions in the nearby mountains and across official border points. In some cases guards had to be bribed, but by all reports that was easy enough. Villagers insisted that millions of leva had been made by village operators, and, indeed, an acquaintance in another village admitted making 400 German marks a day running fuel.

With economic possibilities beyond the black market and subsistence farming limited, many villagers were looking to get out of the village. The migration restrictions described in Chapter 3 were removed after 1989, but village administrators insisted that the rate of village out-migration had not increased; rather, the constraints had shifted from legal to economic ones. There were not many attractive jobs in towns, and the cost of living there, especially rent, was prohibitive. The value of city real estate led many urbanites to rent out extra rooms, and this foreclosed the possibility for villagers to move in with urban connections. One village family I knew well left the village in 1994 after the father got a job with a construction firm. The husband, wife, and two teenage children were living in a small dormitory room hardly big enough for their four beds and one table. Such stories deterred many would-be migrants. Most villagers were also hesitant to leave their agricultural subsistence production, which provided their only security. In fact, the above family left the grandmother in the village to tend to the subsistence plot, and the father returned to do the communal pasturing of sheep and other chores on weekends. So the ability to maintain connections to the village continued to be a factor in out-migration, just as it had under socialism.

A reverse flow of migration back to the villages was one of the projected benefits of land restitution, but it still had not materialized in 1997, even in the wake of near hyperinflation. Most urbanites did not need to come back, since they acquired farm produce from rural relatives. Villagers kept asking me sarcastically where all the urbanites were that were supposed to work the restituted land. As already noted, a few did return, but they hardly evoked admiration. Villagers either assumed some scandalous event had forced them to leave town or questioned their motives for returning. For example, several villagers complained about returnees who came back to buy up resources in the farm auction: "They ran away from here after the 9th. They haven't done any of the work; they went to towns and had light work instead. Now they come back and say they have a right to buy because they were born here. They are not villagers. You are more of a villager than these people. But they will get a share because the people in charge and the liquidators are from town, and they want to defend the rights of townsfolk for their own benefit." Urbanites were in a no-win situation: staying away, they confirmed villagers' insistence that they were too lazy and well-heeled to work the land; coming back, they provoked the rage of villagers who resented their claims on village property. This double bind itself may help explain why urbanites were not more interested in taking up farming on restituted land, but ultimately the same reasons villagers hesitated to adopt private farming explain urban disinterest as well.

The importance of agriculture was a product of socialist conflicting complementarity, but it was maintained by the transition. Economic crises, especially unemployment and inflation, increased the importance of subsistence production. As we saw in Chapter 2, the subsistence economy was thoroughly enmeshed in the cooperative farm system, so increasing subsistence needs actually enhanced allegiance to cooperative farming. Under such conditions, the attack on the farm by antisocialists inspired rural support for the Socialist Party (Creed 1995b). The socialist government responded by supporting cooperatives politically, but its economic policies (or the lack thereof) eventually undermined cooperative production. It is ironic that decollectivization drove many villagers to the Socialist Party when, as was mentioned in Chapter 2, the Communist Party may have been on the verge of beginning its own decollectivization reforms in 1988. This outcome then underlines the importance of the timing of transition in relation to prior reform programs. Had it occurred after more radical decollectivizing reforms by the Communist Party, or for that matter, before the beneficial effects of domestication, the political conclusions drawn by villagers during the early transition might have been quite different. But such interpretations are never permanent anyway, and the events of 1996–97 have already provoked new ones.

CONCLUSION

By 1994 many villagers had understandably become cynical about the transition, including many of those who had supported the UDF. One middle-aged man was so disenchanted as to accuse the UDF of being part of a communist conspiracy. In his scenario, recounted with conviction and strongly seconded by his wife, the communists saw the writing on the wall in 1989 and realized that single-party rule could not be sustained. So they constructed the UDF as a front to play the role of an opposition. This accounts for why many members of the UDF had communist backgrounds. The communists still controlled everything, but the UDF did the dirty work, taking the blame for the problems created by the transition and thereby enhancing the popularity of the communists. In this conspiratorial view, all politicians were communists, much like before, and as he put it, "They haven't learned anything new or forgotten anything old." During the two ensuing years of reckless Socialist Party stewardship, many village socialists became equally disheartened. In 1997 I heard numerous calls for the violent elimination of all politicians, who, as one such commentator put it, "are all the same, all scoundrels, and all working together to fill their own pockets."

Nevertheless, I see many of Bulgaria's political and economic problems in the 1990s as a result of the bipolar opposition between socialist and antisocialist forces, not their collusion. There are several reasons for this, all of which have been central to this analysis. Socialism was an interconnected system, bound together through a proliferation of conflicting and complementary interdependencies. It was defined in opposition to the rest of the world and, indeed, much of the rest of history. Even as it evolved in directions more similar to capitalism, the reform mechanism kept changes within a socialist paradigm. Because of its intense integration, the socialist system collapsed quickly, sealing it historically and reinforcing its identity as a system. These characteristics make the Bulgarian past seem discontinuous, self-contained, and immediate, ensuring that reflections on change or development in the postcommunist era evoke a before-and-after distinction. In Zamfirovo I was commonly asked to participate in such exercises: "You were here before. Now you see what it's like. Which is better?" My attempts to point out positive *and* negative changes were often recast by my audience as validating either socialist or postcommunist life, depending on which changes they thought were more important. Such discourse helps maintain binary political divisions and opposition. In other words, the debate about the present reproduces the divisions of the past.

The details of such discussions, however, also point the way out of this dilemma. Listening to why many villagers think life was better before provides suggestions for ameliorating the present without necessarily reproducing the past. Such possibilities are missed, however, when village opinions are read simply as support for particular parties or policies defined along old binary lines of socialism versus capitalism. One of the important contributions of ethnography in such a case is to bring these concerns to the fore and to disassociate them from rigid political categories. If we can do this, then elements of socialist experience can be tapped to inform and constrain capitalist practice in the postcommunist era. The difficulty, however, is to transcend the limitations of the capitalist-communist dichotomy without threatening our appreciation of socialism as a distinctive social system.

In this chapter I conclude my effort to achieve this goal by focusing on two issues that became primary concerns for villagers in the mid-1990s: their identity as something other than peasants and their commitment to equality. In both cases I characterize the situation under socialism and then demonstrate how concerns around these issues influenced village attitudes toward transition. Both concerns are connected to the agrarian issues at the heart of this analysis. Both factors were also ideologically associated with socialism and became important dimensions of its domestication, but they are not necessarily synonymous with socialism. When separated in this way, they can be treated as rural concerns that need to be addressed in the transition, not simply as socialist legacies to be over-come.

Equality

No potential change disturbed villagers more than the specter of inequal-ity. This quintessentially capitalistic characteristic threatened to radically alter an enduring aspect of village life that predated socialism by many years. In fact, more than a century ago Englishman Edward Dicey (1894:7) published an account of his trip to Bulgaria in which he maintained that

> Bulgaria, as at present constituted approaches as closely as is con-sistent with the imperfection of all human institutions to the ideal state of our latter-day social reformers, in which there are to be no poor and no rich, in which every citizen is to have a share, and to a considerable extent an equal share, in the land of the common-wealth, in which there are to be no privileged classes and no social distinctions, and in which the people, who in the case of Bulgaria are the peasants, are to govern themselves by themselves and for themselves.

Obviously, the essential caveat here is "as closely as is consistent with the imperfection of all human institutions," for Bulgaria was never a classless Utopia. Nearly every village had its *chorbadjii* (rich peasants) up until the socialist period, and then there were the Roma, who were usually landless and always discriminated against. Still, as Table 13 illustrates, the degree of differentiation in Bulgaria throughout and immediately after the inter-war era was fairly limited.[1] As Dicey suggests, and Chapter 1 supports, most Bulgarians were smallholders. Table 13 also suggests that demo-graphic trends discussed in Chapter 3 actually tended to decrease differ-entiation during the interwar period.

Even though most villages had a few rich families, this distinction must be seen as a relative one. It often meant ownership of as little as 10 hec-

1. Furthermore, as Rothschild (1974:330–31) notes, "most of the smallest holdings of less than one hectare were either vineyards and gardens cultivated by persons for whom agricul-ture was a secondary occupation, or intensive tobacco farms. Hence, they are not evidence of agricultural pauperism."

Table 13. Land Distribution in Bulgaria, 1926–46

	Percentage of Holdings		
Hectares	1926	1934	1946
0–1	11.9	13.5	14.9
1–5	45.1	49.6	53.7
5–10	28.0	26.2	24.5
10–20	12.6	9.2	6.2
20–30	1.8	1.1	0.6
30+	0.6	0.4	0.1

SOURCE: Rothschild 1974:330.

tares, and in Zamfirovo, for example, there was no one with more than 15. More important, land wealth did not always translate into significant differences in lifestyle. The larger holders may have hired workers, but Zamfirovo residents questioned the value of this advantage.

> They had more land, but that just meant more work. When it came time for me to think about marriage, I tell you, I hunted for a husband with *less* land because I did not want all that work. What was the point? If you had more land you could hire workers, but nobody around here was rich enough to hire all their labor; they had to work as much as they could and hire the rest. They had a little more money, and maybe they could afford a few things others could not buy, but for me it was not worth it. I found the perfect husband; he had a lot of land, but most of it was forest, which didn't need any work at all. Then when they collectivized I got a job sewing, thank God.

This account mirrors statements reported by Kouzhouharova, Meurs, and Stoyanova (n.d.) from a woman in the village of Olorsk: "They [the rich] worked very much too, but unlike us, they worked their own land"; and from a woman in Momino: "The rich had more land . . . but I don't think they were living better than us." The situation produced and reflected an ethos of egalitarianism that was never significantly challenged by capitalist forces and that may have been sustained by Orthodox Christianity (see Schneider 1990).

This ethos was transformed into state ideology during the socialist period. Both the ideology of communism and the policies of the socialist

state reinforced villagers' commitment to equality, and this in turn provided greater legitimacy for the Communist Party. When I was in the field
in 1987–88, "we are all equal" was one of the most commonly cited characteristic of village life. Even critics of the system sarcastically acknowledged its equality, saying, "We are poor, but we are all equally poor."

Of course, the political power and economic circumstances of every
villager were not identical, even under socialism. Still, in the 1980s it was
difficult to actually assess the overall differences. As the preceding chapters make clear, there were simply too many factors to consider. The official occupations of household members and their salaries or pensions
were just the beginning. Discretionary labor resources and the whole profile of informal resources at a household's disposal were equally—if not
more—determinant and, unfortunately, more analytically elusive. A conversation involving myself, a retired skilled craftsman who worked part-
time for the cooperative farm, and a young truck driver for the farm made
this point nicely. The truck driver pointed to the retiree and commented,
"People like him, they work very little—only a couple hours a day. The
rest of the time they stay at home, and they get bigger salaries than I do
for working all day." To which the older man retorted, "True, you are on
the job all day, but most of the time you are doing your own personal
work and using the farm's truck to haul fertilizer, hay, and everything
else." The driver smiled and did not refute the characterization. Such
resources also had to be gauged against the requirements of the household. Having more labor in a three-generation household did not necessarily mean a higher standard of living if much more labor had to be
expended to maintain it. Finally, there was the general difficulty of eval-
uating economic differentials in a context where cash was often of less
value than important personal connections and where there were limits
imposed on material consumption by an economy of shortage.

Everything was further complicated by changes over time. Household
possibilities were affected by the domestic cycle. More important, the context in which these factors operated and which ultimately defined their
utility also changed. The primary process in this regard was political and
economic reform. Clearly, agricultural reforms enhanced the utility of the
three-generation household. At the same time, other reforms eroded the
value of political clout in the village and increased the utility of informal
relations, restricting the privileges of the political elite. This is a local
example of the evolution Böröcz (1989) suggests for eastern Europe as a
whole. Böröcz cogently points out how the political transitions from a

"plan-command system" in the 1950s to the "plan-bargain economy" of the reform era transformed the class structure, creating multiple class positions and a degree of flexibility. All these contingencies make a class analysis of the village population in 1987 less than useful. Instead, the situation calls to mind the Swiss alpine community described by McGuire and Netting (1982), where numerous factors maintained community equality.

The focus of class analysis should not be simply difference but rather the differences that make a difference. In other words, focusing on class is a way to see how differential access to power and resources significantly shapes people's lives. In the village of Zamfirovo in the 1980s such political and economic inequality was not a major factor shaping villagers' lives. Most villagers had more money than they could spend on the limited goods available. Even the political power of local communist leaders, so important to socialist states, had diminished as a result of reforms and conflicting complementarity, which forced accommodations at every turn. As noted throughout this book, villagers ignored dictates from local leaders, including the Communist Party secretary, leading old-timers to actually comment on the limited power these officials had as compared to the past (see Chapter 2). This was exemplified by the replacement of the village party secretary in 1988 with a very young man of little experience—the position no longer carried its past power. Thus, if we use Böröcz's (1989:305) concept of "control over the labor of others" as a central criterion of class, most Zamfirovo residents end up in the same boat. To find significant differentiation, we would have to look at the villagers as a group, compared to the upper echelons of the party/state apparatus—a worthy project, but one beyond the parameters of this analysis.

There were a few exceptions to village equality. Several Roma families lived in quite squalid conditions in the "Gypsy Quarter" of the village (although other village Roma lived in conditions similar to the average Bulgarian).[2] Less impoverished but still significantly disadvantaged were elderly villagers with no family or informal connections. As declining health diminished their subsistence cultivation, these individuals were forced to live solely on their pensions, and their situation could become quite desperate. It became even more so in the transition, as the purchasing power of their pensions dropped precipitously. At the other extreme

2. For information on the plight of Bulgarian Roma, see Helsinki Watch (1991) and Silverman (1996).

of the continuum were village political leaders who had, through past political positions, established connections of continuing economic value to the village; such connections sustained their privileged position even after their political power over the village population dwindled. Since these individuals often used their influence to promote relatives, maintaining control across generations, they were commonly referred to by villagers as "the mafia." Actually, this group included various factions that at times cooperated and at other times competed for leadership positions. Villagers complained that "the mafia" did not have to work hard because they all had cushy jobs and could tap so many resources through theft, but in other ways their lifestyle was not greatly different from the average villager's. Furthermore, while the value of their connections did not totally disappear with the decline in local political authority, it did dissipate. The best illustration came from an argument I witnessed between two women in 1988. One was the wife of a retired village leader who had retained a part-time position in village administration. She had asked her neighbor for a favor, which the neighbor politely refused. This provoked a critical comment and the neighbor lost her patience: "You cannot expect people to fulfill your every request just because you are married to Dimitur. Things are different now. You have to get used to it." Still, Dimitur's wife continued to get some favors from villagers working directly under her husband. Certainly, part of his declining influence had to do with his age and partial retirement, but it also reflected the general decline in official political power.

The deterioration of political authority opened up a space for informal networks to exert more influence. While the importance of informal capital might, therefore, have provided a potential basis for differentiation, it failed to do so because nearly everyone was involved in informal relations. Furthermore, villagers resisted being involved in one-sided affairs reminiscent of patron-client relations. Connections had to be mutually beneficial to both parties and equally so. One informant explained his hesitation to ask a relative for assistance by saying, "We are embarrassed to ask him. He has already done a lot for us and there is nothing we can do for him. So we will not ask him for anything else." The same sentiment further explains some of the ambivalent attitudes toward theft described in Chapter 5. Theft was sometimes ignored until it reached the point of creating significant inequality, whereupon criticism and censure were brought to bear.

The commitment to equality was also a dominant theme in villagers' criticisms of perestroika. Several surmised it was going to lead to wealth differentials that, as one informant put it, "we are not supposed to have in our system." He phrased the same critique in terms of personal possibilities, saying he could not benefit from the reforms because his household was low on labor—the implication being that others should not benefit either (Creed 1991:56). Walliman and Stojanov (1989:365) make a similar observation about the self-management reforms in industry described in Chapter 4. Given the responsibility to disperse their own wage fund, "most brigades continue[d] to adhere to the norm of equality and to close ranks against the disciplining of individuals." Reforms dependent on such differentiation were not successful.

Given this commitment to equality, we can see why many villagers did not greet the potential transition to capitalism, a system of notorious inequality, with open arms. In 1992, some villagers clearly saw the transition as a referendum on equality. When I asked one woman worker in the cooperative farm for her opinion of the changes, I got a defense of equality instead: "Why do we have to have rich and poor? Why? Why can't everybody have a little bit? What's wrong with that? That mother-fucking Gorbachev is to blame for this mess." Other villagers were visibly tormented by emerging inequality: "I can't face the idea of telling my kid that he cannot have something when other children have it. We are used to everybody being the same and having the same things. I simply can't tell him that we are too poor. It doesn't make sense. These are the same friends he played with before as equals." Such complaints clearly indicate the beginnings of differentiation. Indeed, most villagers reported that things had improved for a number of villagers during the transition, but as one informant working in the town hall phrased it, "They are a handful, that's all. For everybody else it's worse than before. Is this democracy, for life to get worse for 99 percent so 1 percent can do better?"[3]

The commitment to equality was not universal; some villagers actually derided it as old-fashioned. In any case, the concept of equality in the village should not be equated with asceticism. Many villagers were acquisitive, and some seemed to have a good dose of bourgeois materialism. Indeed, it was the prospect of actualizing this desire that made the transition potentially appealing to many in 1989. From a situation in which money was usually not the limiting factor, the bountiful market of capital-

---

3. The conceptual linking of democracy and economic equality was common in the village after 1989.

ism appeared truly utopian. The concomitant arrival of inflation and unemployment, however, negated this interpretation. Thus, in 1995 when I
asked villagers whether it was better to have goods in the stores and not
be able to afford them or better not to have them at all, most villagers
thought for a while and concluded it was better not to have them around
at all. Under socialism, materialism was restrained in ways that allowed it
to coexist with a commitment to equality. Consumption was obviously constrained by the economy of shortage, which had an especially severe impact on consumer goods. Even for goods that were available, concerns of
practicality often limited consumption. For example, even though modern houses provided a degree of status, no one went through the difficulty
and expense of extensive home improvement unless they had a son they
expected or hoped would bring his wife to live there. As late as 1995 there
was still no evident conspicuous consumption by villagers who were pur-
portedly doing better in the transition. Indeed, in the early transition, as
in the socialist system, evident inequality was likely to invoke accusations
of corruption or to be attributed to personal connections rather than
individual ability. In such a context, some of the status benefits of capitalist consumption were absent, or even reversed.

The impact of these considerations was intensified by the village context. One villager said he was not going to improve his house because it
seemed inappropriate when neighbors were having such difficulties. One
elderly villager allowed for some inequality, but thought it should be limited. "Let there be private economy, and competition. I am in agreement.
But there's no reason why there should be such a big difference between
higher and lower. Some difference, of course, but not a gigantic difference. We have to live together." Villagers were individualistic in many
ways, but they were still keenly aware of where they stood vis-à-vis each
other. Such concerns were less evident in bigger, more anonymous cities,
where economic differentiation exploded in the early 1990s and conspicuous consumption, especially of automobiles, flourished.

Perhaps inspired by urban successes, some of the capitalist reformers of
the 1990s targeted the cultural value of equality as a major handicap to
capitalist development. However, they confused cause and effect, or they
attempted to find a one-way relationship where a more dialectical one
prevailed. Whatever the origins of ideas about equality, they were sustained and reinforced by socialist practice, the complexity of which I have
tried to relate in this book. Only by providing villagers with viable economic alternatives can the commitment to equality be altered. This does

not mean simply introducing differentiation with a few beneficiaries but creating a system in which all villagers see possibilities for economic improvement. While the postcommunist system succeeded in destroying many aspects of the socialist system, it was slow to provide *viable* replacements for the masses, at least any that could outlive the Serbian embargo. A small class of the newly rich could be found in many villages by the mid-1990s—making differentiation increasingly central to village life and an important focus of future research. Whether it becomes a motivation for villagers to pursue new possibilities or a basis of resistance depends on the degree of opportunity in a larger political and economic context.

Like so much else being attributed to the collapse of communism, the attack on equality was actually under way for some time in communist Bulgaria. It was evident in the reforms I have discussed for both agriculture and industry, and it became blatant with the advent of restructuring. On October 12, 1987, the Communist Party newspaper, *Rabotnichesko delo,* ran a front-page article entitled "The Worker Salary: Restructuring Excludes Leveling." The economist who wrote the article stated that the reorganization of production would have to exclude wage leveling and encourage greater financial differentials between workers. The fact that this appeared in the party newspaper shows that the party had already given up the ideal of equality and was jockeying to maintain power in the unstable period of the "second socialist revolution" (Zaslavskaya 1990). However, the intensive attack on equality associated with perestroika was too brief to shape the perception of socialism, and the differentiating potential of earlier reforms was limited by systemic constraints and local practice. For antisocialists and evangelical capitalists these failures underlined the necessity of more assertive and uncompromising measures to break through the commitment to equality.

Given its role in the reception of transition, equality may provide the basis for a more comparative analysis of politics throughout eastern Europe, with varying degrees of differentiation before and during socialism accounting for differences in postsocialist political sentiments. This is not the place to pursue such a comparison, but on the most superficial level it would certainly distinguish Bulgaria from Hungary, Poland, and Romania, where there was significant rural class stratification in the interwar period. It would also distinguish socialist Bulgaria from the economic differentiation facilitated by reform under Hungarian socialism (Szelényi 1988, Lampland 1995) and the increasing rural class stratification promoted by private agriculture in socialist Poland (Nagengast 1991). Aware of such regional differences, Zamfirovo residents often invoked equality as part of their national identity.

Rural Identities

Clearly the concern over inequality had more than economic motives. Besides its connection with nationality, classlessness interacted with kinship, gender, residence, political sentiment, occupation, and perhaps other concerns to shape the very identities of Zamfirovo residents. To fully understand village actions in the 1990s, we must appreciate how the transition affected these other elements of identity as well. Such an analysis would require another book, and I doubt by this point that many readers are willing to grant me that indulgence. So I will focus here only on residence and occupation. During the years of socialism, one's employment became increasingly pivotal to individual identity. This also occurred in capitalist countries, but the motivation was different. Under socialism occupation became central to identity not because it defined one's primary contribution to the economy or one's class position but because it reflected one's connection to the state. As the socialist state took over more and more dimensions of society, social identities increasingly revolved around one's relationship to the state. For a few this meant their role as dissidents; for many more it highlighted their Communist Party membership; but for most it focused attention on their occupation as state employees.

So while socialism in Bulgaria maintained the importance of agriculture in all the ways discussed heretofore, it ironically displaced agriculture from the identities of villagers. The expansion of nonagricultural occupations and the distinction between professional (cooperative) and subsistence (personal) farming distanced villagers from the increasingly demeaning association with agriculture *as an occupation.* Few villagers in the late 1980s, especially those of working age, considered themselves farmers; their identities were linked instead to their nonagricultural jobs in small enterprises or village administration, bringing them closer to the proletarian ideal of communism. Those working for cooperative farms saw themselves as "tractor drivers" or "combine operators" rather than as farmers or peasants. This brought villagers squarely into the modern project, while agriculture itself was increasingly cast as a retrograde activity.

Even older folks who had been "peasants" all their lives suddenly became "pensioners," like other state retirees.

Everyone in a village, however, remained undeniably a "villager," which constantly threatened their claim to modernity. This is reflected linguistically, in that the common translation of the English word "peasant" is *selyanin,* from the word *selo,* which means "village." This cultural association made it difficult to dissociate increasingly pejorative connotations of "peasant" from the mere fact of village residence (and thus makes the term *selyanin* inherently ambiguous in contemporary Bulgarian). Here, however, the cooperative farm provided salvation: the dominant agrarian activity of a village was carried out by the cooperative farm, freeing villagers to develop identities not centrally focused on farming. They could maintain their important (and often inescapable) village identity without its negative agrarian connotations. At the same time, their personal agricultural activities allowed them to stay in nonfarming occupations where their salaries alone would have been inadequate. In this way, subsistence agriculture merely supplemented their identities, just as it subsidized household, cooperative, village, and national economies. What it meant to be a villager shifted.

Urbanites who had never lived in a village or who had left it before alternate identities began to emerge hardly recognized these nuances. This made it difficult for them to appreciate the potential meaning of decollectivization for rural residents. With the elimination of cooperative farms and the restitution of land to former owners, the cultural and physical burdens of agriculture would no longer be borne by an institution but by individual households. Furthermore, without cooperatives there would be no mechanism to ensure owners access to mechanical assistance, nor could they be assured of affording necessary supplies, such as chemical fertilizers (see Meurs and Spreeuw, n.d.). Besides, since owners were expecting only small amounts of land, any economy of scale seemed unlikely. In such a context, decollectivization seemed to be forcing them back into arduous small-scale manual labor—a process many villagers saw as repeasantization. Moreover, these reconstituted peasants could not expect to reclaim their interwar status. The parallel agricultural disengagement of both socialist and capitalist development ensured that "peasant" remained a negative category in the transition. Thus, the private farmer's claim in Chapter 6 that villagers supported cooperatives because they did not want to work was accurate with one important qualification—they did not want to do *peasant* work.

Simultaneously, many of the nonagricultural enterprises in villages and neighboring towns were closing or slowing down, making the transition from worker to peasant seem all the more inevitable. This concern, which some had traced to socialist reforms during the 1980s (see Chapter 4), seemed more likely to develop from antisocialist policies by the 1990s. Villagers were losing their nonagricultural occupations and having to do more subsistence farming, both for themselves and for their unemployed urban relatives. Given that the additional work tended to be small-scale and manual, the transition seemed to be returning the entire village (maybe all of rural Bulgaria) to a premodern condition. This was most evident in the increased number of villagers plowing with a donkey in the spring of 1997—a procedure considered comically primitive back in 1987. So while the occupational bases of nonagricultural identities disintegrated, the cultural value of their identity as villagers was also threatened. Hence, the combination of economic trends, their social consequences, and the cultural interpretation of both not only fueled rural antagonism toward the urban framers of decollectivization but also prompted resistance to transition in general, increasing support for the Socialist Party. Ironically, this increased favor put the Socialist Party in the position of directing the transition after the 1994 elections, a job that eroded the very basis of their support.

The transition threatened villagers' sense of self in other ways as well. It moved Bulgaria into the global arena, where villagers felt they were disadvantaged. Whether from 500 years under the Turkish yoke or 40 years under Soviet hegemony, villagers were skeptical of their ability to adapt or compete in the capitalist world. A villager returning from his first trip to the West in 1995 explained it this way: "How can we ever be part of Europe. I've been to Vienna and I tell you when you get back to Romania, Serbia, and Bulgaria, you are in a different world. We are so far behind. We are all just aborigines here." A similar sentiment was often conveyed with the term "wild": "We are wild. What can you do with such a wild tribe?"[4] The negative consequences were captured in a favorite proverb repeated by villagers as the capstone to any criticism of the country: "A simple people [make] a weak state." As an outsider, by contrast, I was impressed with the resourcefulness and stamina of Bulgarian villagers and credit them with domesticating socialism. Of course, they also recognized

4. This provides an interesting counterpoint to the rhetoric of transition based on "civil society."

their talents and often countered assertions of inferiority with strong national pride. Still, being thrown from the socialist bloc into the larger global arena was disconcerting, especially when they envisioned entering the new world order as reconstituted peasants. Identification with the village and place of residence remained, but the possibility of class differentiation seemed to threaten this basis of community as well. Of course, family identities were less threatened, but for many this continuity only highlighted the decline of alternatives. Clearly, these threats to modern village identities complement political and economic factors in explaining why the villagers of Zamfirovo were hesitant to give up the cooperative farm and why they came to view the transition with ambivalence.

Domesticating Transition?

Zamfirovo residents are not innately conservative. Many welcomed the prospect of change in 1989 as long overdue. But they wanted change that took their concerns and desires seriously, that responded to their cultural and economic interests. For many villagers this was the very promise of democracy—to institutionalize and formalize, and thereby expand, what had previously been informal local influence. That some of their concerns were connected to the socialist system, such as their commitment to equality and cooperativism, should not surprise anyone having read the preceding chapters. Villagers not only managed to adjust to socialism but also adjusted socialism to their own requirements and needs. The resulting articulation between the Bulgarian state and Zamfirovo households provided a degree of self-actualization for villagers missed in macro-level views of socialist society. Agriculture was central to these arrangements not simply because of the rural milieu but because its importance to the totalizing state made it a powerful tool for villagers (re)working the socialist system. Villagers were able to use this tool to their maximum advantage even while removing themselves from negative agrarian identifications—a truly ingenious achievement.

Villagers had also survived the worst of communist authoritarianism and curtailed the power of the party, so that by 1988 the Communist Party was more annoying than frightening, at least for villagers. Sure, they felt the constraints of the system, but having significantly domesticated it through everyday practice over four decades, they were hesitant to trade it in for a new, perhaps less tractable, replacement. By the late 1980s the reform dynamic and local practice in a context of conflicting complementarity had tamed Bulgarian socialism to the point that it was bearable, if still far from ideal. Unfortunately, such domestication also increased the contradictions between ideology and practice and diminished the system's capacity to drive economic development, rendering it more vulnerable on several fronts.[5] Thus, in a horrible twist of fate, as socialism became more tolerable, it became less viable.[6] This, of course, verifies the earlier lessons of reform from Hungary and Poland in 1956 and from Czechoslovakia in 1968, but it does so in a different manner. The Bulgarian example shows how quotidian local practice in a context of conflicting complementarity transformed the system without grand designs or radical agendas. The results rendered the system susceptible to spectacular attacks from more aggrieved opponents and political opportunists, although not from the village artisans of domestication themselves, many of whom did not want the revolutionary outcome they helped make possible.

When the interests of villagers are treated generically as communist legacies, they are dissociated from the people who hold them and piled onto a discredited symbol that can be easily dismissed by politicians. The resulting failure of transition leaders to consider or address rural concerns reminded villagers of the early years of socialism, which they recalled so negatively. This, in turn, provoked anxiety about the future and led them to embrace domesticated socialism as a means of defense against would-be capitalist excesses. According to most villagers I knew, this resistance was not intended to resuscitate either single-party rule or central planning. Instead, by mobilizing around arrangements that were important to improving their life under socialism, such as the symbiotic relationship between personal and cooperative farms, villagers hoped to defend these arrangements and prevent the transition from re-creating past difficulties. They appealed to socialism and the Socialist Party to exercise influence over the anticipated development of capitalism—in other words, they attempted to use socialism to domesticate capitalism. Socialist governments, however, failed to protect villagers from economic crises, provoking widespread cynicism. Still, this political shift does not neces-

5. For a discussion of the importance of internal contradictions in provoking the transition, see Staniszkis (1991:2–4).

6. The Romania case suggests that socialism also became less viable as it got *less* tolerable. If processes of socialist amelioration and deterioration intersect in the collapse of communism, they still set their constituent societies on different trajectories of transition.

sarily indicate an abandonment of the socialist practices and ideas described here: it may merely reflect village uncertainty about how to maintain them. The economic hardships of 1996–97 made villagers more ambivalent about the transition than ever. Consequently, some became even more convinced of the superiority of past arrangements, but they had lost faith in the ability of the Socialist Party to sustain or revive them. These nuances are missed by those who never recognized the domestication of socialism and who retain mutually exclusive views of communism and capitalism. A real transition hinges on overcoming this opposition through ethnographic appreciations and expositions of local interests in their historical contexts.

Socialism created a distinctive historical context, the complexity of which I have tried to capture for a single Bulgarian village. The social relations of socialism, the systemic interdependencies of the economy, and the cultural identities developed over forty years cannot be erased as easily as Marxist-Leninist political philosophy or party institutions. This context is the one in which transition proceeds; there is no other place to start, and there are no other materials to use. As Millar and Wolchik (1994:28) put it, "there is no such thing as a clean slate." Certainly, the past always influences the present, but by generating such intense integration within the state, so intricately balanced through conflicting complementarity, and so ideologically and historically distinctive, socialism produced an extremely robust history. This in turn made the transition more difficult than anyone expected. In Bulgaria by the mid-1990s there was still no clear destination in sight. As one villager expressed it in 1995, "We have no system in Bulgaria, no capitalism, and no socialism. We are without a system." His complaint captures the ambiguity of the transition, but the cause might just as easily be attributed to the presence of *both* systems—a robust socialist past interacting with an unforgiving global capitalism. If so, some hybridity may result by default, whether recognized as such or not. To refuse this possibility is to deny the everyday power of Bulgarian villagers—a conclusion the previous pages render imprudent.

Bibliography

Documents

All cited archival materials are held in what was the Mihailovgrad County Archives (now Montana County Archives), stock numbers 374, 177, 819, 60K, 180, 462K, and 71K. Other village and farm documents were held in the Zamfirovo town hall, although some of them may eventually be forwarded to the archives. Some statistical data came from the Mihailovgrad (Montana) Central Statistical Bureau.

Books and Articles

Achagu, Guchips M.
  1985   "Ukrepvane na ikonomicheskoto sustoyanie na TKZS v planinskite i po-luplaninskite rayoni na Bulgariya v kraya na 50-te i prez 60-te godini," *Istoricheski pregled* 41:44–56.
Agócs, Peter, and Sándor Agócs
  1994   "'The Change Was but an Unfulfilled Promise': Agriculture and the Rural Population in Post-Communist Hungary," *East European Politics and Societies* 8:32–57.
Arendt, Hannah
  1966   *The Origins of Totalitarianism*. New York: Harcourt, Brace and World.
Atanasov, Atanas
  1990   "Trudovo-kooperativnite zemedelski stopanstva v Bulgariya (1958–1960g.)," *Istoricheski pregled* 46:41–54.
Bates, Daniel G.
  1994   "What's in a Name? Minorities, Identity, and Politics in Bulgaria," *Identities* 1:201–25.
  1995   "Uneasy Accommodation: Ethnicity and Politics in Rural Bulgaria," in David A. Kideckel, ed., *East European Communities: The Struggle for Balance in Turbulent Times*. Boulder, CO: Westview Press, 137–57.
Baylis, Thomas A.
  1971   "Economic Reform as Ideology: East Germany's New Economic Mechanism," *Comparative Politics* 3:211–29.

Beck, Sam
  1976   "The Emergence of the Peasant-Worker in a Transylvanian Mountain
          Community," *Dialectical Anthropology* 1:365–75.
Begg, Robert, and Mieke Meurs
  n.d.   "Writing a New Song: State Policy and Path Dependence in Bulgarian
          Agriculture." Unpublished manuscript.
Bell, John D.
  1977   *Peasants in Power: Alexander Stamboliski and the Bulgarian Agrarian Na-
          tional Union, 1899–1923.* Princeton: Princeton University Press.
Bell, Peter D.
  1984   *Peasants in Socialist Transition: Life in a Collectivized Hungarian Village.*
          Berkeley and Los Angeles: University of California Press.
Berent, Jerzy
  1970   "Causes of Fertility Decline in Eastern Europe and the Soviet Union,"
          Population Studies 24:35–58; 247–92.
Bićanić, Ivo
  1990   "Unofficial Economic Activities in Yugoslavia," in Maria Łoś, ed., *The
          Second Economy in Marxist States.* New York: St. Martin's Press, 85–100.
Billaut, Micheline
  1988   "Le mouvement coopératif en Bulgarie," *Revue des Etudes Slaves* 60:481–
          91.
Böröcz, József
  1989   "Mapping the Class Structures of State Socialism in East-Central Eu-
          rope," *Research in Social Stratification and Mobility* 8:279–309.
Boyd, Michael L.
  1990   "Organizational Reform and Agricultural Performance: The Case of
          Bulgarian Agriculture, 1960–1985," *Journal of Comparative Economics*
          14:70–87.
Brisby, Liliana
  1960   "Bulgaria's Economic Leap Year," *World Today* 16:35–46.
Brown, J. F.
  1970   *Bulgaria Under Communist Rule.* New York: Praeger.
Buchanan, Donna A.
  1991   "The Bulgarian Folk Orchestra: Cultural Performance, Symbol, and the
          Construction of National Identity in Socialist Bulgaria." Ph.D. disserta-
          tion, University of Texas, Austin.
  1995   "Metaphors of Power, Metaphors of Truth: The Politics of Music Profes-
          sionalism in Bulgarian Folk Orchestras," *Ethnomusicology* 39:381–416.
  1996   "Wedding Musicians, Political Transition, and National Consciousness
          in Bulgaria," in Mark Slobin, ed., *Retuning Culture: Musical Changes in
          Central and Eastern Europe.* Durham, NC: Duke University Press, 200–
          230.
Burawoy, Michael
  1985   *The Politics of Production.* London: Verso.
Burawoy, Michael, and János Lukács
  1992   *The Radiant Past: Ideology and Reality in Hungary's Road to Capitalism.* Chi-
          cago: University of Chicago Press.

Burks, R. V.
1973   "The Political Implications of Economic Reform," in Morris Bornstein,
        ed., *Plan and Market: Economic Reform in Eastern Europe*. New Haven: Yale
        University Press, 373–402.
Byrd, William A., and Ling Quingsong, eds.
1990   *China's Rural Industry: Structure, Development and Reform*. Oxford: Oxford
        University Press.
Cassel, Dieter, and Ulrich Cichy
1987   "The Shadow Economy and Economic Policy in East and West," in Ser-
        gio Alessandrini and Bruno Dallago, eds., *The Unofficial Economy: Conse-
        quences and Perspectives in Different Economic Systems*. Brookfield, VT:
        Gower, 127–46.
Castells, Manuel, and Alejandro Portes
1989   "World Underneath: The Origins, Dynamics, and Effects of the Infor-
        mal Economy," in Alejandro Portes, Manuel Castells, and Lauren A.
        Benton, eds., *The Informal Economy: Studies in Advanced and Less Developed
        Countries*. Baltimore: Johns Hopkins University Press, 11–37.
Cernea, Michael
1978   "Macrosocial Change, Feminization of Agriculture and Peasant Women's
        Threefold Economic Role," *Sociologia Ruralis* 18:107–24.
Chan, Anita, Richard Madsen, and Jonathan Unger
1984   *Chen Village: The Recent History of a Peasant Community in Mao's China*.
        Berkeley and Los Angeles: University of California Press.
Cole, John
1981   "Family, Farm, and Factory: Rural Workers in Contemporary Romania,"
        in Daniel N. Nelson, ed., *Romania in the 1980s*. Boulder, CO: Westview
        Press, 71–116.
Comisso, Ellen
1991   "Property Rights, Liberalism, and the Transition from 'Actually Exist-
        ing' Socialism," *East European Politics and Societies* 5:162–88.
Cousens, S. H.
1967   "Changes in Bulgarian Agriculture," *Geography* 52:12–22.
Crampton, Richard J.
1981   "Bulgarian Society in the Early 19th Century," in Richard Clogg, ed.,
        Balkan Society in the Age of Greek Independence. London: Macmillan, 157–
        204.
1987   *A Short History of Modern Bulgaria*. Cambridge: Cambridge University
        Press.
1988   "'Stumbling and Dusting Off,' or an Attempt to Pick a Path Through
        the Thicket of Bulgaria's New Economic Mechanism," *Eastern European
        Politics and Societies* 2:333–95.
Creed, Gerald W.
1990   "The Bases of Bulgaria's Ethnic Policies," *Anthropology of East Europe Re-
        view* 9:12–17.
1991   "Between Economy and Ideology: Local Level Perspectives on Politi-
        cal and Economic Reform in Bulgaria," *Socialism and Democracy* 13:45–
        65.

1993   "Rural-Urban Oppositions in the Bulgarian Political Transition," *Südosteuropa* 42:369–82.
1995a   "Agriculture and the Domestication of Industry in Rural Bulgaria," *American Ethnologist* 22:528–48.
1995b   "The Politics of Agriculture: Identity and Socialist Sentiment in Bulgaria," *Slavic Review* 54:843–68.
Danilov, Viktor
1989   "The Issue of Alternatives and History of the Collectivisation of Soviet Agriculture," *Journal of Historical Sociology* 2:1–13.
Davies, Robert
1979   "Informal Sector or Subordinate Mode of Production?: A Model," in Ray Bromley and Chris Gerry, eds., *Casual Work and Poverty in Third World Cities.* New York: John Wiley and Sons, 87–104.
Dicey, Edward
1894   *The Peasant State: An Account of Bulgaria in 1894.* London: John Murray.
Dobreva, Stanka
1994   "The Family Farm in Bulgaria: Traditions and Changes," *Sociologia Ruralis* 34:340–53.
Dobrin, Bogoslav
1973   *Bulgarian Economic Development Since World War II.* New York: Praeger.
Douglass, William
1975   *Echalar and Murelaga: Opportunity and Rural Exodus in Two Spanish Basque Villages.* New York: St. Martin's Press.
Dunn, Stephen P., and Ethel Dunn
1988   *The Peasants of Central Russia.* Prospect Heights, IL: Waveland Press. (Reprint of 1967 edition.)
Entwistle, E. W.
1972   "Agrarian-Industrial Complexes in Bulgaria," *Geography* 57:246–48.
Erlich, Alexander
1960   *The Soviet Industrialization Debate, 1924–1928.* Cambridge: Harvard University Press.
Feiwel, George R.
1977   *Growth and Reforms in Centrally Planned Economies: The Lessons of the Bulgarian Experience.* New York: Praeger.
1979   "Economic Reform in Bulgaria," *Osteuropa-Wirtschaft* 24:71–91.
1982   "Economic Development and Planning in Bulgaria in the 1970s," in Alec Nove, Hans-Hermann Höhmann, and Gertraud Seidenstecher, eds., *The East European Economies in the 1970s.* London: Butterworths, 215–52.
Fél, Edit, and Tamás Hofer
1969   *Proper Peasants: Traditional Life in a Hungarian Village.* Chicago: Aldine.
Friedl, Ernestine
1963   "Some Aspects of Dowry and Inheritance in Boeotia," in Julian Pitt-Rivers, ed., *Mediterranean Countrymen.* Paris: Mouton, 113–37.
Friedrich, Carl J., and Zbigniew K. Brzezinski
1956   *Totalitarian Dictatorship and Autocracy.* Cambridge: Harvard University Press.

Frydman, Roman, Andrzej Rapaczynski, John S. Earle, et al.
1993   *The Privatization Process in Central Europe.* London: Central European University Press.

Gabor, I. R.
1979   "The Second (Secondary) Economy," *Acta Oeconomica* 22:291–311.

Gergov, Georgi
1984   *Teritorialna struktura na selskoto stopanstvo v Bulgariya.* Sofia: Nauka i Izkustvo.

Giurova, Svoboda
1989   "Trudnosti i greshki pri masovoto kooperirane na selyanite v Plevenski okrug," *Istoricheski pregled* 45:56–67.

Gleick, James
1987   *Chaos: Making a New Science.* New York: Penguin.

Grant, Bruce
1995   *In the Soviet House of Culture: A Century of Perestroikas.* Princeton: Princeton University Press.

Greenwood, Davydd
1976   "The Demise of Agriculture in Fuenterrabia," in J. Aceves and W. Douglass, eds., *The Changing Faces of Rural Spain.* New York: Schenkman, 29–44.

Grossiaux, Jean-François
1987   "Prix de la fiancée et dot dans les villages Yougoslaves," in Georges Ravis-Giordani, ed., *Femmes et patrimoine dans les sociétés rurales de l'Europe Méditerranéenne.* Paris: Editions du Centre National de la Recherche Scientifique, 291–305.

Grossman, Gregory
1982   "The Second Economy of the USSR," in V. Tanzi, ed., *The Underground Economy in the United States and Abroad.* Lexington, MA: Lexington Books, 245–69.
1989   "Informal Personal Incomes and Outlays of the Soviet Urban Population," in Alejandro Portes, Manuel Castells, and Lauren A. Benton, eds., *The Informal Economy: Studies in Advanced and Less Developed Countries.* Baltimore: The Johns Hopkins University Press, 150–70.

Grozev, Vulko
1981   "Major Transformations in Agriculture," in Georgi Bokov, ed., *Modern Bulgaria: History, Policy, Economy, Culture.* Sofia: Sofia Press, 283–98.

Habermas, Jürgen
1986   "The New Obscurity: The Crisis of the Welfare State and the Exhaustion of Utopian Energies" (trans. Phillip Jacobs), *Philosophy and Social Criticism* 2:1–18.

Hajnal, John
1965   "European Marriage Patterns in Perspective," in D. V. Glass and D. E. C. Eversley, eds., *Population in History: Essays in Historical Demography.* Chicago: Aldine, 101–43.

Halperin, Rhoda H.
1990   *The Livelihood of Kin: Making Ends Meet "The Kentucky Way."* Austin: University of Texas Press.

Halpern, J. M., and R. A. Wagner
  1984   "Time and Social Structure: A Yugoslav Case Study," *Journal of Family History* 9:229–44.
Hammel, Eugene A.
  1968   *Alternative Social Structures and Ritual Relations in the Balkans.* Englewood Cliffs, NJ: Prentice-Hall.
Hann, C. M.
  1985   *A Village Without Solidarity: Polish Peasants in Years of Crisis.* New Haven: Yale University Press.
  1993   "From Production to Property: De-collectivisation and the Family-Land Relationships in Contemporary Hungary," *Man* 28:299–319.
Haraszti, Miklos
  1978   *A Worker in a Worker's State.* New York: Universe Books.
Havel, Václav
  1985   "The Power of the Powerless," in John Keane, ed., *The Power of the Powerless: Citizens against the State in Central-Eastern Europe.* Armonk, NY: M.E. Sharpe, 23–96.
Helsinki Watch
  1991   *Destroying Ethnic Identity: The Gypsies of Bulgaria.* New York: Helsinki Watch.
Hirszowicz, Maria
  1980   *The Bureaucratic Leviathan: A Study in the Sociology of Communism.* New York: New York University Press.
Ho, Samuel P. S.
  1979   "Decentralized Industrialization and Rural Development: Evidence from Taiwan," *Economic Development and Cultural Change* 28:77–96.
Hockenos, Paul
  1990   "Can Hungary's Left Resurrect Itself in the Midst of a Conservative Revolution?" *In These Times* 14 (7):11.
Höhmann, Hans-Hermann
  1982   "Economic Reform in the 1970s—Policy with No Alternative," in Alec Nove, Hans-Hermann Höhmann, and Gertraud Seidenstecher, eds., *The East European Economies in the 1970s.* London: Butterworths, 1–16.
Holmes, Douglas
  1989   *Cultural Disenchantments: Worker Peasantries in Northeast Italy.* Princeton: Princeton University Press.
Hristov, V.
  1941   "Gorskoto stopanstvo na Bulgariya," *Stopanski problemi* 6 (4–5):156–64.
Humphrey, Caroline
  1983   *Karl Marx Collective: Economy, Society and Religion in a Siberian Collective Farm.* Cambridge: Cambridge University Press.
  1991   "'Icebergs,' Barter, and the Mafia in Provincial Russia," *Anthropology Today* 7 (2):8–13.
Ivanov, Kostadin
  1972   "Some Problems of Formation and Distribution of Income in the

Agroindustrial Complexes," *East European Economics* 11:64–79. (Reprint of 1971 edition.)

Ivanova, Radost
1984   *Bulgarskata folklorna svatba.* Sofia: Bulgarska Akademiya na Naukite.

Jackson, Marvin R.
1988   *Bulgaria's Attempt at "Radical Reform." Berichte des Bundesinstituts für ost-wissenschaftliche und internationale Studien,* no. 2. Cologne: Bundesinstituts für ostwissenschaftliche und internationale Studien.

Jelavich, Barbara
1983   *History of the Balkans.* Vol. I, *18th and 19th Centuries.* Cambridge: Cambridge University Press.

Johnson, Paul
1989   *Redesigning the Communist Economy: The Politics of Economic Reform in Eastern Europe.* Boulder, CO: East European Monographs (distributed by Columbia University Press, New York).

Jones, B. D., and Dimiter A. Jankoff
1957   "Agriculture," in L. A. D. Dellin, ed., *Bulgaria.* New York: Praeger, 287–312.

Kaneff, Deema
1992   "Social Constructions of the Past and Their Significance in the Bulgarian Socialist State." Ph.D. dissertation, University of Adelaide.
1995   "Developing Rural Bulgaria," *Cambridge Anthropology* 18 (2):23–34.
1996   "Responses to 'Democratic' Land Reforms in a Bulgarian Village," in Ray Abrahams, ed., *After Socialism: Land Reform and Social Change in Eastern Europe.* Providence, RI: Berghahn Books, 85–114.

Karcz, Jerzy F.
1973   "Agricultural Reform in Eastern Europe," in Morris Bornstein, ed., *Plan and Market: Economic Reform in Eastern Europe.* New Haven: Yale University Press, 207–43.

Kearney, M.
1995   "The Local and the Global: The Anthropology of Globalization and Transnationalism," *Annual Review of Anthropology* 24:547–65.

Keliyan, Maya
1991   "Selskostopanskata kooperatsiya," *Sotsiologicheski pregled* 1991 (4):1–9.

Kenedi, János
1982   *Do it Yourself: Hungary's Hidden Economy.* London: Pluto Press.

Kertesi, Gábor, and György Sziráczki
1985   "Worker Behaviour in the Labour Market," in Peter Galasi and György Sziráczki, eds., *Labour Market and Second Economy in Hungary.* Frankfurt: Campus Verlag, 216–45.

Kideckel, David A.
1979   "Agricultural Cooperativism and Social Process in a Romanian Commune." Ph.D. dissertation, University of Massachusetts, Amherst.
1982   "The Socialist Transformation of Agriculture in a Romanian Commune, 1945–1962," *American Ethnologist* 9:320–40.

1993   *The Solitude of Collectivism: Romanian Villagers to the Revolution and Beyond.*
        Ithaca: Cornell University Press.
1995   "Two Incidents on the Plains in Southern Transylvania: Pitfalls of Priva-
        tization in a Romanian Community," in David A. Kideckel, ed., *East
        European Communities: The Struggle for Balance in Turbulent Times.* Boulder,
        CO: Westview Press, 47–63.
Kligman, Gail
1988   *The Wedding of the Dead: Ritual, Poetics, and Popular Culture in Transyl-
        vania.* Berkeley and Los Angeles: University of California Press.
1992   "The Politics of Reproduction in Ceauşescu's Romania: A Case Study in
        Political Culture," *East European Politics and Societies* 6:364–418.
n.d.   *The Politics of Duplicity: Women's Bodies and the State in Ceauşescu's Ro-
        mania.* Berkeley and Los Angeles: University of California Press. Forth-
        coming.
Kolev, Aleksandur, and Ivan Olovanski
1977   *Razvitie na kooperativnata sobstvenost v selskoto stopanstvo na NRB prez etapa
        na izgrazhdane na razvito sotsialistichesko obshtestvo.* Sofia: Zemizdat.
Konrád, George, and Ivan Szelényi
1976   "Social Conflicts of Under-Urbanization," in Mark G. Field, ed., *Social
        Consequences of Modernization in Communist Societies.* Baltimore: Johns
        Hopkins University Press, 162–78.
Kopeva, Diana, Plamen Mishev, and Keith Howe
1994   "Land Reform and Liquidation of Collective Farm Assets in Bulgarian
        Agriculture: Progress and Prospects," *Communist Economies and Economic
        Transformation* 6:203–17.
Korbonski, Andrzej
1975   "Political Aspects of Economic Reforms in Eastern Europe," in Zbigniew
        M. Fallenbuchl, ed., *Economic Development in the Soviet Union and Eastern
        Europe.* New York: Praeger, 8–30.
1989   "The Politics of Economic Reforms in Eastern Europe: The Last Thirty
        Years," *Soviet Studies* 41:1–19.
Kornai, János
1980   *Economics of Shortage.* Amsterdam: North-Holland Publishing.
Kouzhouharova, Veska, Mieke Meurs, and Rositsa Stoyanova
n.d.   "From Cooperative Village to Agro-Industrial Complex: The Rise and
        Fall of Bulgarian Collective Agriculture." Unpublished manuscript.
Krumov, Ventsislav
1986   "Nyakoi konfliktni momenti pri brigadnata organizatsiya na truda ot
        nov tip," *Sotsiologicheski pregled* 7:1–10.
Kyuranov, Chavdar
1987   "Generalization and Conclusion," in Chavdar Kyuranov, ed., *Dneshnoto
        Bulgarsko semeistvo.* Sofia: Nauka i Izkustvo, 407–23.
Laird, Roy D., and Betty A. Laird
1988   "The Zveno and Collective Contracts: The End of Soviet Collectiviza-
        tion?" in Josef C. Brada and Karl-Eugen Wädekin, eds., *Socialist Agricul-*

ture in Transition: Organizational Response to Failing Performance. Boulder, CO: Westview Press, 34–44.

Laky, T.
1980   "The Hidden Mechanisms of Recentralization in Hungary," *Acta Oeconomica* 24:95–109.

Lampe, John R.
1986   *The Bulgarian Economy in the Twentieth Century*. New York: St Martin's Press.

Lampe, John R., and Marvin R. Jackson
1982   *Balkan Economic History, 1550–1950: From Imperial Borderlands to Developing Nations*. Bloomington: Indiana University Press.

Lampland, Martha
1995   *The Object of Labor: Commodification in Socialist Hungary*. Chicago: University of Chicago Press.

Langazov, Dosiu
1984   *Malkoto Bulgarsko selo*. Sofia: Partizdat.

Lewin, Moshe
1988   *The Gorbachev Phenomenon: A Historical Interpretation*. Berkeley and Los Angeles: University of California Press.

Lomnitz, Larissa Adler
1988   "Informal Exchange Networks in Formal Systems: A Theoretical Model," *American Anthropologist* 90:42–55.

Łoś, Maria
1990   "Dynamic Relationships of the First and Second Economies in Old and New Marxist States," in Maria Łoś, ed., *The Second Economy in Marxist States*. New York: St. Martin's Press, 193–230.

Lowenthal, Richard
1970   "Development vs. Utopia in Communist Policy," in Chalmers Johnson, ed., *Change in Communist Systems*. Stanford: Stanford University Press, 33–116.

Ludzhev, Dimitur
1989   "Preustroystvoto na kooperativnoto dvizhenie v Bulgariya (9 Septemvri 1944 g.—nachaloto na 50-te godini)," *Istoricheski pregled* 45:3–16.

Marcus, George E.
1995   "Ethnography in/of the World System: The Emergence of Multi-sited Ethnography," *Annual Review of Anthropology* 24:95–117.

Marinov, Hristo Todorov
1985   *Pasporti, adresna registratsiya, zhitelstvo: sbornik ot zakoni, ukazi, pravilnitsi, naredi instruktsii i drugi*. Sofia: Nauka i Izkustvo.

Markov, Georgi
1984   *The Truth That Killed* (trans. Liliana Brisby). New York: Ticknor and Fields.

McGuire, Randall, and Robert McC. Netting
1982   "Leveling Peasants?: The Maintenance of Equality in a Swiss Alpine Community," *American Ethnologist* 9:269–90.

McIntyre, Robert J.
1975   "Pronatalist Programmes in Eastern Europe," *Soviet Studies* 27:366–80.
1980   "The Bulgarian Anomaly: Demographic Transition and Current Fertility," *Southeastern Europe* 7:147–70.
1988a   *Bulgaria: Politics, Economics and Society.* London: Pinter Publishers.
1988b   "The Small Enterprise and Agricultural Initiatives in Bulgaria: Institutional Invention Without Reform," *Soviet Studies* 40:602–15.
1989   "Economic Change in Eastern Europe: Other Paths to Socialist Construction," *Science and Society* 53:5–28.
Meurs, Mieke, and Darren Spreeuw
n.d.   "Rational Peasants in Eastern Europe: Household Decisions About Organizational Form During the Agarian Transition," in Derek Jones and Jeffrey Miller, eds., *The Bulgarian Economy: Lessons from Reform During Early Transition.* Forthcoming.
Migev, Vladimir
1990   "Tendentzii v razvitieto na TKZS i na politikata na durzhavata spryamo tyah (1951–1953g.)," *Istoricheski pregled* 46:5–17.
Mihailov, Il.
1941   "Nashite obshtinski gora," *Bulgarsko stopanstov* 3 (10–11):131–33.
Millar, James R., and Sharon L. Wolchik
1994   "Introduction: The Social Legacies and the Aftermath of Communism," in James R. Millar and Sharon L. Wolchik, eds., *The Social Legacy of Communism.* New York: Woodrow Wilson Center Press and Cambridge University Press, 1–28.
Mitchell, Katharyne
1992   "Work Authority in Industry: The Happy Demise of the Ideal Type," *Comparative Studies in Society and History* 34:679–94.
Mitsuda, Hisayoski, and Konstantin Pashev
1995   "Environmentalism as Ends or Means? The Rise and Political Crisis of the Environmental Movement in Bulgaria," *Capitalism, Nature, Socialism* 6:87–111.
Molloff, J. S.
1933   "Bulgarian Agriculture," in O. S. Morgan, ed., *Agricultural Systems of Middle Europe.* New York: Macmillan, 41–85.
Mosely, Philip E.
1940   "The Peasant Family: The Zadruga or Communal Joint Family in the Balkans and its Recent Evolution," in Caroline Ware, ed., *The Cultural Approach to History.* New York: Columbia University Press, 95–108.
Moser, Caroline
1978   "Informal Sector or Petty Commodity Production: Dualism or Dependency in Urban Development?" *World Development* 6:1041–64.
Moskoff, William
1978   "Sex Discrimination, Commuting and the Role of Women in Rumanian Development," *Slavic Review* 37:440–56.
Mouzelis, Nicos
1976   "Greek and Bulgarian Peasants: Aspects of Their Sociopolitical Situa-

tion During the Interwar Period," *Comparative Studies in Society and History* 18:85–105.

Nagengast, Carole
1991   *Reluctant Socialists, Rural Entrepreneurs: Class, Culture, and the Polish State.* Boulder, CO: Westview Press.

New York Times
1/12/84 "Drugs Dulling Golden Youth in Yugoslavia," by David Binder, p. A7.

Nichols, John
1974   *The Milagro Beanfield War.* New York: Holt, Rinehart, and Winston.

Nolan, Peter
1976   "Collectivization in China: Some Comparisons with the USSR," *Journal of Peasant Studies* 3:192–220.

Ofer, Gur
1977   "Economizing on Urbanization in Socialist Countries: Historical Necessity or Socialist Strategy," in Alan Brown and Egon Neuberger, eds., *Internal Migration: A Comparative Perspective.* New York: Academic Press, 277–303.
1980   "Growth Strategy, Specialization in Agriculture and Trade: Bulgaria and Eastern Europe," in Paul Marer and John Michael Montias, eds., *East European Integration and East-West Trade.* Bloomington: Indiana University Press, 283–313.

Oren, Nissan
1971   *Bulgarian Communism: The Road to Power, 1934–1944.* New York: Columbia University Press.
1973   *Revolution Administered: Agrarianism and Communism in Bulgaria.* Baltimore: Johns Hopkins University Press.

Pasvolsky, Leo
1930   *Bulgaria's Economic Position.* Washington, DC: The Brookings Institution.

Petkov, Krastyu
1985   *Sotsiologiia na truda,* Vol. 1. Sofia: Profizdat.
1987   "General and Specific Features in the Transition to Self-Management," in Krastyu Petkov, ed., *The Transition to Self-Management in the Socialist Countries.* Sofia: Georgi Dimitrov Research Institute for Trade Union Studies, 8–25.

Petrov, Goran
1940   *Selo Smolyanovtsi, Ferdinandsko: polozhenie duh i problemi.* Ferdinand: Nauka.

Pitassio, Armando
1989   "Reform Politics in Bulgaria," *Telos* 79:204–16.

Potter, Sulamith Heins, and Jack M. Potter
1990   *China's Peasants: The Anthropology of a Revolution.* Cambridge: Cambridge University Press.

Pryor, Frederic L.
1992   *The Red and the Green: The Rise and Fall of Collectivized Agriculture in Marxist Regimes.* Princeton: Princeton University Press.

Rabotnichesko delo
10/12/87 "Rabotnata zaplata: preustroystvoto izkliuchva uravnilovka," by Todor Dudov, pp. 1, 3.

Rev, Istvan
  1987   "The Advantages of Being Atomized: How Hungarian Peasants Coped
          with Collectivization," *Dissent* 34:335–50.
Roberts, Bryan
  1976   "The Provincial Urban System and the Process of Dependency," in A.
          Portes and H. Browning, eds., *Current Perspectives in Latin American Re-
          search*. Austin: University of Texas Institute of Latin American Studies,
          99–131.
  1989   "Employment Structure, Life Cycle, and Life Chances: Formal and In-
          formal Sectors in Guadalajara," in Alejandro Portes, Manuel Castells,
          and Lauren A. Benton, eds., *The Informal Economy: Studies in Advanced
          and Less Developed Countries*. Baltimore, MD: Johns Hopkins University
          Press, 41–59.
Roth, Klaus
  1989   "On Folk and Popular Literature in Post-Liberation Bulgaria," *The An-
          thropology of East Europe Review* 8:20–21.
Rothschild, Joseph
  1959   *The Communist Party of Bulgaria: Origins and Development, 1883–1936*.
          New York: Columbia University Press.
  1974   *East Central Europe Between the Two World Wars*. Seattle: University of
          Washington Press.
Ruble, Blair A.
  1991   "Stepping off the Treadmill of Failed Reforms?" in Harley D. Balzer, ed.,
          Five Years That Shook the World: Gorbachev's Unfinished Revolution. Boulder,
          CO: Westview Press, 13–29.
Rupp, Kalman
  1983   *Entrepreneurs in Red: Structure and Organization Innovation in the Centrally
          Planned Economy*. Albany: State University of New York Press.
Ruskova, Liulyana
  1987   *Vzaimootnosheniya selo-grad: sotsialni i prostranstveni problemi*. Sofia: Bulgar-
          ska Akademiya na Naukite.
Sabel, Charles F., and David Stark
  1982   "Planning, Politics, and Shop-Floor Power," *Politics and Society* 11:439–75.
Salzmann, Zdenek, and Vladimir Scheufler
  1986   *Komárov: A Czech Farming Village*. Prospect Heights, IL: Waveland Press.
          (Reprint of 1974 edition.)
Sampson, Steven L.
  1983   "Rich Families and Poor Collectives: An Anthropological Approach to
          Romania's 'Second Economy,'" *Bidrag til öststatsforskning* 11:44–77.
  1987   "The Second Economy of the Soviet Union and Eastern Europe," *The
          Annals of the American Academy of Political and Social Science* 493:120–36.
Sanders, Irwin T.
  1949   *Balkan Village*. Lexington: University of Kentucky Press.
Sanjek, Roger
  1982   "The Organization of Households in Adabraka: Toward a Wider Per-
          spective," *Comparative Studies in Society and History* 24:57–103.

Schneider, Jane
   1980   "Trousseau as Treasure: Some Contradictions of Late Nineteenth Cen-
          tury Change in Sicily," in Eric Ross, ed., *Beyond the Myths of Culture*. New
          York: Academic Press, 81–119.
   1990   "Spirits and the Spirit of Capitalism," in Ellen Badone, ed., *Religious
          Orthodoxy and Popular Faith in European Society*. Princeton: Princeton Uni-
          versity Press, 24–54.
Schroeder, Gertrude E.
   1982   "Soviet Economic 'Reform' Decrees: More Steps on the Treadmill," in
          U.S. Congress, Joint Economic Committee, *Soviet Economy in the 1980s:
          Problems and Prospects*, vol. 1. Washington, DC: U.S. Government Print-
          ing Office, 65–88.
   1991   "The Soviet Economy on a Treadmill of Perestroika: Gorbachev's First
          Five Years," in Harley D. Balzer, ed., *Five Years that Shook the World: Gor-
          bachev's Unfinished Revolution*. Boulder, CO: Westview Press, 31–48.
Schwartz, M., R. Bar-El, R. Finkel, and A. Nesher
   1986   *Moshav-Based Industry in Israel*. Working Paper Series of the Settlement
          Study Centre, Rehovot, Israel, no. 16. Jerusalem: Ahva Coop Printing
          Press.
Scott, James C.
   1985   *Weapons of the Weak: Everyday Forms of Peasant Resistance*. New Haven: Yale
          University Press.
Shanin, Teodor
   1971   "Cooperation and Collectivization: The Case of Eastern Europe," in Pe-
          ter Worsley, ed., *Two Blades of Grass*. Manchester: Manchester University
          Press, 263–74.
Sigurdson, Jon
   1977   *Rural Industrialization in China*. Cambridge: Harvard University Press.
Sik, Endre
   1988   "Reciprocal Exchange of Labour in Hungary," in R. E. Pahl, ed., *On
          Work: Historical, Comparative and Theoretical Approaches*. Oxford: Basil
          Blackwell, 527–47.
Silverman, Carol
   1983   "The Politics of Folklore in Bulgaria," *Anthropological Quarterly*, 56:55–
          61.
   1984   "Pomaks," in Richard Weeks, ed., *Muslim Peoples: A World Ethnographic
          Survey*, vol. 2, 2d ed. Westport, CT: Greenwood Press, 612–16.
   1996   "State, Market, and Gender Relationships Among Bulgarian Roma,
          1970–90," *Anthropology of East Europe Review* 14:4–15.
   n.d.   "The Contemporary Bulgarian Village Wedding." Unpublished manu-
          script.
Simić, Andrei
   1973   *The Peasant Urbanites: A Study of Rural-Urban Mobility in Serbia*. New York:
          Seminar Press.
Singelmann, Joachim
   1995   "Agricultural Transformation and Social Change in an East German

County," in David A. Kideckel, ed., *East European Communities: The Strug-gle for Balance in Turbulent Times*. Boulder, CO: Westview Press, 65–83.

Siulemezov, Stoyan
1986   *Istoriya na kooperativnoto dvizhenie v Bulgariya*. Sofia.

Sklar, June L.
1974   "The Role of Marriage Behaviour in the Demographic Transition: The Case of Eastern Europe Around 1900," *Population Studies* 28:231–47.

Smith, M. Estellie
1989   "The Informal Economy," in Stuart Plattner, ed., *Economic Anthropology*. Stanford: Stanford University Press, 292–317.

Smollett, Eleanor
1980   "Implications of the Multicommunity Production Cooperative (Agro-Industrial Complex) for Rural Life in Bulgaria or the Demise of the Kara Stoyanka," *Bulgarian Journal of Sociology* 3:42–56.

1985   "Settlement Systems in Bulgaria: Socialist Planning for the Integration of Rural and Urban Life," in Aidan Southall, Peter J. M. Nas, and Ghaus Ansari, eds., *City and Society: Studies in Urban Ethnicity, Life-Style and Class*. Leiden: Institute of Cultural and Social Studies, University of Leiden, 257–79.

1989   "The Economy of Jars: Kindred Relations in Bulgaria—An Explora-tion," *Ethnologia Europaea* 19:125–40.

1993   "America the Beautiful: Made in Bulgaria," *Anthropology Today* 9 (2):9–13.

Sofia News
6/28/90 "Black or White?" by Ani Ivancheva, pp. 8–9.

Sokolovsky, Joan
1990   *Peasants and Power: State Autonomy and the Collectivization of Agriculture in Eastern Europe*. Boulder, CO: Westview Press.

Staniszkis, Jadwiga
1991   *The Dynamics of the Breakthrough in Eastern Europe: The Polish Experience*. Berkeley and Los Angeles: University of California Press.

Stark, David
1989   "Bending the Bars of the Iron Cage: Bureaucratization and Informaliza-tion in Capitalism and Socialism," *Sociological Forum* 4:637–64.

1990   "Privatization in Hungary: From Plan to Market or From Plan to Clan," *East European Politics and Societies* 4:351–92.

Statisticheski Godishnik
1939   *Statisticheski godishnik na Tsarstvo Bulgariya 1939*. Sofia: Glavna Direktsiya na Statistikata.

1977   *Statisticheski godishnik na Narodna Republika na Bulgariya 1977*. Sofia: Ko-mitet po Edina Sistema za Sotsialna Informatsiya pri Ministerskiya Suvet.

1982   *Statisticheski godishnik na Narodna Republika na Bulgariya 1982*. Sofia: Ko-mitet po Edina Sistema za Sotsialna Informatsiya pri Ministerskiya Suvet.

1983   *Statisticheski godishnik na Narodna Republika na Bulgariya 1983.* Sofia: Ko-
        mitet po Edina Sistema za Sotsialna Informatsiya pri Ministerskiya
        Suvet.
1993   *Statisticheski godishnik na Republika Bulgariya 1993.* Sofia: Natsionalen Sta-
        tisticheski Institut.
Statisticheski Sbornik
1969   *Statisticheski sbornik: okrug Mihailovgrad.* Mihailovgrad: Okruzhen otdel
        da Durzhavnoto Upravlenie za Informatsiya.
Stavrev, Svetoslav
1988   "Motivatsiya za samoupravlenie i za uchastie v upravlenieto," *Sotsio-
        logicheski Pregled* 3:28–42.
Stillman, Edmund O.
1958   "The Collectivization of Bulgarian Agriculture," in Irwin Sanders, ed.,
        Collectivization of Agriculture in Eastern Europe. Lexington: University of
        Kentucky Press, 67–97.
Stillman, E. O., and R. H. Bass
1955   "Bulgaria: A Study in Satellite Non-Conformity," *Problems of Communism*
        4:26–33.
Stoilov, Atanas
1987   "Bulgaria," in Krastyu Petkov, ed., *The Transition to Self-Management in the
        Socialist Countries.* Sofia: Georgi Dimitrov Research Institute for Trade
        Union Studies, 26–39.
Stokes, Gale
1993   *The Walls Came Tumbling Down: The Collapse of Communism in Eastern Eu-
        rope.* New York: Oxford University Press.
Swain, Nigel
1981   "The Evolution of Hungary's Agricultural System Since 1967," in Paul
        Hare, Hugo Radice, and Nigel Swain, eds., *Hungary: A Decade of Eco-
        nomic Reform.* London: George Allen and Unwin, 225–51.
1985   *Collective Farms Which Work?* Cambridge: Cambridge University Press.
Szelényi, Ivan
1988   *Socialist Entrepreneurs: Embourgeoisement in Rural Hungary.* Madison: Uni-
        versity of Wisconsin Press.
Taaffe, Robert N.
1977   "The Impact of Rural-Urban Migration on the Development of Commu-
        nist Bulgaria," in Huey Louis Kostanick, ed., *Population and Migration
        Trends in Eastern Europe.* Boulder, CO: Westview Press. 157–79.
Tanov, Atanas
1986   "Agriculture in the Economy of the People's Republic of Bulgaria," *Eco-
        nomic Thought* 3:44–55.
Taras, Ray
1984   *Ideology in a Socialist State: Poland, 1956–1983.* Cambridge: Cambridge
        University Press.
Thirkell, John
1985   "Brigade Organization and Industrial Relations Strategy in Bulgaria,
        1978–1983," *Industrial Relations Journal* 16:33–43.

Todorov, Nikolai
  1977   "The Genesis of Capitalism in the Balkan Provinces of the Ottoman
          Empire in the 19th Century," in N. Todorov, ed., *La ville balkanique sous
          les Ottomans (XV-XIXes)*. London: Variorum Reprints, 313–24. (Reprint
          of 1970 edition.)
  1983   *The Balkan City, 1400–1900*. Seattle: University of Washington Press.
Todorova, Maria
  1990   "Myth-Making in European Family History: The Zadruga Revisited," *East
          European Politics and Societies* 4:30–76.
  1992   "Discussant Comments" delivered at the National Convention of the
          American Association for the Advancement of Slavic Studies. Phoenix,
          Arizona, November 19–22.
  1996   "The Ottoman Legacy in the Balkans," in L. Carl Brown, ed., *Imperial
          Legacy: The Ottoman Impact on the Balkans and the Middle East*. New York:
          Columbia University Press, 45–77.
Totev, Anastas
  1984   "Sotsialno-biologicheski balans na naselenieto i otrazhenieto mu vurhu
          demografskite strukturi," and "Migratsiya na naselenieto v Bulgariya," in
          Minko Minkov, ed., *Harakteristika na Bulgarskoto naselenie: trudovi vuz-
          mozhnosti i realizatsiya*. Sofia: Nauka i Izkustvo, 107–11, 116–22.
Troxel, Luan
  1993   "Socialist Persistence in the Bulgarian Elections of 1990–1991," *East Eu-
          ropean Quarterly* 26:407–30.
Tsentralno statistichesko upravlenie
  1988   *Empirichno sotsiologichesko izsledvane "gradut i seloto—86,"* Tom I. Sofia:
          Tsentralno Statistichesko Upravlenie.
Vasary, Ildiko
  1987   *Beyond the Plan: Social Change in a Hungarian Village*. Boulder, CO: West-
          view Press.
Vayda, Andrew P., Anthony Leeds, and David B. Smith
  1962   "The Place of Pigs in Melanesian Subsistence," in Viola E. Garfield, ed.,
          *Symposium: Patterns of Land Utilization, and Other Papers. Proceedings of the
          Annual Spring Meeting of the American Ethnological Society, 1961*. Seattle:
          University of Washington Press, 69–74.
Verdery, Katherine
  1983   *Transylvanian Villagers: Three Centuries of Political, Economic, and Ethnic
          Change*. Berkeley and Los Angeles: University of California Press.
  1991   "Theorizing Socialism: A Prologue to the 'Transition,'" *American Eth-
          nologist* 18:419–39.
  1994   "The Elasticity of Land: Problems of Property Restitution in Transyl-
          vania," *Slavic Review* 53:1071–109.
Wädekin, Karl-Eugen
  1982   *Agrarian Policies in Communist Europe: A Critical Introduction*. The Hague:
          Allenheld, Osmun and Co.
Walliman, Isidor, and Christo Stojanov
  1988   "Workplace Democracy in Bulgaria: From Subordination to Partnership
          in Industrial Relations," *Industrial Relations Journal* 19:310–21.

1989   "The Social and Economic Reform in Bulgaria: Economic Democracy
        and Problems of Change in Industrial Relations," *Economic and Indus-
        trial Democracy* 10:361–78.
Whitaker, Roger
1979   "Continuity and Change in Two Bulgarian Communities: A Sociological
        Profile," *Slavic Review* 38:259–71.
Wiedemann, Paul
1980   "The Origins and Development of Agro-Industrial Development in Bul-
        garia," in Ronald A. Francisco, Betty A. Laird, and Roy D. Laird, eds.,
        Agricultural Policies in the USSR and Eastern Europe. Boulder, CO: Westview
        Press, 97–135.
Wolf, Eric R.
1982   *Europe and the People Without History*. Berkeley and Los Angeles: Univer-
        sity of California Press.
Wolff, Robert
1974   *The Balkans in Our Time*. Cambridge: Harvard University Press.
Wyzan, Michael L.
1990   "The Bulgarian Experience with Centrally-Planned Agriculture: Lessons
        for Soviet Reformers?" in Kenneth Gray, ed., *Soviet Agriculture and Food
        Systems: A Comparative Perspective*. Ames: Iowa State University Press.
Yun-Shik, Chang
1991   "The Personalist Ethic and the Market in Korea," *Comparative Studies in
        Society and History* 33:106–29.
Zaslavskaya, Tatyana
1990   *The Second Socialist Revolution: An Alternative Soviet Strategy*. Bloomington:
        Indiana University Press.
Zhivkova, Veska
1989   *Seloto: sotsiologicheski analiz*. Sofia: Partizdat.
1993   *Bulgarskoto selo, 1878–1944 (sotsiologicheski analiz)*. Sofia: Ango Boy.
Zukin, Sharon
1992   "Postmodern Urban Landscapes: Mapping Culture and Power," in Scott
        Lash and Jonathan Friedman, eds. *Modernity and Identity*. Cambridge,
        MA: Blackwell.

Index